Iain Provan is the Marshall Sheppard Profes
College in Vancouver, Canada. He was b
concluding his formal education with a
Cambridge in 1987. He has written a number of books, including commentaries on *Lamentations* (NCB, 1991), *1 and 2 Kings* (NIBC, 1995) and *Ecclesiastes and Song of Songs* (NIVAC, 2001), and *A Biblical History of Israel* (co-authored with Phil Long and Tremper Longman, WJK, 2003). His most recent books are *Convenient Myths: The Axial Age, Dark Green Religion, and the World That Never Was* (2013) and *Seriously Dangerous Religion: What the Old Testament Really Says and Why It Matters* (2014), both published by Baylor University Press. He is married, with four adult children, and his main hobby is fly-fishing.

DISCOVERING GENESIS

Content, interpretation, reception

IAIN PROVAN

First published in Great Britain in 2015

Society for Promoting Christian Knowledge
36 Causton Street
London SW1P 4ST
www.spck.org.uk

British Library Cataloguing-in-Publication Data
A catalogue record for this book is available from the British Library

ISBN 978–0–281–07085–5
eBook ISBN 978–0–281–07086–2

Typeset by Graphicraft Limited, Hong Kong
First printed in Great Britain by Ashford Colour Press
Subsequently digitally printed in Great Britain

eBook by Graphicraft Limited, Hong Kong

Produced on paper from sustainable forests

For Phil and Polly Long
Good friends for such a very long time!

2 Corinthians 4.8–10

Contents

Acknowledgements

I would like to thank seven of my many excellent Regent College teaching assistants over the years for their help in this project. James Smoker and Stacey Van Dyk researched the Bibliography as the project got going; Margie McKerron did a whole lot of work chasing down references, reading the manuscript and bringing the project to a conclusion; Henna Lehtonen and Timothy Tse took time out from other duties to help her; and Jacob Taxis and Amy Anderson generated the Indexes. I would also like to thank the students in my Genesis classes in 2012 and 2013, who helped me to sharpen my thinking about reading the text. I have always found my teaching to benefit my research, and vice versa, and I am glad to have worked in educational institutions where both have been valued – not the least of which has been Regent College, my academic home for the last 18 years. Finally, I am grateful to Philip Law and SPCK for the opportunity to write this particular book. I hope that many people will find it helpful.

Iain Provan
Vancouver, Canada

Abbreviations

Only abbreviations not currently found in the *SBL Handbook of Style* are included here.

BMW	Bible in the Modern World
CTHP	Cambridge Texts in the History of Philosophy
DOML	Dumbarton Oaks Medieval Library
ER	Evangelical Ressourcement
FCBS	Fortress Classics in Biblical Studies
GSC	Geneva Series Commentary
HBISJW	HBI Series on Jewish Women
HBM	Hebrew Bible Monographs
JSRC	Jerusalem Studies in Religion and Culture
LOLA	Library of Liberal Arts
NCE	Norton Critical Editions
OECS	Oxford Early Christian Studies
OTT	Old Testament Theology
PMLA	*Publications of the Modern Language Association of America*
RSMRC	Routledge Studies in Medieval Religion and Culture
STI	Studies in Theological Interpretation
TatC	Texts @ Contexts
TSC	Theology and the Sciences
WPL	Wordsworth Poetry Library

1

Introduction

'In the beginning God created the heavens and the earth.' So the book of Genesis itself begins – a beginning about a beginning in which a Person (God) sets the cosmos in motion. This is where the story starts, by addressing three fundamental human questions: *Was* there a beginning? Are we living in a creation? Who created? The scale of this story, we understand immediately, will be grand; the questions that it seeks to answer will be huge. Why do we encounter the world as an ordered place in which life flourishes? Where do human beings fit into the scheme of things? How are they supposed to live, and what are they supposed to do? Why is there evil in the world, and why is there suffering? What is God doing in the cosmos to rescue it from evil and suffering? How do Abraham and his descendants fit into that plan? The storyteller – traditionally Moses – is nothing if not ambitious. So far as we can tell, those who preceded him were content to pass on smaller accounts of narrower matters – a story about Cain and Abel, for example (now related in Genesis 4), or a genealogy of the descendants of Adam down to Noah and his sons (now found in Genesis 5).[1] Perhaps some stories had already been collected into larger cycles of stories about particular characters, like Jacob.[2] These resources are now gathered up together, however, and woven into a coherent and sustained account of the universe and of ancient Israel's place within it, which continues beyond the confines of Genesis into the remainder of the Pentateuch, and then into the subsequent narrative books of the Old Testament (OT) (Joshua to Kings). Ancient myths, genealogies, etiologies, and other stories – all are deployed in this astonishingly bold project.

The structure of Genesis

These various resources have been incorporated into the book of Genesis by means of a particular structuring device – a repeated pattern of words

---

[1] R. W. L. Moberly, *The Theology of the Book of Genesis* (OTT; Cambridge: Cambridge University Press, 2009), 22–8; B. K. Waltke, *Genesis: A Commentary* (Grand Rapids: Zondervan, 2001), 24–8.

[2] H. Gunkel, *Genesis* (trans. of the 1910 ed. by M. E. Biddle; Macon: Mercer University, 1997), vii–xlviii.

that marks off one section of Genesis from another, often referred to in modern biblical scholarship as the '*toledot* formulae'. In Hebrew, the words are *'elleh toledot*, and these words have been translated into English in a number of ways, including 'these are the generations of', 'this is the family history of', and 'this is the account of'. They always stand at the beginning of the section of the book to which they refer, and they are almost always followed by a personal name, as in Genesis 6.9, 'This is the family history of Noah.' The person named after the 'formula', however, is not necessarily the main character in the section of Genesis that follows it, which is often much more about his *descendants*. The account of Terah's line, for example, hardly mentions Terah himself; it concerns, centrally, Abraham and his family (Genesis 11.27—25.11).

There are 11 *toledot* formulae in total, dividing Genesis into 11 sections (which I shall refer to as 'acts' in an unfolding drama), to which we must add a twelfth – since we must account for the material in Genesis 1.1—2.3 that precedes the first 'formula'. We may outline the structure of the book in the following manner, therefore:

1.1—2.3	(1) Prologue
2.4—4.26	(2) The 'family history' of the heavens and the earth: Adam, Eve, Cain and Abel, down to Seth and Enosh. This is the only exception to the rule about a personal name following *'elleh toledot*. Here the cosmos itself is imagined as the progenitor of the human race, no doubt because Adam emerges from the 'womb' of the ground (Hb. *'adamah*, Gen. 2.7).
5.1—6.8	(3) The family history of Adam down to Noah, prior to the great flood
6.9—9.29	(4) The family history of Noah, whose family survives the flood, down to Shem, Ham and Japheth (and Ham's son Canaan)
10.1—11.9	(5) The family history of Shem, Ham and Japheth: the origins of the nations after the flood, including the account of the scattering at Babel
11.10–26	(6) The family history of Shem
11.27—25.11	(7) The family history of Terah: his son Abraham and his family
25.12–18	(8) The family history of Ishmael, Abraham's 'unchosen' son
25.19—35.29	(9) The family history of Isaac, Abraham's chosen son

36.1–8	(10) The family history of Esau, Isaac's 'unchosen' son
36.9—37.1	(11) A second account of the family history of Esau
37.2—50.26	(12) The family history of Jacob, Isaac's chosen son: the 12 brothers, especially Judah and Joseph

It is important to note that the endpoints of each of the 'acts' marked off by *toledot* formulae represent important transitions in the story of Genesis:

4.26	'At that time men began to call on the name of the LORD' – the beginning of the worship of Yahweh, which prepares us for Noah
6.8	'Noah found favour in the eyes of the LORD' – Noah is identified as a worshipper of Yahweh, which will be crucial in the story of the flood
9.29	'Altogether, Noah lived 950 years, and then he died' – the end of the 'old world' and the point of transition into 'the world and its peoples as we know them now' in Genesis 10 (the descendants of Shem, Ham and Japheth)
11.9	'The LORD scattered them over the face of the whole earth' – the context for the story of the line of Shem
11.26	'Terah . . . became the father of Abram' – the transition into the Abraham story
25.11	'After Abraham's death, God blessed his son Isaac' – the transition from Abraham to his 'unchosen' son, Ishmael
25.18	'His [Ishmael's] descendants settled in the area from Havilah to Shur' – the transition back into the chosen line of Isaac
35.29	'[Isaac] breathed his last and died' – the transition from Isaac into the story of his 'unchosen' son, Esau
36.8	'Esau (that is, Edom) settled in the hill country of Seir' – the *anticipated* transition back to the chosen line of Jacob
37.1	'Jacob lived in the land where his father had stayed, the land of Canaan' – the *actual* transition back to the chosen line of Jacob
50.26	'Joseph died at the age of a hundred and ten' – the transition into the story of the exodus from Egypt

The curiosity in this structure is the double account of Esau's line. Because it disturbs the normal pattern in the book, most commentators have regarded the second account in Genesis 36.9—37.1 as having been inserted into the text after its basic shape had already been established. It is not easy to imagine why this addition might have been made, however. Was it perhaps to bring the total number of 'acts' in the book up to the number 12 – the traditional number of the Israelite tribes? Did it perhaps have something to do with the importance of Edom in biblical thought as a crucial player in the advent of messianic rule in the world?[3] We can only guess.

The *toledot* formulae, then, explicitly indicate the overall structure of the book of Genesis. Within the various acts in the drama, moreover, a plausible case can often be made for the presence of further structuring devices. For example, Bruce Waltke regards the Jacob cycle of stories in Genesis 25.19—35.22 (most of Act 9) as possessing what he calls a 'concentric pattern':

> A Oracle sought; struggle in childbirth; Jacob born (25.19–34)
>   B Interlude: Rebekah in foreign palace; pact with foreigners (26.1–35)
>   C Jacob fears Esau and flees (27.1—28.9)
>   D Messengers (28.10–22)
>   E Arrival in Haran (29.1–30)
>   F Jacob's wives are fertile (29.31—30.24)
>   F′ Jacob's flocks are fertile (30.25–43)
>   E′ Flight from Haran (31.1–55)
>   D′ Messengers (32.1–32)
>   C′ Jacob returns and fears Esau (33.1–20)
>   B′ Interlude: Dinah in foreign palace; pact with foreigners (34.1–31)
> A′ Oracle fulfilled; struggle in childbirth; Jacob becomes Israel (35.1–22)

Waltke also regards the Abraham and Joseph cycles as having the same concentric pattern – like a 'chiastic' pattern, but possessing a double rather than a single centre (F and F′).[4] Certainly chiasmus is a well-established literary reality in the OT, and others have argued for it persuasively in other parts of Genesis. Gordon Wenham has tried to show, for example, that the story of the great flood in Genesis 6.10—8.19 appears in chiastic form (he calls it a 'palistrophe'), the waters rising until God remembers

---

[3] See Obad. 21; Num. 24.18; Amos 9.12 (cf. Acts 15.17).
[4] Waltke, *Genesis*, 19–21. Waltke is building here on earlier work by G. A. Rendsburg, *The Redaction of Genesis* (Winona Lake: Eisenbrauns, 1986), and D. A. Dorsey, *The Literary Structure of the Old Testament: A Commentary on Genesis–Malachi* (Grand Rapids: Baker, 1999).

Noah in Genesis 8.1, after which they begin to recede.[5] Wenham represents the matter thus:

A Noah (6.10a)
  B Shem, Ham and Japheth (10b)
    C Ark to be built (14–16)
      D Flood announced (17)
        E Covenant with Noah (18–20)
          F Food in the ark (21)
            G Command to enter ark (7.1–3)
              H Seven days waiting for flood (4–5)
                I Seven days waiting for flood (7–10)
                  J Entry to ark (11–15)
                    K Yahweh shuts Noah in (16)
                      L 40 days flood (17a)
                        M Waters increase (17b–18)
                          N Mountains covered (19–20)
                            O 150 days waters prevail ((21)–24)
                              P GOD REMEMBERS NOAH (8.1)
                          O′ 150 days waters abate (3)
                        N′ Mountain tops visible (4–5)
                      M′ Waters abate (5)
                    L′ 40 days (end of) (6a)
                  K′ Noah opens window of ark (6b)
                J′ Raven and dove leave ark (7–9)
              I′ Seven days waiting for waters to subside (10–11)
            H′ Seven days waiting for waters to subside (12–13)
           G′ Command to leave ark (15–17 (22))
        F′ Food outside ark (9.1–4)
      E′ Covenant with all flesh (8–10)
    D′ No flood in future (11–17)
  C′ Ark (18a)
  B′ Shem, Ham and Japheth (18b)
A′ Noah (19)

In seeking such smaller structures within Genesis we are, of course, inevitably working at a more hypothetical level than in the case of the larger *toledot*-structure for the whole book. These hypotheses often appear to cast light, however, on otherwise opaque aspects of the text. In the case

[5] G. J. Wenham, 'The Coherence of the Flood Narrative', *VT* 28 (1978): 336–48.

of the flood story, for example, the presence of a palistrophe helps to explain some redundancy in the text. For example, the period of 'seven days' waiting for embarkation in the ark is mentioned twice, in Genesis 7.4 and 7.10, even though it seems that only one period of time is in view. Why? Wenham suggests that this is a matter of literary necessity: the author requires in the first half of the palistrophe a parallel (H and I) to the two seven-day periods in the second, where the ark's inhabitants are waiting for the floodwaters to subside (Gen. 8.10, 12; I' and H'). In narrative reality we are dealing in the first case with one week, and in the second with two weeks, but the chosen structure forces the author to 'duplicate' the first time-period.

The story of Genesis

How does the story of Genesis unfold within this overall structure? Here I am simply going to outline the story, not describe it in any great detail. I shall be unpacking this outline in more depth in Chapters 5—11 below.

The book of Genesis begins, of course, with the story of the early history of the earth as a whole (Gen. 1—11) – often labelled by scholars as 'the Primeval History'. The Prologue in Genesis 1.1—2.3 describes, first, the creation of the world. The earth and everything within it is characterized here as the good creation of a personal God, using the working week (six days, followed by a Sabbath) as its governing metaphor. Creation reaches its apex, first, in the creation of the land animals and human beings on the sixth day, and then in the resting of God on the seventh day. The human creatures are given an especially important role in creation as the 'image-bearers' of God: as well as multiplying in number like the other creatures, they are to 'rule' the earth and 'subdue it' (Gen. 1.28). This is the language of kingship; it denotes that God has delegated governance functions in the cosmos to men and women.

Act 2 of Genesis begins by exploring this human role in creation further. Now, however, the humans are not presented as kings, but as priests – set in God's garden 'to work it and take care of it' (2.15). If in Genesis 1 humans appear 'late' on the scene, arriving to govern a kingdom that has already been created and is functioning well, in Genesis 2 they appear early, before any 'shrub [has] yet appeared on the earth' and before any 'plant [has] yet sprung up' (2.5); they are created in order to enable creation as a whole to function as God intended. Taking Genesis 1 and 2 together, it appears that human beings exist both as the apex and as the centre of creation, created both to govern and to serve in a paradise in which there is 'no shame' (Gen. 2.25). Their relationships with God, with each other and with the other creatures are good.

In Genesis 3, something goes wrong with this good creation. Created by God to live in harmony with him and with each other – to be 'one flesh' (2.24) and to look after each other's interests – human beings lose touch with God and with each other. The man blames God for what has happened ('the woman you put here with me', 3.12), and also blames the woman herself; the woman blames the serpent, who first seduced her into eating the fruit of the forbidden tree (the tree of the knowledge of good and evil, 3.13). In pursuit of immortality, they have grasped at knowledge they should not yet have possessed (3.5). Thus it is, claims Genesis 3, that moral evil entered human experience in God's good world. The consequences are serious. Barred from the tree of life and the garden in which it sits (2.22–24), humans have now lost the path to the immortality they so deeply craved. Now they turn in on themselves, and become locked into a struggle for power – the man seeking to dominate the woman, and the woman desiring to get the better of the man (3.16). The struggle is not just with the other, but also with the dark cosmic forces that tempted them to evil in the first place (3.15). It does not just affect their marriage, either; it affects their family, as well as their ability to gain sustenance from the ground (3.16–19).

In Genesis 4 the family difficulties are illustrated. If husbands and wives are in conflict in Genesis 3, now we also discover that brother hates brother. Cain's jealousy of Abel puts him in a dangerous place, as God warns him that sin 'is crouching at your door; it desires to have you, but you must master it' (4.7). However, Cain ignores the warning and succumbs to evil; he kills his brother, failing to act instead as his 'keeper' (4.9). From this moment onwards, down until Noah's time, evil works its way ever more deeply into human society, even as we read of significant advances in technology and culture (4.17–24). Life goes on; *human beings* go on, being fruitful and multiplying, even in the midst of considerable wrongdoing (Gen. 5). Eventually, however, 'man's wickedness on the earth' is so great that God determines to bring an end to all life – or virtually so. The last statement of Act 3 of Genesis (5.1—6.8) hints that at least Noah may be spared, for he alone 'found favour in the eyes of the LORD' (6.8). It is left to Act 4 to expand on this understated verse, as Genesis 6.9—9.29 go on to describe the unusual boat in which Noah will survive the great flood that is coming – Noah, his family and representatives of all the living things that depend to some extent on dry land (including birds). Some of these animals are taken on board to ensure the survival of their species, others to serve as sacrificial victims in worship after the flood is over (7.2; 8.20).

The rains ultimately fall and the floodwaters rise, until the point at which God remembers Noah (8.1); then they recede. Noah and all those with him disembark from the boat, and life begins anew, with a commitment by God never again to curse the ground, destroy all living creatures or disrupt the normal cycles of nature (8.21–22). This is followed by a covenant between God and Noah that solemnly establishes the matter. Here the creation mandate that was addressed to human beings in Genesis 1 is reissued (9.1, 7), although certain adjustments are made to the resources that human beings may use for food (9.2–3), reflecting the new situation in the world. The commitments that God announces in Genesis 8 and 9 are necessary if the human story is to continue, for human nature (we read) has not changed in the midst of the flood: 'every inclination of his heart is evil from childhood' now as it was before (8.21; cf. 6.5). This truth is immediately illustrated, as Act 4 ends, by the strange story of Noah's sons and their reaction to his 'nakedness' (9.18–29).

Act 5 introduces the family lines of Noah's sons, and it ambitiously attempts to draw a map of the entire ancient world and its peoples (Gen. 10.1—11.9). Act 6 briefly recounts the family line of Shem, the forefather of Abraham. Life still goes on, it tells us; people are still being fruitful and multiplying. Sandwiched between the genealogies here we find a brief account of the happenings at the tower of Babel (11.1–9), which is designed to illustrate that human nature has *indeed* not changed as a result of the great flood. People may still be multiplying, but they are not 'filling the earth' (Gen. 9.1); instead, they have chosen to settle down in one place, with the intention of making 'a name' for themselves. Elsewhere in the OT, it is only God who rightly makes a 'name' for himself (e.g. Isa. 63.11–14). These are human beings, then, striving to be 'like God' in a wrong way – the 'original sin' of Genesis 3. This attempt at human solidarity in opposition to God inevitably fails, and the people involved are scattered 'over the face of the whole earth' (Gen. 11.9).

The Primeval History comes to an end in Genesis 11.26, and we transition immediately in Act 7 into the story of Israel as such. The line of Shem (the 'Semitic' peoples) eventually produces Terah, the immediate ancestor of Abraham, whose story occupies the remainder of Genesis 11.27—25.11. It is significant that Terah's family comes *out of* the same Babylonia in which the famous tower was previously built. God's response to the fragmentation of the human race at Babel, in this story, is to take up one fragment of this race and give it a promise of land and nationhood (Gen.

12.1–2). He will 'make great' Abraham's 'name', even as he opposed those who wanted to make their *own* name great in Babylon. God's ultimate goal, it seems, is that all the earth may still receive the blessing that he originally intended in creation (12.3). Genesis 12.1–13, then, is presented as a response to what happens in Genesis 1—11; the story of Abraham's descendants is bound up with the story of the whole earth.

It is this promise to Abraham that occupies centre stage for most of the remainder of the Pentateuch.[6] The book of Genesis informs us, first, about various things that happened to Abraham and his immediate descendants, Isaac and Jacob, in relation to this promise. The Promised Land is identified in chapters 12 and 13 as Canaan (12.5–7; 13.14–17); the identity of the descendant through whom the promise of nationhood will be realized remains a mystery for a little longer. At first it seems that it might be Ishmael, Abraham's son by the concubine Hagar (Gen. 16). However, by the time that Ishmael's family history is summarized in Act 8 (Gen. 25.12–18), the reader knows that this is not so. Isaac is the chosen son, born to Sarah in her old age and growing up to survive a threat to his life at the hands of his own father (Gen. 22).

The story of Isaac's family is then recounted in Act 9 (Gen. 25.19—35.29). Here it becomes especially clear for the first time in the account of Abraham's descendants that the divine promise is under threat not only from the barrenness of various women in the story (Gen. 18.10–15; 25.21), nor merely from the desires of several of its powerful men (12.10–20). The promise is also under threat from the moral character of God's people themselves – people who, like Cain before them, fail to love their neighbours (and, especially, their brothers). Jacob, Isaac's son, steals first of all his brother Esau's birthright (his inheritance) and then Esau's blessing from Isaac (a blessing that *should* have been given to the firstborn). This leads on eventually to Jacob's exile from the Promised Land (Gen. 28) and an education in cheating in a foreign one (Gen. 29), before he eventually returns, a new man with a new name, and is reconciled with his brother (Gen. 32—33).

After the double account of the family history of Esau that follows in Acts 10 and 11 (Gen. 36.1 to 37.1), the book of Genesis comes to a conclusion in Act 12 with the family history of Jacob (37.2—50.26). The overtly central character in this part of the story, the privileged and irritating Joseph, is so hated by his brothers that they beat him up, throw him

---

[6] D. J. A. Clines, *The Theme of the Pentateuch* (JSOTSup 10; 2nd ed.; Sheffield: Sheffield Academic Press, 1997).

into a pit and later sell him into slavery in Egypt. Brothers, again, fail to love their brother. In Egypt, however, Joseph rises to a position of power, protecting the country from the worst aspects of a serious famine and ultimately encountering his brothers again when they arrive in Egypt in search of food. Reconciliation follows, and thus there is, in a way, a happy ending to the book of Genesis.

However, it is striking that *by* the end of this story we have progressed only a very little further in terms of the earlier divine promise to Abraham. Genesis 46.27 tells us that all the persons of the house of Jacob that came into Egypt were 70 – not exactly as many descendants as the stars of heaven (15.5) or the sand of the sea (22.17). And, of course, these people are in *Egypt* – they are not in Canaan, which is still almost entirely in the possession of the Canaanites (note Gen. 23.17–20; 33.19 for the exceptions). The promise appears to have run aground in the sands of a foreign land. It will require the later departure from Egypt that is described in the book of Exodus, and all the events described thereafter in Leviticus and Numbers, to get Abraham's descendants back even to the borders of the Promised Land, where they still sit as the Pentateuch ends in the book of Deuteronomy. It is not until many generations later, under King David and King Solomon, that the promise is even somewhat fulfilled in all its various aspects, by which time it has become clear that the most important character in Act 12 of Genesis is perhaps not Joseph after all, but his brother Judah (Gen. 38; 49.8–12).

The distinctiveness of Genesis

When measured against the other books in the Pentateuch, Genesis reveals itself to possess some distinctive features. It is almost entirely narrative, whereas the remaining books are characterized by extensive sections that are explicitly instructional and indeed legal in character. The Genesis narratives themselves are focused for the most part on a small extended family or clan, and not on what we might rightly call a people group or a nation (as in Exodus through Deuteronomy). The exception is Genesis 1—11, which tells an even larger story than the remainder of the Pentateuch – the story of the world at large prior to Abraham's time. It is not only the focus of Genesis that is distinctive here, but also the substance; Genesis 1—11 is far more obviously and extensively in dialogue with its ancient Near Eastern context – its literature, rituals and religious perspectives – than the remainder of the Pentateuch, and indeed the remainder of Genesis itself.

When we reach Genesis 12—50, we discover various other features of Genesis that mark it out from the books that follow. For example, we encounter many names and customs that never recur later in the biblical story (e.g. the name 'Mamre', Gen. 13.18; the custom of taking a concubine as a solution to the problem of childlessness, Gen. 16.2). God himself is named using the composite 'Yahweh Elohim' ('LORD God'), which only otherwise appears in the Pentateuch in Exodus 9.30. Some of what the patriarchs believe and do is in fact in explicit contradiction to what the remainder of the Pentateuch teaches. Gordon Wenham notes a number of such examples in his Genesis commentary.[7] Abraham marries his half-sister (Gen. 20.12) and Jacob marries two sisters (29.21–30), whereas Leviticus 18.9, 11, 18 and 20.7 condemn both practices. Judah and Simeon marry Canaanites and Joseph an Egyptian, a practice condemned in Exodus 34.16 and Deuteronomy 7.3. Both Isaac and Jacob give the lion's share of their inheritance to junior sons, a practice contrary to the rules given in Deuteronomy 21.15–17. As to religious practice,

> the patriarchs do indulge in worship practices that later generations regarded as improper. They erect pillars, pour libations over them, and plant trees (28:18, 22; 35:14; 21:33), whereas Deut 12:2–3 condemns worship 'upon the hills under every green tree' and commends the uprooting of pillars and Asherim.

There is, indeed, none of the religious tension in Genesis 12—50 between God's people and their neighbours that marks the later story. It is not without reason, then, that Genesis can be referred to as 'the Old Testament of the Old Testament'.[8] It is a quite distinctive book.

---

[7] G. J. Wenham, *Genesis 16–50* (WBC; Dallas: Word, 1994), xxv, xxxiv.
[8] R. W. L. Moberly, *The Old Testament of the Old Testament: Patriarchal Narratives and Mosaic Yahwism* (OBT: Minneapolis: Fortress, 1992).

2

Strategies for reading 1:
Before the Renaissance

People have been reading the book of Genesis for a very long time – for more than 2,500 years, at a minimum. In the next two chapters we shall consider the main interpretative approaches to the book throughout these centuries, reflecting as we proceed upon how each one illuminates the book. In order to provide some structure to the discussion, I shall subdivide each chapter into two broad periods of time, recognizing that one could easily dispute the boundary dates of each period.

Early reading of Genesis (before AD 476)

Prior to the modern period, Genesis was read in the main by Jews and then by Christians who wanted to know, as they read their Scriptures generally, what they should believe and how they should live. This is certainly true of the period prior to the Middle Ages.

In Judaism this quest for understanding began at least as early as the scribes who worked in the period of 'the Great Assembly' in the later Persian and then the Hellenistic period, drawing their inspiration from the biblical Ezra himself, who in Ezra 7.10 is said to have 'devoted himself to the study ['the interpretation', Hb. *lidrosh*] and observance of the law of the LORD, and to teaching its decrees and laws in Israel'. The quest was then picked up by the Tannaim, who first emerged towards the end of the scribal era and whose teachings are contained in the Mishnah and the Baraita (i.e. Tannaitic traditions not contained in the Mishnah); and then by the Amoraim, who worked during the third to the sixth centuries AD, and whose discussions of and elaborations on the Mishnah are contained in the Gemara. Mishnah and Gemara together constitute the Talmud, the basis of religious authority in Orthodox Judaism, whose statements on its various subjects are of two broad types: *halakhic* (directly relating to questions of Jewish law and practice) and *aggadic* (not directly related to such matters, but exegetical, homiletical, ethical or historical in nature). A particularly important rabbinic text (for our purposes) that arose from this quest for understanding is *Genesis Rabbah*, a fifth-century AD product of certain Palestinian Amoraim that is typically classified as an aggadic midrash. By 'midrash' ('interpretation', from the same Hb. verbal root as *lidrosh* in Ezra 7.10) is meant

> a particular genre of rabbinic literature containing anthologies and compilations of homilies, including both biblical exegesis . . . and sermons delivered in public . . . as well as *aggadot* and sometimes even *halakhot*, usually forming a running commentary on specific books of the Bible.[1]

The biblical Genesis is expounded in some detail in *Genesis Rabbah*.

Beyond these various texts we find still other early examples of intense Jewish interest in the meaning and significance of their Torah, including the book of Genesis. For example, the Aramaic Targums that began to arise in the Persian period in response to liturgical needs in the synagogues not only translated the Hebrew of their source texts, but to some extent also interpreted it. This is certainly true of *Targum Onkelos*, which probably reflects materials already being used in the first-century synagogues, but in its final form dates to the third century AD; and *Targum Neofiti I*, which likewise dates in its final form to the second or third centuries AD. Then again, there is voluminous interpretative material to be found in the Jewish pseudepigrapha (writings where the stated author is not the true author). The book of *Jubilees* is an important example here – a document that recapitulates the contents of the Bible, sometimes staying fairly close to the biblical narrative, but sometimes adding or deleting material or giving new reasons for what is happening in the story.[2] It is likely that *Jubilees* was one of the basic texts written and used by the Qumran sect, and probably it dates from around 104 BC.

Finally we should mention the work of the Jewish and Hellenistic philosopher Philo of Alexandria, who lived from about 25 BC until AD 50, and of the Jewish historian Flavius Josephus, who lived from around AD 37 until sometime after AD 100. Among Philo's writings we find various exegetical works, probably written for a Jewish audience, that are directly relevant to our understanding of early Jewish ways of reading Genesis: his *Exposition of the Pentateuch*, beginning with the creation story and going on to discuss both the patriarchs and the later legal material in the Pentateuch, with a view to showing that the Mosaic law is in harmony

---

[1] M. D. Herr, 'Midrash', *EncJud* 14:182–5.
[2] C. T. R. Hayward, 'Genesis and Its Reception in Jubilees', in *The Book of Genesis: Composition, Reception, and Interpretation* (VTSup 152; ed. C. A. Evans, J. N. Lohr and D. L. Petersen; Leiden: Brill, 2012), 375–404.

with the law of nature; his *Allegorical Interpretation* on certain biblical passages from Genesis, which 'translates' biblical material into philosophical and mystical concepts; and his *Questions and Answers on Genesis and Exodus*, which seeks to provide answers to some difficult questions about these books. These works build on the earlier exegetical approaches of other Egyptian Jews like Aristobulus, Demetrius and Artapanus, and they attempt a reading of the Jewish Scriptures that fits (better than others) certain prevailing intellectual and cultural norms of Philo's day, not least by showing how the central biblical characters in the Torah are each paradigms of human character and behaviour.[3]

For his own part, Josephus wrote one book of relevance to our area of interest, his *Jewish Antiquities*, which he hoped would soften Gentile attitudes towards the Jews by educating Gentiles as to the true nature of Judaism and of Jewish history. In the course of his retelling of that history he interacts somewhat with the book of Genesis, as well as with other Jewish sources (including various aggadic midrashim), producing what 'is meant to be a revised and improved version of the Genesis story ... more accessible, appealing, and easier to relate to for *Ant.*'s primary intended audience'.[4]

Christians, too, read what was now to become (to them) the OT, in pursuit of what they should believe and how they should live. Early Christians like the apostle Paul believed that 'every part of Scripture is God-breathed and useful one way or another – showing us truth, exposing our rebellion, correcting our mistakes, training us to live God's way' (2 Tim. 3.16), and in believing so they were fundamentally thinking about the Old Testament and not the New (which did not yet exist). It is easy to see how this works out in Paul's own letters to various Christian churches in the first-century Roman world, for everywhere he grounds his teaching in these pre-existing Scriptures. For example, he often applies the Ten Commandments to the various ethical situations with which he is confronted in the churches (e.g. Rom. 7.7; 13.9; Eph. 6.2–3). The generations of Christians who came immediately after the apostolic age unsurprisingly followed the apostolic example. Indeed, faced in the second-century AD by a man named Marcion presenting the option of dispensing with the OT entirely and grounding Christian teaching only in the emerging New Testament (NT) documents, they resolutely resisted. They took the view that reception of the OT as Scripture was intrinsically bound up with their acceptance of Jesus Christ as Saviour and Lord, and that they could not have the one without the

---

[3] G. E. Sterling, 'When the Beginning Is the End: The Place of Genesis in the Commentaries of Philo', in Evans, Lohr and Petersen, *Genesis*, 427–46.

[4] C. T. Begg, 'Genesis in Josephus', in Evans, Lohr and Petersen, *Genesis*, 303–29 (323).

other: 'it is axiomatic that authoritative Scripture for the Apostolic Fathers [AD 95–150] were the Hebrew Scriptures', albeit that they were usually read in Greek translation, because so many of the early Gentile Christians could not read Hebrew.[5] Christopher Seitz captures well what these Fathers of the Church believed, in solidarity with their apostolic predecessors:

> The Christian church at its origin received the Scriptures of Israel as the sole authoritative witness . . . These Scriptures taught the church what to believe about God: who God was; how to understand God's relationship to creation, Israel, and the nations; how to worship God; and what manner of life was enjoined in grace and in judgment . . . It is not possible to speak of Christ [in the New Testament] without speaking of him 'in accordance with the Scriptures.'[6]

It was the Scriptures of Israel, they believed, that gave the Church its fundamental orientation to reality – the fundamental story of which it found itself a part, summarized in what has come to be known as 'the Rule of Faith'.[7] For Christian claims to be considered as true, it had to be demonstrated that they were 'in accordance with the [OT] Scriptures'. That is why it is OT references that litter Christian writings throughout the first and second centuries AD, and not references from the literature that would ultimately make up the NT. Irenaeus of Lyons, who flourished around AD 180–99, was in fact the first Christian writer in history to cite and allude to more NT than OT documents.[8]

This is why, even as the NT was gradually becoming 'Scripture' in the early Christian centuries in precisely the same sense that the OT was Scripture, ultimately becoming a settled 'canon' throughout the Western and Eastern Church by the fifth century AD, we find such serious attention being given to OT texts by Christian writers. As early as Clement of Rome, the governing bishop in that city from *c.* AD 92 to 101, we find commentary specifically on the book of Genesis.[9] Both Justin Martyr (*c.*100–65), in his

[5] C. D. Allert, *A High View of Scripture? The Authority of the Bible and the Formation of the New Testament Canon* (ER; Grand Rapids: Baker, 2007), 109.

[6] C. R. Seitz, *The Character of Christian Scripture: The Significance of a Two-Testament Bible* (STI; Grand Rapids: Baker Academic, 2011), 17–18.

[7] Sometimes in modern discussion of this 'Rule' it is (apparently) regarded as if it were quite separate from and even prior to Scripture, but this is a mistake. The Rule of Faith is simply the early Church's brief elaboration of the core message of OT Scriptures in the light of the Christ event that fulfilled them.

[8] Allert, *High View*, 119.

[9] Clement of Rome, *First Letter to the Corinthians* 9.3—11.2, in *The Epistles of St. Clement of Rome and St. Ignatius of Antioch* (ACW 1; ed. J. Quasten and J. C. Plumpe; trans. J. A. Kleist; Mahwah, NJ: Paulist, 1946), 14–16. Other early Christian documents referencing Genesis include the *Epistle of Barnabas* (*c.* AD 130), in *The Didache. The Epistle of Barnabas. The Epistles and The Martyrdom of St. Polycarp. The Fragments of Papias. The Epistle to Diognetus* (ACW 6; ed. J. Quasten and J. C. Plumpe; trans. J. A. Kleist; New York: Newman, 1948), 43, 45, 55, 56–7, 59.

Dialogue with Trypho, and Irenaeus himself (*c*.135–202), in *Against Heresies*, make substantial use of Genesis in their arguments, as do Clement of Alexandria (*fl*.190–215) and Tertullian (*fl*.197–222) in various of their writings. Slightly later in the third century, we find Origen's writings (*fl*.200–54) full of references to and reflections upon the Genesis story (not least in his *Homilies on Genesis*), and in the fourth century the 'Cappadocian Fathers' (Basil the Great, Gregory of Nazianzus and Gregory of Nyssa) are also notable for their commentary. Worthy of especial note as we move into the fifth century is Augustine (354–430), a prolific author who gave considerable attention to Genesis, most importantly in *On the Literal Meaning of Genesis* and in *Two Books on Genesis against the Manichaeans*. This is by no means an exhaustive listing of all the early Christian writers who perused Genesis in pursuit of truth and virtue, but it is sufficient to establish the point that from the beginning to the end of our period Christians held Genesis in the highest esteem as Scripture.

How did these early readers of Genesis, both Jews and Christians, read the book? Many of them were interested in what we might call nowadays a 'literal' or 'historical' meaning, or perhaps the 'plain sense' of the text – the meaning that we might imagine, after reading the text, the original author intended to communicate. In Judaism this manner of approaching the text was and is known as *peshat* – discerning the meaning of a passage by paying careful attention to its language. Of the two great schools of midrashic interpretation that emerged in the first half of the second century AD – those of Rabbi Akiva, on the one hand, and Rabbi Ishmael, on the other – it is the school of Rabbi Ishmael that is the more closely associated with this literal approach, building on the hermeneutical approach of the first-century Hillel before him. Since the purpose of reading Torah was to know how to live in the present, *peshat* was closely associated with *derash*, the homiletical application to the present moment. Even Philo, who is not typically known as a proponent of literal reading, 'takes seriously the historicity of the biblical narrative . . . [and] on occasion . . . even declares his admiration for the literal narrative'.[10] Christians, too, read the text for its plain sense, and indeed Augustine (at least) places a high value on doing so in his writings (for example) against the Manichaeans, when he says of Genesis 2 and 3:

> Of course, if anyone wanted to take everything that was said according to the letter, that is, to understand it exactly as the letter sounds, and could

---

[10] F. O'Fearghail, 'Philo and the Fathers: The Letter and the Spirit', in *Scriptural Interpretation in the Fathers: Letter and Spirit* (ed. T. Finan and V. Twomey; Dublin: Four Courts, 1995), 39–59 (46–7).

avoid blasphemies and explain everything in harmony with the Catholic faith, we should not only bear him no hostility, but regard him as a leading and highly praiseworthy interpreter.[11]

His predecessors certainly often read Genesis in just such a manner. Consider, for example, these words from Gregory of Nyssa concerning Genesis 1.30, on the giving of plants for food to the animals:

Many wild beasts do not eat fruit . . . nevertheless these creatures, when submitting to the laws of nature, [once] ate fruits . . . so the lion is [now] a meat-eater, and the vulture looks for carrion. But vultures were not yet circling above the earth to find carrion when the animals originated . . . The beasts did not yet tear apart prey, since they were not meat-eaters yet . . . So was the first creation.[12]

There is much to be found in this early attention to the literal sense of Genesis that illuminates the book. For example, we often see great attention being given to the detail of Hebrew grammar and syntax, which must be considered as the foundation of all good OT interpretation. This is illustrated in the debate between the schools of Rabbi Akiva and Rabbi Ishmael about the significance of various Hebrew particles as well as verbal forms like the infinitive absolute, with the latter arguing that the Torah speaks in ordinary human language, and therefore resisting the former's tendency to invest each word individually with great theological significance.[13] It is also illustrated in a Christian text like the *Hebrew Questions on Genesis* of Jerome (*c.* AD 347–420), which sets out to address textual and exegetical difficulties in the book, referring as it proceeds both to the Hebrew text and to Jewish interpretation of it.[14] We also discover in this early period serious reflection on the question of *how* the book of Genesis speaks 'literally'. We encounter such reflections in large scale, for example, where the literary genre of Genesis 1 and 2 is being considered – how are these chapters meant to be read? For example, Augustine, in his *Literal Meaning of Genesis*, considers whether it is likely that Genesis 1 intends to communicate to its readers 'the form and shape of heaven', arguing rather that 'the sacred writers knew the truth, but . . . the Spirit of God,

[11] Augustine, *Two Books on Genesis against the Manichaeans*, 2.2.3, in *Saint Augustine on Genesis* (FC 84; ed. T. P. Halton; trans. R. J. Teske; Washington, DC; Catholic University of America Press, 1947), 95.
[12] Gregory of Nyssa, *On the Origin of Man* (ACCS 1:42). On the treatment of Genesis as an historical account in the writings of the Church Fathers, see further S. Rose, *Genesis, Creation and Early Man: The Orthodox Christian Vision* (Platina, CA: Saint Herman of Alaska Brotherhood, 2000).
[13] L. Jacobs and D. Derovan, 'Hermeneutics', *EncJud* 9:25–9 (28).
[14] C. T. R. Hayward, *Saint Jerome's Hebrew Questions on Genesis* (OECS; Oxford: Clarendon, 1995).

who spoke through them, did not wish to teach men these facts that would be of no avail for their salvation'.[15] We also encounter such reflections on a smaller scale, as when Augustine considers the nature of Genesis 2's treatment of the creation of human beings from the dust of the ground:

> Now to think of God as forming man from the slime of the earth with bodily hands is childish . . . we should be compelled to believe that the writer had used metaphor rather than that God is contained in the structure of members such as we know in our bodies.

The literal sense includes the metaphorical.

Such literal reading remains important throughout all the succeeding centuries. At the same time, the literal sense was not the only one of interest to early Jews and Christians, not least because both sets of readers understood the Pentateuch, and indeed all of Scripture, as comprising a unified, self-consistent and divinely communicated text that revealed truth and exhorted virtue. Especially where coherence was under threat, therefore, either within Scripture or between Scripture and other recognized guides as to what should be believed and practised, both Jewish and Christian readers were apt to move beyond the literal sense to other levels of meaning.

In Judaism these further levels were comprehended through the exegetical methods known as *remez* (getting at the implied meaning) and *sod* (getting at the mystical, allegorical meaning). At times considered dangerous for the uneducated, because of the danger of misinterpretation and indeed heresy, a preference for hidden meanings rather than plainly evident ones in Torah is nevertheless a marked feature of the school of Rabbi Akiva already introduced above. Whereas in the pursuit of scriptural understanding Rabbi Ishmael and his followers would try to offer interpretations of individual texts that stayed within the normal boundaries of human language, Rabbi Akiva and his followers observed no such constraint. They pursued instead the 'inner' or 'spiritual' meaning of texts in Torah, tending to prize it more highly than the literal.[16] Hellenistic Jews were particularly attracted to such an approach, because it offered a readily

---

[15] Augustine, *The Literal Meaning of Genesis*, 2.9.20 (ACW 41 and 42; ed. J. Quasten and W. J. Burghardt; trans. J.H. Taylor; 2 vols; New York: Newman, 1982), 1:59.

[16] I shall often use the word 'spiritual' in this sense in the remainder of this book without any 'scare quote marks', just as I shall use 'plain sense' and 'literal' without such marks. This is not to be taken by the reader to mean that I like the word 'spiritual' when it is used to refer to the kind of reading also indicated by words like 'allegorical'. In fact I dislike it intensely, since it gives the impression that literal reading cannot at the same time be spiritual reading. As such, the term has Gnostic overtones. However, I also dislike the proliferation of scare quote marks.

comprehensible way, to Greeks and to Romans, of harmonizing biblical teaching with prevailing philosophical and ethical norms; the Stoics had already adopted this approach to the ancient Greek myths. Philo provides us with the most notable example of the approach. Wishing to impress the authority of Scripture upon both Jews and Gentiles by demonstrating that beneath its symbolic language lies profound truth, he draws a sharp distinction between what is obvious in Scripture and what (much more importantly) is not. Of the events surrounding the serpent in Genesis 3, for example, he says that

> these things are not mere fabulous inventions, in which the race of poets and sophists delights, but are rather types shadowing forth some allegorical truth, according to some mystical explanation. And anyone who follows a reasonable train of conjecture will say with great propriety, that the aforesaid serpent is the symbol of pleasure, because in the first place he is destitute of feet, and crawls on his belly with his face downwards. In the second place, because he uses lumps of clay for food. Thirdly, because he bears poison in his teeth, by which it is his nature to kill those who are bitten by him. And the man devoted to pleasure is free from none of the aforementioned evils; for it is with difficulty that he can raise his head, being weighed down and dragged down, since intemperance trips him up and keeps him down. And he feeds, not on heavenly food, which wisdom offers to contemplative men by means of discourses and opinions; but on that which is put forth by the earth in the varying seasons of the year, from which arise drunkenness and voracity, and licentiousness . . . Owing to which conduct, he too, carries about poison in his teeth, no less than the serpent does; for his teeth are the ministers and servants of his insatiability, cutting up and smoothing everything which has a reference to eating, and committing them, in the first place to the tongue, which decides upon, and distinguishes between the various flavours, and, subsequently, to the larynx. But immoderate indulgence in eating is naturally a poisonous and deadly habit . . .[17]

Early Christian readers also often moved beyond the literal sense of the biblical text, and for much the same kinds of reason. The Bible must be read in consistency with itself, with the faith of the Church at large, and with what was known from other sources to be true and good. Indeed, having lauded the interpretation of the literal sense in the passage cited above from his *Literal Meaning of Genesis*, Augustine immediately goes on to say this:

---

[17] Philo, *On the Creation of the World* 157–9, in *The Works of Philo* (trans. C. D. Yonge; Peabody, MA: Hendrickson, 1993), 3–24 (22).

But if there is no way to understand what is written in a devout manner worthy of God without believing it to be set forth figuratively and enigmatically, we have the authority of the apostles . . . to explain all these figures of things in accord with the catholic faith.

This was the view of many others in the post-apostolic Church as well, and Origen is perhaps the best-known case.[18] His treatment in his fifth homily on Genesis of the story of Lot's wife in Genesis 19.17–26 illustrates his approach well. He is concerned as he reads this passage that the punishment does not fit the crime. 'Do we think there was so much evil in this transgression, that the woman, because she looked behind her, incurred the destruction which she appeared to be fleeing by divine favor?'[19] His solution follows:

> But because 'the law is spiritual' and the things which happened to the ancients 'happened figuratively,' let us see if perhaps Lot, who did not look back, is not the rational understanding and the manly soul, and his wife here represents the flesh. For it is the flesh which always looks to vices, which, when the soul is proceeding to salvation, looks backward and seeks after pleasures. For concerning that the Lord also said: 'No man putting his hand to the plow and looking back is fit for the kingdom of God.' And he adds: 'Remember Lot's wife.' But the fact that 'she became a little statue of salt' appears to be an open indication of her folly. For salt represents the prudence which she lacked.

In the judgement of most modern readers of Genesis, early non-literal or spiritual reading of the book is nowhere near as illuminating as early plain-sense reading. In its defence, and precisely because these early readers were concerned with the *coherence* of Scripture, both intellectually and morally, it sometimes produces considerable insight into *connections* between texts that modern readers, often operating in more atomistic mode, tend to overlook. There is an integrative impulse in spiritual reading that reappears, in fact, in modern narrative criticism, which often draws the insights of ancient readers about spiritual reading into new

---

[18] It is generally the case that those who were members of the catechetical and theological 'school' of Alexandria (e.g. Origen, Athanasius, the Cappadocian Fathers and Cyril of Alexandria) emphasized the importance of the *sensus spiritualis*; while members of the 'school of Antioch' (e.g. John Chrysostom and Theodore of Mopsuestia) attached more importance to the *sensus litteralis*. The distinction should not be overplayed, however, not least because these 'schools' never existed in any concrete sense. They represent simply a convenient way of referring to similar emphases found among different authors.

[19] Origen, *Genesis Homily 5*, in *Homilies on Genesis and Exodus* (FC 71; ed. H. Dressler; trans. R. E. Heine; Washington, DC: Catholic University of America Press, 1947), 114.

proposals about the literal sense. Modern readers tend to agree, however, with those ancient readers who were the most cautious in moving beyond the literal sense, and they worry about the extent to which, in that process, the text tends to lose its own voice and to become subordinate to the voice of the reader.

Origen's reading of the story of Lot's wife is a case in point. He understands very well what the plain sense of the text is, but he is puzzled by it, because he thinks that the fate of Lot's wife is out of all proportion to her fault: 'For what great crime was it, if the concerned mind of the woman looked backward whence she was being terrified by the excessive crackling of the flames?' It is a fair question; but it leads Origen immediately *away* from the text rather than deeper *into* it. It produces an interpretation, in fact, that is probably very distant from any sense ever intended by its author, and one that has much more to do with Greek rather than Hebrew perceptions about spirituality. It is an interpretation, moreover, that involves citing one NT text entirely out of context (Rom. 7.14, 'We know that the law is spiritual; but I am unspiritual, sold as a slave to sin'), generalizing from another without offering any justification for doing so (Gal. 4.24, referring to the story of Hagar and Sarah), and associating two further NT texts with his overall argument (Luke 9.62; 17.31–32), even though neither one appears to fit it very well. And finally, it is an interpretation that contributes to a pernicious line of argument all the way down through Christian history that characterizes the righteous path through life in terms of maleness (and rationality), and the path to destruction in terms of femaleness (and irrationality), entirely departing from the biblical idea that the full image of God in human beings embraces both male and female.

In sum, the horizon of the interpreter in this case entirely obliterates the horizon of the text – and not just the OT text, but also various NT texts as well. A better response to Origen's puzzlement would have been to dig down deeper into the literal sense of the text, counting it possible that he had not yet understood that sense as well as he might. Is it actually the case that the author *tells* us that Lot's wife suffers her fate because of her wickedness in looking back? In fact, this is not the case. It is perfectly open to the reader of the plain sense to read the angels' words in the story as concerning the need for haste ('move really fast and don't stop'), and to read Lot's wife simply as failing to move quickly and resolutely enough. She is not necessarily wicked; at most she has exercised only poor judgement. Perhaps she has not even done that, for the innocent are often caught up with the guilty in the biblical story, which leads on to considerable biblical reflection on the theme of theodicy: how far is suffering explicable in terms of moral fault? The story of Lot's wife contributes to that wider biblical discussion – if it is allowed to do so.

Medieval reading of Genesis (*c.* AD 476–1350)

Medieval readers of Genesis followed and developed the lines of interpretation laid down for them in the preceding centuries. Plain-sense reading continued, but it remained the case that the literal sense was not the only sense of interest to the readers of Genesis, especially when the internal coherence of Scripture was under threat, or when the plain sense appeared to be in conflict with what was known from or taught in other authoritative sources of information. A few examples will suffice to illustrate.[20]

Saadiah Gaon (AD 882–942) is often regarded as the founding father of medieval Jewish philosophy – the first to attempt, specifically, to reconcile the Bible and rabbinic tradition with what reason more broadly was considered to have established. He was deeply committed to the literal sense of the text. Nevertheless, in his influential work, *Sefer ha-Emunot ve-ha-De'ot*, Saadiah argues that biblical statements that appear to contradict the results of rational enquiry (or indeed the evidence of the senses) must be interpreted in another manner, since sense perception, reason and revelation cannot contradict each other.[21] The abandonment of the literal sense is also justified where one biblical text is contradicted by another, or where rabbinic tradition qualifies the apparent meaning of a biblical text. Here, then, we encounter a fairly controlled approach to non-literal approaches to reading.

More committed still to the literal sense of the text was the later school of Rashi (AD 1040–1105). Rashi himself was certainly content to cite ancient rabbinic midrashim, but he sharply distinguished these interpretations from the plain meaning of the biblical texts in question; his successors were even more emphatic on this point. As in the earlier period, this more literal reading of texts is typically associated with a deep commitment to the elucidation of grammatical and linguistic matters. One of the most important of the medieval Jewish exegetes of the Bible,

---

[20] For further discussion of Jewish interpretation of Genesis in this period, see B. L. Visotzky, 'Genesis in Rabbinic Interpretation', in Evans, Lohr and Petersen, *Genesis*, 579–606, who considers various significant rabbinic texts and commentaries, including 'the Babylonian Talmud (sixth century), Tanhuma Genesis (seventh to ninth century), Pirqe Rabbi Eliezer (ninth century), 'Abot de Rabbi Nathan (ninth century), and the commentary of Rabbi Solomon ben Isaac (also known as Rashi, France, eleventh century)' (581).
[21] A. S. Halkin et al., 'Saadiah (ben Joseph) Gaon', *EncJud* 17:606–14.

for example, was Abraham Ibn Ezra (1089–1164), whose introduction to his commentary on the Pentateuch refers to its being 'bound by the cords of grammar and approved by the eye of reason',[22] and who contributed greatly through his work to linguistic research. This is not to deny that he too, however, was just as determined as Saadiah Gaon to ensure that revelation be not understood as standing in conflict with reason, including the narrative sections of the Pentateuch, which 'must be interpreted in accordance with natural and psychological verisimilitude'.[23] Yet he rejected the exegetical validity of midrashic expansions that are not anchored in the biblical text, and remained conservative in his embrace of non-literal approaches.

Other medieval Jewish readers, influenced in particular by Islamic Neoplatonic and Aristotelian philosophers, adopted a much friendlier approach to non-literal reading. They distinguished between the 'inner' and 'apparent' meanings of words and teachings, and regarded the latter as allegories pointing to philosophical truth that the educated (but not the masses) could unlock. Among these was Moses Maimonides, one of the greatest of the post-Talmudic Jewish scholars (1135–1204). His famous *Guide for the Perplexed* was in fact written for educated Jews who were troubled by some of what they read in Scripture, and in this work he makes effective use of spiritual reading where he thinks it will be helpful to the reader. In writing of Eve and the serpent in Genesis 3, for example, he states:

> The following is . . . a remarkable passage, most absurd in its literal sense; but as an allegory it contains wonderful wisdom, and fully agrees with real facts, as will be found by those who understand all the chapters of this treatise. When the serpent came to Eve he infected her with poison; the Israelites, who stood at Mount Sinai, removed that poison; idolaters, who did not stand at Mount Sinai, have not got rid of it.[24]

Here the 'inner' meaning is not just a meaning that has been or can be generated alongside the 'apparent' one, and which may in certain prescribed circumstances be preferred. The inner meaning is, in fact, considered superior to the apparent, because it is only the former that establishes what Maimonides calls 'real truth':

---

[22] U. Simon and R. Jospe, 'Ibn Ezra, Abraham ben Meir', *EncJud* 9:665–72 (666).

[23] Simon and Jospe, 'Ibn Ezra', 666.

[24] Maimonides, *The Guide for the Perplexed* 2.30 (trans. M. Friedlander; 2nd ed.; New York: Dover, 1904), 217.

In every word which has a double sense, a literal one and a figurative one, the plain meaning must be as valuable as silver, and the hidden meaning still more precious: so that the figurative meaning bears the same relation to the literal one as gold to silver ... [The] hidden meaning ... is profound wisdom, conducive to the recognition of real truth.[25]

Maimonides himself thought that it was important to place some limits on allegorizing in pursuit of his Neoplatonic and Aristotelian view of the world; for example, he accepted the Genesis claim that the world is a created (rather than an eternal) entity. Others went further, however, allegorizing even where Maimonides had refrained from doing so. Conflict inevitably ensued with those for whom the literal sense was fundamentally important, and for whom the reshaping of Jewish faith and practice in line with Greek philosophy was problematic. The trouble that followed towards the end of the twelfth and throughout the thirteenth century is often referred to as the 'Maimonidean Controversy'. At the heart of this controversy lay the charges that Maimonides and those like him engaged in indiscriminate allegorization of the Scriptures while denying the historicity of various biblical persons and events, and that they held that only the simple, and not the educated, need observe various commandments. These charges, although overstated in many cases, certainly reflected substantive reality in others. For example, Jacob b. Abba Mari Anatoli (1194–1296), a translator into Hebrew of some of the works of the Islamic philosopher Averroes (1126–98) – who in turn was in large measure responsible for the renewed interest in Aristotle in the West in the twelfth century and afterwards – interpreted the major characters of the Genesis story allegorically, rather than historically.

> Abraham and Sarah symbolized form and matter; Lot and his wife symbolized the intellect and the body; Isaac symbolized the active soul, and his wife Rebecca the intelligent soul; Leah symbolized the perceptive soul, and her sons the five senses; Leah's daughter Dinah represented sensations induced by imagination; Joseph symbolized practical reason, while Benjamin symbolized theoretical reason.[26]

In the Christian world we find very similar tensions playing themselves out. For example, Peter Abelard (1079–1142), the pre-eminent Christian philosopher of the twelfth century, follows very much in the footsteps of Augustine in offering commentary on the six days of creation in Genesis 1. He provides literal-historical, moral and allegorical readings of

---

[25] Maimonides, 'Introduction', in *Guide*, 6.
[26] H. H. Ben-Sasson, R. Jospe and D. Schwartz, 'Maimonidean Controversy', *EncJud* 13:371–81 (378).

the chapter, while also drawing the text into connection with the science of his own day. His avowed main emphasis, however, lies upon the first of these kinds of reading, which he regards as having been somewhat neglected: 'Although many men put together many allegorical or moral interpretations of Genesis, among us [Latin Christians] the insightful intellect of most blessed Augustine alone undertook to explicate the literal-historical in this matter.'[27] These comments are directed to his former lover, Heloise, whose own interest in literal-historical reading is clear elsewhere in the documentary evidence.

Indeed, there is evidence from throughout the late eleventh and twelfth centuries that some Christian exegetes, in pursuing such an interest, approached Jewish scholars like Rashi for help.[28] Certainly Rashi's influence is very apparent in the later *Postillae Perpetuae* of Nicholas of Lyra (1270–1340), which he composed between 1322 and 1330. These writings form a continuous commentary on the entire Bible, and they prioritize the literal sense, consigning the other senses to appendices. Rashi is often cited by name by Nicholas, as is Andrew of St Victor, a Christian OT exegete and English abbot (1110–75), who was the first Western Christian scholar to draw on Jewish texts in a systematic manner when writing his own commentaries (including one on Genesis), all of which (unusually for a medieval Christian exegete) dealt only with the literal sense. The *Postillae* of Nicholas became widely available in the libraries of Western Christendom shortly after his death, and greatly influenced later Protestant thinkers like John Wycliffe and Martin Luther (especially in his work on Genesis). A strong emphasis on the literal sense is also to be found in the thinking of the man whose work would become the cornerstone of post-Reformation Roman Catholicism, Thomas Aquinas (1125–1274): 'Nothing necessary for faith is contained under the spiritual sense which is not elsewhere put forward by the Scripture in its literal sense.'[29]

At the same time, the non-literal reading of biblical texts was everywhere to be found among medieval Christians, and often predominated, just as allegorical reading dominated medieval European culture in general:

[27] 'Dedication Letter to the Commentary on the Six Days of Creation', quoted from *Letters of Peter Abelard: Beyond the Personal* (ed. J. M. Ziolkowski; Washington, DC: Catholic University of America Press, 2008), 62.
[28] C. J. Mews and M. J. Perry, 'Peter Abelard, Heloise and Jewish Biblical Exegesis in the Twelfth Century', *JEH* 62 (2011): 3–19.
[29] Thomas Aquinas, *Summa Theologiae* 1.1.10 (trans. Fathers of the English Dominican Province; 5 vols; Westminster, MD: Christian Classics, 1948), 1:7.

The concentration of allegory in the air in the Middle Ages was heavy. Readers and hearers were exposed to it from various sources, and many probably followed simple allegories on the literal and on the figurative levels as naturally as we understand editorial cartoons.[30]

The entire world could itself be viewed as a vast allegory. It is no surprise, then, that we find Peter Abelard's great opponent, Bernard of Clairvaux (1090–1153), resisting what he thought of as Abelard's rationalism and emphasizing the spiritual sense of the text. This is best exemplified, perhaps, in Bernard's sermons on the Song of Songs. In this way of approaching the text, the literal sense is of little importance; what is important is to understand how the text speaks of the ecstatic union of the human soul with God. Bernard happened to deploy this style of reading in line with the official teaching of the Church, but this was by no means true of everyone. The Cathars or Albigensians of the thirteenth century, for example, deployed it in order to deny the literal interpretation of the miraculous events of Jesus' life and death. This resulted in the so-called Albigensian Crusade, launched by Pope Innocent III in 1209 – a military campaign designed to eliminate the heretics. The question as to the appropriate boundaries of allegorical interpretation was thus being raised in a pointed way among Christians in the thirteenth century, just as it was being debated also within Judaism. What counted as 'good reading' of Scripture?

The English Franciscan monk Roger Bacon (*c.*1214–94) – a contemporary of Thomas Aquinas – reflects intensely on this question in his *Opus Majus, Opus Minus* and *Opus Tertium* (1267–8).[31] He is by no means against the spiritual reading of Scripture – searching the Bible for truths to be believed, or blessings to be hoped for, or virtues to be practised. However, the Bible's spiritual meaning can only properly be based upon its literal sense; and he is profoundly concerned about the ability of many of his contemporaries to articulate that literal sense in a competent manner. They are not well educated to begin with, he claims. They lack knowledge of ancient languages apart from Latin, and therefore they cannot properly access the authors from whom they draw all their knowledge. They need to be reading at least Greek and Hebrew, and Arabic as well. They also know little of mathematics, alchemy, chemistry, physics, experimental sciences or moral philosophy – all are ignored, in favour of what Bacon terms 'speculative philosophy'. They have little interest in

---

[30] P. E. Beichner, 'The Allegorical Interpretation of Medieval Literature', *PMLA* 82 (1967): 33–8 (33).
[31] R. Bacon, *The Opus Majus of Roger Bacon* (trans. R. B. Burke; Philadelphia: University of Pennsylvania Press, 1928), and T. Witzel, 'Roger Bacon', NCE 13:111–16.

new knowledge, unlike Bacon himself, who was a genuinely experimental scientist thoroughly interested in such subjects as astronomy, agriculture and medicine, and researching into such matters as the reflection of light and the composition and effects of gunpowder. The lack of a general education is problematic when it comes to reading Scripture well, and the lack of more than an elementary knowledge of Hebrew and Greek, in particular, is problematic. Most scholars, charges Bacon, depend upon the Latin Bible, and the Latin text upon which they depend is corrupt. And so, he maintains, the literal sense of the biblical text has fallen into doubt. Therefore, there must also be doubt about its spiritual meaning.

In such a context, Bacon's plea is not only for more emphasis upon, and more accurate reading of, the Bible; it is also for more openness to the world as it is opening up to empirical enquiry, and less dependence upon medieval tradition. He is looking for a surer foundation than this tradition – in science, and in original and properly established texts, both biblical and otherwise. His view of the Bible in terms of its role in promoting knowledge is particularly interesting. It must have its own *independent* role in doing this, he asserts, which requires that its correct text should be established so that its literal sense can be clear and its spiritual meaning may then be grasped – not only by the educated, but also by the great mass of the illiterate, to whom the educated in the Church can then mediate it. It is indeed one of Bacon's great concerns that the poor educational practices he sees around him lead on inevitably to what he considers a quite false method of preaching, in which preachers content themselves with wordy and abstract sermons which 'stimulate the hearers to all curiosity of mind, but do not elevate the affection towards good' (*Opus Tertium*).[32] Eloquence, he says, ought to be accompanied by science, and science by eloquence; for 'science without eloquence is like a sharp sword in the hands of a paralytic, whilst eloquence without science is a sharp sword in the hands of a furious man' (*Opus Tertium*).[33] These various emphases on good reading of 'books', whether Bible or creation or indeed other books, and on effective communication of the results of this 'good reading', will also characterize the immediately succeeding centuries.

My comments above about the degrees of illumination offered by literal and non-literal reading of Genesis in the pre-medieval period largely apply also to the medieval period, and not much more needs to be said about this, except to underline the way in which the ancient integrative

---

[32] Witzel, 'Roger Bacon', NCE 13:114.
[33] Witzel, 'Roger Bacon', NCE 13:114.

impulse in reading Scripture often produced insights into the text that have remained important in subsequent centuries. Robert Alter's reading of Genesis 38 in *The Art of Biblical Narrative* (1981), for example, in arguing for conscious literary artistry in the redactor who put the Joseph story together, notes a number of connections between the chapter and its surrounding context. For example, there are two 'goings down' described in Genesis 37—39 (38.1, 'Judah left his brothers and went down'; 39.1, 'Joseph had been taken down to Egypt'), both concerning the 'death' of sons (Joseph, allegedly, and Er and Onan, actually).[34] 'Recognition' is a recurrent motif, not just in Genesis 37—38, but also in chapters 42 and 45. In Genesis 37.32–33 Jacob recognizes the garment shown to him by his sons as Joseph's garment, and in chapter 38 Judah recognizes the seal, cord and staff as his own (38.25–26). In both stories we find also the common symbol of the kid goat (the brothers slaughter one in order to deceive in Gen. 37.31; Judah sends one to 'the woman' in Gen. 38.20, in order to redeem a pledge). And finally, Genesis 38 is a tale of exposure through a lack of sexual restraint; chapter 39 is a tale of seeming defeat and ultimate triumph through sexual self-discipline.

In reading Genesis 37—39 in this integrated manner, Alter acknowledges that several of these insights are found in pre-modern Jewish commentary on Genesis, from both the early and the medieval periods. The medieval Jewish exegete Obadiah Sforno (*c.*1475–1550) already notes that both the 'goings down' concern the 'death' of sons. The common symbol of the young goat, and the common speech of recognition, are already noted in *Genesis Rabbah*. Alter might actually have expanded on the connections with *Genesis Rabbah*, since that text also notes the parallel between the two 'goings down', as well as the contrast between Joseph's sexual continence and Judah's sexual incontinence. What is clear, anyway, is that ancient readers who have approached Genesis believing that it is an interconnected unity have seen different things in the text than those who have approached it as a patchwork of disparate documents (a particularly modern tendency, as we shall see); and some of these things have been judged by modern scholars actually to be 'there' in the literal sense, not just in a further spiritual sense.

---

[34] R. Alter, *The Art of Biblical Narrative* (London: Allen & Unwin, 1981).

3

Strategies for reading 2: From the Renaissance until the present

As we begin to move from the Middle Ages towards the modern period, we still find many readers of Genesis who are interested in spiritual readings that extend beyond (and sometimes well beyond) the plain sense of the text. In Judaism, the reverberations of the 'Maimonidean Controversy' were still being felt all the way through the fourteenth to the seventeenth century, with strong support on each side of the question. In Christianity, likewise, significant attention was still being given in many quarters to the 'deeper meaning' of the biblical text. This is certainly true in what became in this period the Roman Catholic Church (in distinction to the various Reformed Churches), even among those who were initially sympathetic to various Reformation emphases, like Erasmus of Rotterdam. As we transition from the middle of the seventeenth century into modernity proper, however, we increasingly find that an emphasis on the literal sense dominates intellectual discussion of the Bible.

Renaissance and Reformation (*c.* AD 1350–1648)

The immediate background that needs to be appreciated here lies in Renaissance humanism – an intellectual, literary and scientific movement of the fourteenth to the sixteenth century in Christian Europe, which aimed at basing every branch of learning on the literature and culture of classical antiquity. It looked back to the origins of things in order to renew the present, and indeed its very battle cry was *ad fontes* ('back to the sources'). Dante Alighieri (1265–1321) was the movement's great precursor in Italy, combining in his *Divine Comedy* both classical and Christian materials. However, the person who arguably actually initiated the humanistic movement and led it on to success was Francesco Petrarch (1304–74). Italian 'revivalists' like Petrarch were soon followed by a generation of itinerant teachers and their students, who journeyed from city to city and spread the enthusiasm for antiquity to ever-widening circles, exciting in particular a massive quest for ancient texts. By about 1430 practically all the Latin works now known to us had been collected, and scholars could devote themselves to the revision of the texts. Under the fifteenth-century Medici rulers Cosimo (1429–64) and Lorenzo the Magnificent (1469–92), Florence became pre-eminently the seat of the new learning. Humanism was also favoured by the popes in Rome, most notably Pope Nicholas V, who founded the Vatican Library, which in the number and value of its manuscripts (particularly Greek manuscripts) surpassed all others.

It was inevitable that this general movement 'back to the sources' would involve the Bible, not least because in the fourteenth and fifteenth centuries others had come to share Roger Bacon's earlier concerns about the state of biblical studies in the Church. One aspect of this specifically biblical quest involved the comparison of the Latin Vulgate texts with those written earlier in Greek and Hebrew. This task was facilitated in the fifteenth century and beyond by an increased flow of ancient manuscripts from the East, arriving with scholars fleeing Constantinople after its fall to the Ottoman Turks in 1453, or with merchants and travellers who had traversed the Ottoman Empire. It was further facilitated by a renewed interest and competence in Hebrew and Greek among Western European scholars, often depending in the former case on Jewish teachers like Elias Levita (1469–1549), who taught Hebrew to a number of Christian scholars and also published a Hebrew grammar and dictionary. The sixteenth century saw the publication of two important printed editions of the Bible arising out of the resulting work: the Complutensian Polyglot, the printing of which began in 1514, and which included the texts of the Bible printed in their original languages; and Erasmus's famous 1516 edition of the NT.

The Renaissance that produced all this work on the correct *text* of the Bible did not restrict itself to this kind of enquiry about it. To go back to the sources was also to go back and look carefully at the content of the corrected biblical text and (in line with Bacon's concerns) to establish its literal sense, its plain meaning. So it is that in the Renaissance we see careful and renewed attention being given to the content of biblical texts, by scholars now reading them in their original languages. We see, for example, discussion of the puzzle that there are different names for God in the Hebrew of Genesis 1—2, and of the idea that the Pentateuch might not after all be a unified book, but perhaps a combination of different sources. Both discussions later become important in developing theories about the composition of the Pentateuch. An interesting player in these later discussions is Benedictus Pererius (1535–1610), a well-known Jesuit theologian who was one of Galileo's teachers and through whose writings many in the seventeenth century, including probably Thomas Hobbes, became familiar with the problems of the composition of the Pentateuch. Pererius is interesting not just for his work on the biblical text, however, but for his explicit articulation of the principle of interpretation that 'no interpretation of Scripture should contradict what is known from philosophy' (which at that time included what we call 'science').

The connection here with Galileo reminds us of one of the important environmental factors with respect to Bible-reading in the Renaissance – that it was being carried out in the context of burgeoning exploration of the natural world, which was itself raising disturbing questions about previous interpretations of Scripture, if not about the authority of Scripture itself. In respect of this challenge, the move 'back to the sources' could be helpful to those interested in integrated learning, if its consequence was to remind the scholar to ask questions about the genre of ancient texts. We see this move well illustrated in the commentary of John Calvin (1509–64) on Genesis, when in chapter 1.16 he confronts the problem of the 'greater and lesser lights' in view of what the developing science of astronomy has to say. Here Calvin accepts that Genesis 1 is a non-scientific account of the creation of the world – a description of creation such as could be understood by a normal Israelite, rather than a description corresponding to current (sixteenth-century) scientific knowledge. Ancient texts need not be expected to speak about the natural world in modern Renaissance ways.[1]

Conversely, however, the move back to the sources could convince readers that what the sources had to say in fact called the reader's present articulation of truth and manner of life into question. An important instance of this reality comes to us from the early decades of the sixteenth century, when the humanistic movement in Germany was reaching its zenith. Johann Reuchlin (1455–1522), a polymath well known for his philosophical and Hebrew works, was asked for his opinion on the case of a certain Johann Pfefferkorn, a converted and baptized Jew who had declared the Talmud to be a deliberate insult to Christianity and had pro-cured from the emperor a mandate suppressing Hebrew works. Reuchlin, on scientific and legal grounds, expressed his disapproval of such an action, and Germany became embroiled in conflict. On the one side were the Reuchlinists, the self-styled fosterers of the arts and of the study of humanity; on the other, those whom the humanists termed 'the obscur-antists' and whose lack of culture and ignorance they mercilessly ridiculed.

---

[1] J. Calvin, *Commentaries on the First Book of Moses Called Genesis* (GSC; ed. and trans. John King; London: Calvin Translation Society, 1847), 1:86–7.

In so doing they paved the way in Germany for the Reformation – precisely in their critique (in Bacon's words) of 'weak and unreliable authority, continuance of custom, regard to the opinion of the unlearned, and concealing one's own ignorance, together with the exhibition of apparent wisdom'. When it came down to a decision, however, the majority of these humanists (including Reuchlin) set themselves in opposition to the Reformation. They had not foreseen, while they were doing their work, this kind of ending to their story; and faced with the disintegration of the Church, they drew back.

Martin Luther, famously, did not draw back. His own profound sense of the whole Bible as a text from the past that could and should stand over against church tradition and theological thinking and criticize it led him in the end to become the catalyst for a new and powerful Christian movement that distanced itself from many older ways of being and doing. At the heart of this movement lay a considerable emphasis on the plain meaning of the biblical text, as articulated by its original, ancient authors. It was here, Luther proclaimed, that the theological value of the Bible was to be found, not in what was hidden in the text about Christ and the Church. Unsurprisingly, this led him to a generally negative view of the allegorizing approach that he felt had prevented him for so long from attaining his new perspective: 'I have often declared that I greatly abhor allegories', he once famously wrote, 'and condemn the fondness for them.'[2] John Calvin follows a similar line.[3] This strong antagonism towards allegorical reading, allied with a profound commitment to plain reading, was widely shared in the magisterial Reformation. In its scope it represented a new departure in Christian reading of the OT, including the book of Genesis, and it was a perspective that was increasingly shared in Protestant Europe and its colonies during the succeeding centuries.

One of the consequences of this fundamental commitment to reading biblical texts according to what are considered the 'normal rules' of interpretation, and with serious attention to the reality that biblical texts come to us from the past, was inevitably and increasingly that the focus of interpretation shifted within Protestant circles in the first instance to the past, even if the ultimate intention remained the explication of the text in relation to the present. Here we see, then, the beginnings of what some call the historical-critical and others the grammatical-historical project

---

[2] M. Luther, *Lectures on Genesis: Chapters 26–30* (ed. J. Pelikan and W. A. Henson; trans. G. V. Schick and P. D. Pahl; 55 vols; St Louis: Concordia, 1968), 5:345.

[3] E.g. J. Calvin, *Commentary on the Harmony of the Evangelists, Matthew, Mark, and Luke* (trans. W. Pringle; 3 vols; Edinburgh; Calvin Translation Society, 1846), 3:62–3.

that we shall consider in greater detail in the next section of this chapter. Already in the Reformation period, we find questions arising, for example, about the authorship of this or that biblical text, or its date. The attempt to read the Pentateuch in historical context raised the question in Luther's mind as to whether Moses had really written all of it; similarly, Calvin was not at all persuaded about the Davidic authorship of many of the psalms. These were *traditions* about parts of the Bible that empirical enquiry with an historical mindset appeared to call into question. Similarly, we find questions arising about the *genre* of this or that text – what kind of text is it, and what is the author really trying to say to his contemporaries (and therefore to us) through it? These are modern-sounding questions; but they were already being asked in the pre-modern period.

So it is that the nature of the book of Genesis as a document from the past begins in this period to be illuminated to a greater extent than ever before, as Rabbi Ishmael's conviction all those centuries earlier that Torah speaks in ordinary human language comes to be more widely shared than before (especially in the Christian world), and readers seek ever more to solve puzzles in the text within the bounds of its plain meaning as a text from the past, and to eschew resort to other levels of meaning. It is precisely the distancing of the text from the reader in this way that allows the reader, in fact, to see things in (and behind) the text that have not previously been seen.

Modern reading of Genesis (*c.* AD 1648 until the present)

Scholars debate when modernity began, but the year 1648 has a lot to be said for it. The first half of the seventeenth century in Europe was marked by terrible warfare across the continent, inspired in large measure by religious differences among Christians arising in the aftermath of the Reformation. With the Peace of Westphalia in 1648, and the end of the English Civil War shortly thereafter, a new era began in Europe, marked among other things by a deep desire that peace and quiet should continue to prevail. For increasingly many, this meant breaking any strong connection between the state and religion, which involved, in turn, removing the Bible from its exalted status in Protestant states as the divine Word that regulated public life – or at least weakening its hold. The state should no longer concern itself with many of the matters that are of interest to the Church, and should no longer organize itself on the basis of Christian dogma (which must inevitably divide), but on the basis of universal reason (which is common to all). One of the ways in which this liberal political goal could be advanced was to seek to undermine the authority of the Bible by way of reason, along the lines laid down by Baruch Spinoza (1632–77): the Bible read according to its plain sense, it could be argued, was not worthy of the reasonable person's assent.

As a result of increasingly fervent intellectual attacks of this kind, by the time we reach the eighteenth century we find that the Bible has lost its significance for philosophical thought and for the theoretical constitutional foundations of political ideals in England and then elsewhere. Ethical rationalism, now increasingly shaping the entire modern world, has taken over the public realm and has become the measure of the truth and relevance of the Bible itself. This is a world, then, in which for the first time in history the Bible (including the book of Genesis) is being read by many readers who are not themselves Jews and Christians reading it to discover what they should believe and how they should live. It is being read for quite another reason, namely to ensure that it does not and cannot challenge the control of those who are now seeking to run society in a new and (from their perspective) enlightened manner.

Whether possessing such an agenda or not, Bible readers in the seventeenth and eighteenth centuries who were committed to the literal sense of the text found themselves in circumstances that now required some reassessment as to how, exactly, the Bible should be read. These were not merely political circumstances. They had to deal, also, with ever-increasing amounts of information, increasingly widely disseminated as the number of printers and their output increased throughout Europe, which challenged previous ways of reading. In the middle of the seventeenth century (in 1653) it was still just about possible for a man named Jacob du Bois to write a book on cosmology in which part of his argument, in favour of an earth-centred solar system, was that this idea was 'biblical'. The eighteenth century, on the other hand, saw the Bible largely lose this kind of cultural pre-eminence in Europe, at least so far as science, chronology, ancient history, linguistics, geology, geography, and so on, are concerned. The Bible had ceased to be, for many people, the one document in which all knowledge could be assumed to be rooted, even where it might retain its authority with respect to matters of religious faith and morals. It had become, even more clearly than in any preceding period, a document from the past that at least to some extent must be studied according to the procedures employed in studying any ancient text, *in order to see* which kind of knowledge, and how much of it, it could add to the modern knowledge-pool.

The nineteenth and twentieth centuries saw only the acceleration of these trends. Indeed, the extent of the historical analysis to which the Bible became subject in these centuries is truly astonishing. This was the period in which the Bible itself ceased to be the only real substantive source of information about the non-Graeco-Roman ancient world, for example – the period of the deciphering of Egyptian hieroglyphics and of Mesopotamian cuneiform; of better access to the key texts of the Eastern religions, and to the world of so-called 'primitive' religions. This was also the age in which science came into its own as a discipline distinct from philosophy, gradually proceeding to dominate the world of the university; the age, specifically, of Darwinian evolution. Information and ideas were produced at ever-increasing speeds and indeed *disseminated* at ever-increasing speeds, as first steam-powered presses produced more and more books more cheaply; then newspapers became widely affordable; transportation and communications by rail and sea improved; and regular postal services took off, allowing greater scholarly contact than ever before. In sum, the context in which the Bible has been read by modern readers is quite different from that of pre-modern readers.

It is not surprising, then, that in parts of the world with a Protestant heritage very different ways of reading the Bible in general, and Genesis in particular, have arisen in the modern period, when compared to the preceding periods. Reading according to the literal sense has simply become more challenging than it was before, if recourse to spiritual reading to resolve problems is to be disallowed. New ways of doing things have had to be created. In turn, this Christian scholarship (at least in the sense that these are its cultural roots, if not necessarily in a directly confessional sense) has deeply influenced scholarly Jewish reading of the Bible, at least in the West. We see this direction of influence already in the work of Moses Mendelssohn (1729–86), the German Jewish philosopher at the root of the Jewish Enlightenment (the Haskalah), who in his commentary on the Torah draws on the work of both Robert Lowth (1710–87) and Johann Gottfried von Herder (1744–1803) on Hebrew style. The influence of 'Christian' modernity on much Jewish reading became still more evident in the succeeding periods, even as the conclusions of modern Gentile scholarship were often rejected by Jewish scholars.

Source criticism

If the OT is indeed to be read in a normal manner as a document from the past, then it was inevitable that in the modern period an interest in *sources* would arise – the attempt to reconstruct the documents that might underlie at least some of our current OT narrative texts. The most famous theory to arise in modern OT studies as a result is known as the Documentary

Hypothesis regarding the Pentateuch (or, strictly, the Hexateuch – the Pentateuch plus Joshua). This hypothesis is associated above all with the name of Julius Wellhausen (1844–1918), although he had important precursors in scholars like Jean Leclerc, Wilhelm de Wette and, most importantly, Karl Heinrich Graf. Wellhausen's thesis was that the Hexateuch had been fashioned out of four main documentary sources, known as J, E, D and P. The narrative sources J and E derived from the time of the Israelite monarchy, and were combined some time before the religious reform of King Josiah of Judah by an editor. The source D (for 'Deuteronomy') was the very law book on the basis of which Josiah carried out his reform, and had been composed shortly beforehand. The source P ultimately provided the framework for the entire Pentateuch, and was bound up with the reconstitution of Judaism after the exile.

Associated with this source analysis was a particular reconstruction of the allegedly real history of Israel that lies behind the current biblical story, for placing the sources in this (correct) chronological order was thought to solve many puzzles in the text.[4] As applied to Genesis, the Documentary Hypothesis resulted in now-famous distinctions between, for example, the 'two' creation stories placed side by side in Genesis 1 and 2, and the two interwoven sources running throughout the flood story in Genesis 6—9. The reading of Genesis in this mode was in fact little interested in the form of Genesis as we actually find it on the page. Its focus lay on what was to be discovered underneath.

The careful attention to textual detail typically displayed by source critics has proved of lasting value in the study of Genesis, revealing aspects of the text that any reading of it must take into account. Source criticism as such, however, has not endured well the criticisms levelled at it over the course of time. Scepticism has arisen about our ability to reconstruct documentary sources lying behind Genesis with much objectivity, not least because many of the criteria used by source critics in this endeavour have come into question. Is repetition, for example, necessarily an indication of multiple sources or editors, or can it not be understood as an aspect of literary artistry? More than this, however, it did not take long in the aftermath of Wellhausen's work for some OT scholars to become weary of an exercise that took attention away from the book of Genesis (and other books) that we actually have and (only) into the history of its development. Already in 1938, Gerhard von Rad could say in his *Form-Critical*

---

[4] See J. Wellhausen, *Prolegomena to the History of Israel* (reprint of the 1885 ed.; Atlanta: Scholars, 1994).

Problem of the Hexateuch, 'So far as the analysis of source documents is concerned, there are signs that the road has come to a dead end. Some would say that we have already gone too far.'[5] The intervening years have only seen a further decline of interest in this kind of reading strategy, although it is still represented in the literature.[6]

Form criticism

The Europe of the eighteenth and nineteenth centuries that produced classical source-criticism was above all one that believed in the 'creative individual genius' who emerges from among the mass of human beings and who, by the force of his personality and charisma, imposes himself on the general consciousness, bringing something new to the human experience. Wellhausen's thinking about the documentary sources behind the Pentateuch reflects this reality, with its pronounced emphasis on the creativity of their authors, albeit that he allowed that they used older, disconnected myths, songs and stories in their work. The emerging Europe of the early twentieth century, on the other hand, was one in which an emphasis on novelty and individualism was giving way in many quarters to an emphasis on the larger social nexus within which individuals inevitably operate, and within which their freedom of thought and action is constrained. It is in this context that we already find early dissatisfaction with source-critical endeavour, and the emergence of form criticism, associated in the first instance in OT studies with Hermann Gunkel (1862–1932).

With respect to a book like Genesis, Gunkel's interest lay in the deep roots of the tradition – deeper still than large-scale documentary sources.[7] He wanted to know more about the social background of the tradition (in German, its *Sitz im Leben*), particularly in the oral stage of the tradition's development before (he assumed) it was written down. He was indeed convinced that our biblical authors, rather than creating their texts *de novo*, often simply fixed in writing oral material whose ground rules were partly or wholly already set in the tradition. With respect to

---

[5] G. von Rad, 'The Form-Critical Problem of the Hexateuch', in *From Genesis to Chronicles: Explorations in Old Testament Theology* (ed. K. C. Hanson; trans. E. W. Trueman Dicken; FCBS; Minneapolis: Fortress, 2005), 1–58 (1).

[6] Note recently, e.g., Y. Lin, 'Re-reading Genesis 1–3 in the Light of Ancient Chinese Creation Myths', in *Genesis* (TatC 1; ed. A. Brenner, A. C. C. Lee and G. A. Yee; Minneapolis: Fortress, 2010), 65–80. For a helpful discussion of many of the reasons why the Hypothesis has widely fallen into disfavour, see R. N. Whybray, *The Making of the Pentateuch: A Methodological Study* (JSOTSup 53; Sheffield: Sheffield Academic, 1987), 43–131.

[7] H. Gunkel, *Genesis* (trans. of the 1910 ed. by M. E. Biddle; Macon: Mercer University, 1997), passim.

Genesis, he understood these oral traditions – short, self-contained and independent of each other – as having been passed down from earlier times in family groups, or by professional storytellers, or during religious festivals at various ancient Israelite sanctuaries. In due course they evolved into 'novellas' (like the Joseph story in Genesis 37—50), or 'legend cycles', (like the Jacob story in Genesis 25—35). It was these novellas and legend cycles that were then collected to form the primary material identified by Wellhausen as the sources J and E, such that Wellhausen's 'authors' were really as much collectors as authors. Form criticism as practised, especially in countries like Germany, was often just as little interested in the final form of Genesis as source criticism; it, too, focused on what was to be discovered underneath, and often only on fragments of texts. It could, however, become interested in larger-scale sections of biblical text, and even in whole books. Typically it was seen as complementary to source criticism; but for some, it became an *alternative* way of understanding the formation of our biblical books, rendering the hypothesis of large-scale documentary sources unnecessary.

One of the enduring contributions of the form-critical reading of Genesis has been the emphasis on the question of genre – already a feature of pre-modern reading of the book, as we have seen, but now greatly more developed. What is suggested about the origin and nature of the Genesis creation and flood stories, for example, when we set them in the broader literary context of the ancient Near East and consider analogous texts? Such a question helps the reader to avoid anachronism in reading – imposing modern expectations on texts that cannot bear their weight. It reminds us that we must always read texts according to the conventions that operated in the culture in which the texts were produced, rather than those in our own. This is not to say that form criticism as often practised is without its own problems. It often adheres to unnecessarily narrow ideas of oral tradition and how it works, and (like source criticism) tends towards a focus on what is behind the text that *distracts* us from the text that we have rather than *illuminating* it. It is for this very reason that already in 1938 von Rad could say of both source and form criticism together that

> scholars, especially the younger ones, are weary of research in hexateuchal studies . . . On almost all sides the final form of the Hexateuch has come to be regarded as a starting-point barely worthy of discussion, from which the debate should move away as rapidly as possible in order to reach the real problems underlying it.[8]

---

[8] Von Rad, 'Form-Critical Problem', 1.

Redaction criticism

As interesting and important to modern scholars as source and form criticism came to be in the first part of the twentieth century, by its middle decades we find many people's focus of interest shifting away from the earlier stages of biblical tradition back towards its later or perhaps even final stages – from early oral traditions and written sources to what later editors or redactors *did* with their sources. What was the redactor's agenda, his theology, the message that he was trying to communicate to his readers, as he shaped and edited the earlier material? Redactors, in this way of thinking, are not simply rather mindless functionaries, sticking bits and pieces of text or tradition together in a haphazard and rather clumsy way without any overall plan – an impression of the past that source and form critics could certainly create. Redactors are creative authors in their own right.

A significant figure in establishing redaction criticism as a central discipline of OT studies was the already-mentioned Gerhard von Rad (1901–71), who pioneered redaction-critical study of the Hexateuch. Affirming the work of both source critics and form critics in qualified terms, his interest lies in the redactor whom he thinks gives the Hexateuch its basic shape, the redactor J – not simply Wellhausen's creative genius, and not only Gunkel's collector of traditions, but a man rooted in tradition who is nevertheless on a mission of his own, and who in pursuing it lays down the basic lines of the biblical narrative that all his successors follow. In stressing the deliberateness of those who produced our biblical texts in their current forms, and indeed their artistry, redaction criticism at the same time puts the question of perspective or agenda firmly at the centre of our business in reading them. *Why* is this or that part of Genesis shaped in just this way, and not in that other way? What do those who put the book together mean to say in construing the tradition they inherit in this particular way? The redaction-critical appreciation for 'perspective' in the current form of the text differentiates redaction critics quite sharply, in the end, from source and form critics, who have typically regarded perspective as something that corrupts the original purity of texts as witnesses to historical or sociological reality, and whose goal has been to get behind 'perspective' to 'reality'. And this sharp distinction exists even though many redaction critics themselves appear not to have noticed it, or at least have chosen not to draw attention to it.

Insofar as redaction criticism builds on the kind of historically reconstructive work carried out by source and form critics that has widely come to be regarded as problematic for the reasons mentioned above, it must also share in their weaknesses. That is to say, particular redactional hypotheses may well be vulnerable to the criticism that their starting points in the process of textual composition they claim to be describing are in fact quite beyond demonstration and somewhat weak. Nevertheless, the lasting contribution of redaction criticism has been to help us see that our biblical texts are indeed written from a point of view, with a particular message to communicate – even if we are not able to reconstruct fully or even partially the sources or traditions that the redactors inherit.

Rhetorical criticism

Rhetorical criticism is redaction criticism's close cousin. It is also interested in what our biblical authors are doing with the tradition they inherit in order to communicate their particular message to an audience. It is focused in particular, however, on how rhetoric is deployed to accomplish this goal. The use and study of rhetoric by Bible readers predates by many centuries the modern period, of course, but the beginnings of rhetorical criticism as a modern reading method are widely associated with the 1969 essay by James Muilenburg (1896–1974), entitled 'Form Criticism and Beyond'.[9] From the title we gain the correct impression that Muilenburg thought of rhetorical criticism as building on form criticism, the latter being interested in the way that conventions of speech had shaped texts over time, and the former focusing on how the authors who produced the texts in their final forms had employed conventions of speech – the art of rhetoric – to communicate their own message to their own audiences. How does the present text work, rhetorically? How is it arranged in order to achieve its rhetorical purpose? How are aesthetics deployed, in particular, to *help* the text to 'work'?

In asking such questions Muilenburg is pushing back against a hostility towards art, and indeed the art of rhetoric, that is already found in antiquity in Socrates and Plato, who stressed truth and logic over against rhetorical flourish, and in all those in that tradition who have tended to disregard the literary form in which a biblical text finds itself in the pursuit of more important realities behind or underneath the text. Since rhetorical criticism is best suited for the study of poetic texts or perhaps NT letters, it does not have much to do directly, under that name, with the reading of the book of Genesis; but it *does* have a considerable amount to do with reading

---

[9] J. Muilenburg, 'Form Criticism and Beyond', *JBL* 88 (1969): 1–18.

Genesis under the different name of narrative criticism, to which we shall return shortly.

Structuralism and post-structuralism

On the way to narrative criticism we need to pause to consider both structuralism and post-structuralism. Structuralism pushes in a very different direction from both redaction and rhetorical criticism, in that here the long-standing preoccupation with authorial intent in the modern period of biblical studies is abandoned. The focus of interest falls instead upon the deep structures of thought in texts that transcend individual authors and determine their writing – universally recurring features in fictional narratives of all cultures and ages that reveal an individual text's most fundamental meaning irrespective of its author's conscious intentions.

Perhaps the most famous example of the application of a structuralist reading to Genesis is the 1971 essay of Roland Barthes (1915–80) entitled 'The Struggle with the Angel'.[10] In this essay Barthes discusses Jacob's struggle at Peniel in Genesis 32.22–32 with a man or an angel who turns out at the climactic moment to be God. Reading the story against the background of folk-tale plots in general, Barthes characterizes Jacob as the hero who is on a quest (one of the commonest of all folk-tale plots) and God as the originator of his quest. At the moment of the struggle, a number of narrative developments are possible; but unusually and unexpectedly Jacob recognizes that the opponent who has waylaid him and has attempted to prevent him from accomplishing his mission is none other than the originator (God) himself. This precise pattern of story is rare; in fact, says Barthes, only narratives relating an act of blackmail typically possess this paradoxical form. Structurally, then, the biblical story seems to break a general rule of folk-tale grammar; theologically, the fact that the same supernatural protagonist is both the originator and the opponent implies the kind of radical monotheism that will not permit the existence of an opposing spiritual power.

In short, Barthes' structural analysis reveals how and why Genesis 32.22–32 is a 'tale of the unexpected'. This is a good example of the way in which structuralist reading can illuminate biblical texts by setting them, not just against an ancient Near Eastern background, but against the background of human culture more generally. Biblical storytelling, on this view, is a subset of human storytelling, not only addressing the same

---

[10] R. Barthes, *Image, Music, Text: Essays Selected and Translated by Stephen Heath* (London: Fontana, 1977), 125–41.

human concerns, but also both following and diverging from similar patterns. This is indeed why it is still capable of addressing modern people existentially, even when they stand at some distance both chronologically and culturally from the originating points of biblical literature.

Even if structuralism represents a step away from reading strategies such as redaction criticism, because it is not particularly interested in authors but only in texts, it is still an approach rooted in the modern rather than the postmodern world. Structuralists still believe in metanarratives: in overarching stories about reality, including human reality. They may have given up on the Jewish and Christian metanarratives that previous generations of readers of Genesis have typically embraced. They are still convinced, however, that systematic knowledge of reality is possible, as scientific method brings the biblical literature under its scrutiny – knowledge, for example, of what makes humans beings fundamentally 'tick', as indicated by what their stories share in common. Postmodernity, conversely, declares itself incredulous towards metanarratives; and in literature, this paradigm shift in respect of reality in general is reflected in the shift from structuralism to post-structuralism, most famously associated with Jacques Derrida (1930–2004). For what marks out post-structuralists is that they are much less interested in *texts* than they are in *readers*, and in the act of reading.

Structuralism, in killing the author, already raises the reader to prominence; post-structuralism now attempts to finish the job, or at least to explore further the implications. This lack of interest in textual meaning takes milder and stronger forms. At the milder end of the spectrum are to be found those interested in reader-response criticism or reception theory; at the stronger end are to be found the deconstructionists. Post-structuralists at their most moderate ask: is it mainly the text that directs the act of reading, or is it more the reader or the community of readers that determines the meaning of a text? They tend to ask at their most radical: does the text direct the act of reading *at all*, or is it the reader or the community of readers that *entirely determines* the meaning of a text? Wherever on the spectrum they find themselves, they are certainly interested in the reader who to some extent creates meaning by deciphering words and sentences, filling in the gaps in the story, relating parts to the whole, selecting and organizing, anticipating and modifying expectations.

These themes come out very clearly in Genesis studies with the advent of narrative criticism. Deconstructionists tend to be among the most pessimistic of these post-structuralist readers, and indeed the furthest away from their Jewish and Christian forebears, as a consequence not only of their incredulity towards metanarratives, but also of their lack of any

eschatology that allows readers to 'live happily ever after'. In deconstruc-
tionism, the pilgrim reader does not merely find the path to knowledge
challenging but in the end fruitful; he or she finds it instead to be a dead
end. There is no confidence as to what reading can achieve. All texts –
indeed, all human communications – ultimately deconstruct or undermine
themselves, falling to pieces (at least as objective entities) in the reader's
hands and failing to provide the information that might enable the reader
to adjudicate between competing interpretations. Modern optimism about
recovering 'the meaning' of a text through the application to it of scientific
method has here completely evaporated.

   Deconstructionist approaches to biblical texts do not so much illuminate
them as render them incomprehensible. Post-structuralism in its milder
forms, however, is helpful, insofar as it forces readers to think hard
about their reading and the kinds of things that influence it, creating self-
consciousness about what they bring to the task. It makes us aware, for
example, that we are *in fact* filling in the gaps in a biblical narrative in a
certain way, even if we may not even have noticed the gaps before because
we have never had an alternative reading held in front of us. The subject
and the object are in dialogue with each other in reading a text like Genesis:
it is not simply a matter of the object addressing us in a monologue.
Readers *participate* in the act of reading.

Narrative criticism

The last three decades of the twentieth century saw significant developments in biblical interpretation, as the trend continued towards grappling
with the final form of the biblical text and eschewing, in all or in part,
the kind of excavative scholarship that had marked the earlier segments
of the modern period. Highly influential in terms of its impact on reading
biblical narrative in particular was Robert Alter's already-mentioned book,
The Art of Biblical Narrative (1981). Alter's reading of Genesis 38 in the
context of the Joseph story provides us with helpful insight into his overall approach.

   He begins by asking: what role does literary art play in the shaping
of biblical narrative? Genesis 38 serves as a case study in pursuit of his
affirmation that its role is crucial. It is an interesting passage not least
because of the way in which modern source, form and redaction critics
have handled it. Noting that a story about Judah is strangely located
between Genesis 37 and 39, they have routinely explained it as a secondary
addition to an original Joseph narrative that disturbs the flow of that
narrative; that is why it doesn't 'make sense'. Alter mercilessly parodies this

insufficient explanation for the existence of Genesis 38, arguing that it involves the implausible belief that 'the redactors were in the grip of a kind of manic tribal compulsion, driven again and again to include units of traditional material that made no connective sense, for reasons they themselves could not have explained'.[11] Setting out to achieve a more satisfactory account, Alter draws attention to a number of interesting connections between Genesis 38 and its context that suggest consciousness and artistry in the redactor who put the whole Joseph story together. Noting various ways in which pre-modern readers had already observed some of these connections, he proposes, not that readers should abandon all belief in a historical process behind our texts, but that they should certainly recognize the conscious literary art that is being deployed in pursuit of a profound unity in the final form of the text.

A growing belief among biblical exegetes in the decades since the publication of Alter's book that perhaps biblical authors and editors were more generally of the kind that Alter has in mind in Genesis 37—50 has resulted now in a vast body of narrative-critical studies of various parts of the Bible, including the book of Genesis. In the process, many of the phenomena of the texts understood by previous generations of modern scholars as 'gateways' into the world behind the text – the world of oral forms and written sources – have been reinterpreted in terms of literary art. Such studies have drawn on insights both from earlier work in the OT and from the world of literary studies more generally concerning how texts 'work' and seek to persuade their readers; how they are fashioned in terms of plot, point of view, characterization and rhetorical structure; and how authors, readers, narrators and implied readers are involved in the appropriation of the text. With respect to Genesis 37—50 itself, such narrative-critical endeavour has not only provided a greatly more satisfying resolution of the 'difficulties' in the text than that of which Wellhausen was capable – and these chapters have long been recognized as problematic for the Documentary Hypothesis[12] – but it has also helped us to see that we are dealing here with a story that is much more importantly about Judah than it is about Joseph. We shall return to this specific point in the final chapter of this book.

---

[11] R. Alter, *The Art of Biblical Narrative* (London: Allen & Unwin, 1981), 20.

[12] Wellhausen himself 'admitted that there are particular difficulties involved in the dissection of what had been described as "this smooth-flowing story"' (Whybray, *Making of the Pentateuch*, 118). The difficulties have only become ever more apparent with the passing of time, as a growing number of scholars have tied themselves in logical and methodological knots in pursuit of a convincing source-critical account. For some examples, see Whybray, *Making of the Pentateuch*, 54–5, 89–90, 118–19.

Social scientific criticism

It was not only literary studies that began to have a great impact on biblical interpretation in the 1980s and beyond, but also social scientific studies. This impact was no doubt especially facilitated by the ongoing 'secularization' of biblical studies in this time period, as more and more of the 'professional' readers of the Bible in the expanding modern Western universities ceased to share the overall theological perspective of either the Jewish or the Christian readers who had preceded them, and as inbuilt (perhaps only culturally residual) resistance to 'relocating' the Bible in a much less humanistic frame of reference than previously more completely dissipated. It was only as this happened that the Bible could easily be conceived of as an object of study within the realm of human sciences whose ultimate goal (as Claude Lévi-Strauss once put it) 'is not to constitute, but to dissolve man', or (in the words of Michel Foucault) to decentre the subject 'in relation to the laws of its desire, the forms of its language, the rules of its actions, or the play of its mythical and imaginative discourse'.[13]

Pertaining to the OT in particular, the work of Norman Gottwald on the sociology of ancient Israel illustrates well how a book like Genesis can be read within this frame of reference.[14] Like the structuralists, Gottwald is not very interested in the particularities of the biblical texts, but rather in the deep structures (the social totality of Israelite society) out of which they emerge. Thus, his examination of ancient Israel is not based on individuals and their achievements – on the kinds of realities upon which the biblical narratives themselves focus. He examines Israelite religion, in particular, as one aspect of a wider network of social relations in which it has intelligible functions to perform, and he looks at changes in religious behaviour and thought as aspects of change in the wider network of social and economic relations. This leads him to the radical idea that the early Israelites comprised a mixed multitude of Canaanite people, emergent from within Canaanite society rather than entering Canaan from the outside, and that the religion of Yahweh was a crucial instrument by which the identity of this new people 'Israel' was formed and through which it was maintained. These conclusions represent, of course, a major shift away from traditional understandings of the emergence of early Israel, and indeed a very different manner of approach to biblical texts than the one chosen by the narrative critics, who are reading Genesis not so much for

---

[13] C. Lévi-Strauss, *The Savage Mind* (Chicago: Chicago University Press, 1967), 247; M. Foucault, *The Archaeology of Knowledge* (trans. A. M. Sheridan-Smith; London: Tavistock, 1972), 13.

[14] N. K. Gottwald, *The Tribes of Yahweh: A Sociology of the Religion of Liberated Israel, 1250–1050 BCE* (Maryknoll, NY; Orbis, 1979).

what they hope to find beneath or behind the text, but for what they hope to find *in* it.

Gottwald's work illustrates nicely both the ways in which social scientific criticism can illuminate biblical texts, and the problems attaching to the endeavour. There is much that is deeply insightful in his book, as he seeks to show how deeply and intimately connected are Israelite social organization and theology, and to contrast this with Canaanite social organization and theology. The Pentateuch does not just propose ideas (about God, the world, and so on); those ideas are deeply connected to social practices, which reflect answers to questions like, 'how should I treat my neighbour?' and 'what is the good society?' Cosmology and theology are always deeply bound up with anthropology, ethics and politics, in just such a manner. At the same time, it is clear that Gottwald's approach to his subject matter is deeply reductionistic, ignoring the biblical text's own testimony about important aspects of Israel's history in pursuit of a thesis about what 'really happened', in which his own modernist and materialist perspective appears to play a too-dominating role. In the end, and in important ways, Gottwald does not illuminate the text at all; he suppresses it.

Feminist criticism

Another of the social realities that marked the closing decades of the twentieth century and the opening decades of the twenty-first was the influx of female scholars into university domains that had previously been dominated almost exclusively by men. With them came the feminist perspectives that were being broadly developed in all sorts of ways throughout Western culture. It was inevitable that such perspectives would be brought to bear in the universities also on the Bible. Perhaps the driving question that feminists were asking of literature in general was and remains: what difference does it make if the reader of a literary work experiences it as a woman rather than as a man? The importance of generating such readings is affirmed, in pursuit of the feminist agenda – readings that can be based on the text itself, or that might arise out of resistance to the text, or that even challenge as 'male' the very way in which reading has traditionally been carried out (that sees the procedures, assumptions and goals of criticism as complicit in the attempt to preserve male authority). In all such readings we find at the centre of the exercise a woman who is self-consciously reading as a woman and valuing that female perspective and approach to the text as highly if not more highly than a male perspective or approach.

As applied to the OT in particular, feminist criticism can produce readings that are markedly hostile to the biblical tradition, such as some of those offered in her later years by Mary Daly (1928–2010). For Daly, originally a practising Roman Catholic, the whole Judaeo-Christian tradition ultimately came to represent a male structure designed by men for men: 'when god is male the male is god', as she so famously put it. Other readings have stopped short of that kind of hostility. We may note, for example, the various essays in *Feminist Interpretation of the Bible* (1985), edited by Letty Russell (1929–2007).[15] Although there is keen recognition throughout this volume that the Bible was shaped by males living in a patriarchal culture, most of the contributors adopt reading strategies that in different ways dispute Mary Daly's view that 'the medium is the message', and they find it worthwhile still to read the Bible as feminists. This includes Cheryl Exum, who believes that 'within the admittedly patriarchal context of the biblical literature, we find strong countercurrents of affirmation of women', and who offers a study of the matriarchs of Genesis 12—50 along such lines.[16]

If biblical texts are always written from a point of view and, whether in their deep structures or in their explicit intentionality, promote a certain vision of the world (as suggested by the various modern reading strategies already discussed), then one of the questions that must inevitably arise is, 'where do women fit into this vision?' Feminist criticism presses that question on all readers of a text like Genesis, and in the process raises important issues concerning not only the text in itself, but also the way in which it has been read through the ages. It illuminates the text in itself, in its perspectival nature and in its 'interests', and it illuminates the history of reading, opening up space for new readings that might not even have occurred to previous generations of readers – not because the text is not capable of being read in that way, but simply because the commitments and prejudices of the readers concerned have blinded them to the possibility.

Canonical criticism

Brevard Childs (1923–2007) is the primary name associated with canonical criticism, and with his work (and that of his followers and developers) we come full circle in the story of biblical interpretation in the modern period.[17] Modern biblical criticism arose in the context of a discussion in

---

[15] L. M. Russell (ed.), *Feminist Interpretation of the Bible* (Philadelphia: Westminster, 1985).

[16] J. C. Exum, '"Mother in Israel": A Familiar Figure Reconsidered', in Russell, *Feminist Interpretation*, 73–85 (74).

[17] See, e.g., B. S. Childs, *Introduction to the Old Testament as Scripture* (Philadelphia: Fortress, 1979); and *Biblical Theology of the Old and New Testaments: Theological Reflection on the Christian Bible* (Minneapolis: Fortress, 1992).

the post-Reformation period in Europe about the relationship between Bible and Church, which tended to drive a wedge between the two. One casualty of that discussion in many quarters was any idea that 'canon' had much to do with good biblical interpretation. Free historical investigation of the Bible, unfettered by church tradition and theology, was to be the way ahead for right-thinking Bible readers. The canon, it was agreed, represented an imposition on the biblical literature by the Church. Childs, however, sets out to put canon back at the centre of biblical interpretation, by arguing that it is not in fact best understood as an arbitrary, late imposition on the biblical texts by religious authorities, alien to and distorting of the essence of the Bible. Canon is best understood as a complex historical process within ancient Israel, and then within the Church, which entailed the collecting, selecting and ordering of texts to serve a normative function as Scripture within the continuing religious community. It is intrinsically bound up with the biblical texts as we have them, and should be taken seriously by all those who study them. It is precisely the disregarding of this canonical shaping by modern historical-critical interpretation that has in large measure led to the inability of historical critics to relocate the text in any modern religious context. Childs' approach, on the other hand, while not wishing to bypass 200 years of critical research, demands that historical-critical tools be used to illuminate the canonical text as we have it, rather than for some other purpose.

A good example of his approach is his treatment of Genesis 22.1–19, the story of Abraham's near-sacrifice of Isaac. Beginning with source-, form- and redaction-critical readings, he moves on to examine the way in which the text has been shaped over a long period of time in such a way that it provides the reader and the community of readers with important guidance as to how it should finally be read. This leads him in turn to examine the NT's use of the story and the history of its exegesis in the pre-modern and Renaissance and Reformation periods, before turning to ask: how does one move, then, to theological reflection on both testaments? In just such a way does Childs try to take seriously all the history of critical scholarship that lies behind him, but also the witness of the text itself and the interpretation of the text through the ages, while insisting that the final reading must be a canonical one. In so doing, he does not so much offer fresh illumination of a text like Genesis as offer a framework in which many previously illuminating readings, whether pre-modern, modern or postmodern, can be brought together into fruitful conversation.

4

The world of Genesis: Locating
the text in its time and place

As the last two chapters illustrate, people have been reading the book of
Genesis for a very long time, and in all sorts of ways. As those who stand
now at the far end of the long line of readers throughout the ages, how ought
we to read it? I have already hinted at an answer to this question in the fore-
going, not least in my comments about what is illuminating in past reading.
Now I shall offer an explicit proposal, which begins with this suggestion:
that if the history of the reading of Genesis has taught us anything, it is that
the literal sense of the text is of primary importance in understanding
what the book has to say, and that this literal sense is intrinsically bound
up with the historical, social and religious context in which it first came
to be. Therefore, we must attempt to locate Genesis in its time and place.

Of course, in the case of a book like Genesis we are no doubt dealing
with an entity whose individual parts may well have 'come to be' at differing points over a very long time. Even in a modern period that has tended
towards scepticism with respect to the possibility that the written or oral
sources behind Genesis could have long pre-dated the period of the Israelite
monarchy, there has been general agreement until very recently that a
significant amount of this material does derive from well before the Exile.
Whether the scepticism about very old sources is even justified is an
interesting question, not least on the matter of whether the Moses to whom
the foundational Israelite tradition is attributed could have produced
it. Israelite tradition itself explicitly holds that Moses was literate (e.g.
Exod. 17.14), and there is nothing obviously anachronistic about this claim.
A Moses who was a product of the royal Egyptian nursery would have
been trained in the Egyptian scribal tradition, and would possibly have been
bilingual, growing up in a culture that was already producing literature,
including narrative literature.[1] It is not at all unreasonable, then, to believe
that written tradition, as well as oral tradition, could have existed in the
time of Moses and could have been transmitted to subsequent generations

---

[1] See further I. W. Provan, V. P. Long and T. Longman III, *A Biblical History of Israel* (2nd ed.;
Louisville: Westminster John Knox, 2015), ch. 3.

as the primary 'Israel tradition' that we find reflected in the Pentateuch. As Norman Whybray noted several decades ago, as he reflected on the question of the originating dates of written biblical sources in particular,

> no dates subsequent to the events described can be ruled out *a priori*: there was nothing in the circumstances of Israel at any period which would have made it impossible for narratives about past or contemporary events to be composed in writing.[2]

Be that as it may, it has certainly been the standard modern view (and one with which I concur) that the materials now found in our present book of Genesis were composed in and reflect different moments in Israel's past, and not just the moments in which the book was coming into its final form, which has usually been understood as occurring during the sixth century BC or shortly thereafter. It becomes theoretically possible, then, for the reader of Genesis to enquire into and discover the *various* historical, social and religious contexts in which *parts* of Genesis first came to be, and disciplines like source and form criticism were first designed precisely in order to accomplish this.

However, this is not how I intend to treat the question of historical, social and religious context. The reason is that I share the scepticism of others as to our ability to reconstruct with much objectivity either the documentary or oral sources lying behind Genesis, and in any case I am less interested in the sources that might lie behind the book than I am in the book itself. I suspect that I am among the majority of readers at least on this latter point, and probably nowadays on the former point as well. Instead, I am going to explore this larger question: suppose that (as seems likely) the Genesis tradition, albeit rooted in much earlier times, was receiving its final shape during the sixth and fifth centuries BC; what may we say about the historical, social and religious context, more narrowly or more widely conceived, that might illuminate what the book as a product of that time has to say? What may we say about 'the world of Genesis' – the world that the text both implies and also addresses, with all its redactional perspective, rhetorical device and narrative art?

Before the sixth century: old religion

Our story must necessarily begin (for reasons that will become clear) well before the sixth century BC. It begins when so-called 'complex societies'

---

[2] R. N. Whybray, *The Making of the Pentateuch: A Methodological Study* (JSOTSup 53; Sheffield: Sheffield Academic, 1987), 236.

arose in the ancient world – societies comprising cities of thousands, rather than just villages containing a few hundred, in which people occupied specialized roles (e.g. fisherman, potter, priest) rather than simply being (all of them) farmers.[3] These societies have left behind them voluminous archaeological evidence in the form of pyramids, temples and palaces, and graves and their contents, as well as written texts, so we know a considerable amount about what people back then thought and believed, as well as how they acted. This is so right from the appearance of the Bronze Age civilizations that arose in the fourth millennium BC in Mesopotamia and Egypt onwards. What do we learn from these Near Eastern civilizations about life and thought in ancient times?

We learn, first, that religion in such complex societies involved the worship of many gods and goddesses, often with a high god presupposed in the background. There were gods of sun and moon, and of love, and of many other aspects of existence besides. Indeed, these divinities were regarded throughout the ancient Near East as being thoroughly bound up with the various aspects of existence – astral bodies and natural forces (like storms) – rather than standing 'outside' the cosmos. They were woven into the very fabric of a cosmos that they themselves did not create and could certainly not ignore, being destined to certain tasks within the whole system.

These many gods were envisaged, second, as taking up earthly residence in temples within the emerging city-states, which were themselves thought to reflect the order of the cosmos. An ancient Near Eastern temple was primarily conceived of as the palace of a god within such a city-state. As such, it was a place designed primarily for the performance of rituals by a priestly class created for that purpose. A deity's presence in a temple was marked by an image or cult statue, in which the reality of the deity was embodied. The rituals enabled this image to function as a god, mediating worship from the people to the god and revelation from the god to the people. To keep the god happy as a result of the rituals was to ensure peace and prosperity for the city-state as a whole; but since it was difficult to know how, precisely, always to keep the god happy (at least in Mesopotamia), the Mesopotamian religious system was significantly marked by anxiety. The anxiety was less in Egypt only because the pharaoh was so closely identified with divinity (as we shall see in a moment) that people did not have to worry so much about what the gods were thinking. They already knew. It is important to note that the major temples in these ancient

---

[3] This section depends heavily on the longer account in my book *Convenient Myths: The Axial Age, Dark Green Religion, and the World That Never Was* (Waco: Baylor University Press, 2013), 97–105, to which the interested reader is further directed.

city-states were not designed for what modern people might call worship, involving many ordinary adherents of a religion. Ordinary people tended rather to worship their family and ancestral gods, who would be more likely to be interested in them (and might perhaps advocate for them to the great gods). These were the 'nearby' gods, possessing a temple or shrine in the neighbourhood. Uncertainty also plagued these more local forms of religion.

Crucial to these ancient societies, third, was kingship, regarded throughout the ancient Near East as a gift of the gods to human beings. Kings were believed to have been chosen by the gods and adopted as their sons, rising therefore to some level of divinity. In Egypt this level of divinity was particularly high: the pharaoh's acts were regarded as being the very acts of a god. It was the ancient Near Eastern king who above all communed with the gods and mediated the power of the gods to his city and beyond, discerning the divine will and putting it into practice, so as to ensure that there was order in that part of the cosmos over which he had control (his kingdom).

The shape of ancient society more generally, fourth, inevitably reflected the governing beliefs about the gods, city-states and temples, and kings. The cities in which the (at least) semi-divine kings ruled were regarded as primordial and built for the gods, and the temples were certainly also regarded as built for them. The gods were everything. Ordinary human beings, on the other hand, were almost nothing. This is reflected in our ancient Mesopotamian sources in particular, which consistently portray human beings in general as having been created to labour for the gods. In other words, humanity represented slave labour, created as a cosmic afterthought to meet the needs of deity. These ancient complex societies were, then, highly stratified, hierarchical societies – despotic societies – in which there was little inbuilt dynamic for change. The cosmos they reflected had been this way from the beginning, and it would continue to be this way in the future. Everything was structured to maintain order, with the despot-king at the apex of the societal pyramid.

All of this is what we see, in general terms (and allowing for variation), as we reach the Bronze Age in the ancient Near East. We also know something about similar ancient civilizations that emerged subsequently in other parts of the world: in the Indus Valley around 2600–2000 BC (the Harappan civilization), in China around 1800 BC (the Shang civilization) and in Greece. Some of the similarities probably have nothing to do with direct influence, but others probably do. Certainly the ancient Near East exerted a mighty influence upon Greece, for example, in such matters as art, literature and religion, and through Greece later upon Rome. The religious similarities, in particular, are so striking that Robert Parker can say that

Greek religion belongs to the class of ancient polytheisms: one can in very general terms compare the religions of Rome, of Egypt, of the ancient Indo-Iranians [i.e. the peoples who ultimately settled in what is now Iran, Pakistan and India], and most of the religions of the ancient Near East.[4]

It is this 'class of ancient polytheisms' that we may helpfully classify, for our purposes, as 'old religion'.

The sixth and fifth centuries: an age of revolt

The sixth and fifth centuries BC represent one of the most remarkable periods in human history. All across the ancient world we begin to see the rejection of 'old religion' and the embrace of new religious and philosophical outlooks that solidify eventually into what we now tend to call 'world religions'. In the West we find developments taking place in Greece that are highly significant for the future of Western culture: the rise of pre-Socratic philosophers such as Thales (624–546) and Pythagoras (582–496) in the sixth century, soon to be joined by others such as Heraclitus (535–475) and Parmenides (510–440), and then the great thinkers emerging out of Athens in the fifth and fourth centuries: Plato (427–347) and his student Aristotle (384–322). In the East, in China, the sixth century is the century of both Confucius (551–479) and also Lao-tse (probably a contemporary of Confucius), the founder of Daoism. Both men sought in the East something similar to what the Greek philosophers were seeking in the West: to define a way of life, rationalistically and humanistically, that was somewhat independent of the traditional beliefs about gods, spirits, and forces of nature.

This interest in ultimate reality behind all the particularities of things (and behind all the particular gods as well) finds expression also in India in the sixth and fifth centuries, which is one of the most formative periods for Hinduism and Buddhism, as well as Jainism. The Upanishads were being composed as the foundation of the Hindu perspective; Siddhartha Gautama (precise dates uncertain) was founding the first Buddhist community; and Mahavira (*c.*599–527) was walking the path to enlightenment as leader of the Jains. All three religions are interested in the same question as is being explored in Greece and in China in different ways: what is real and ultimately significant in the world, in the midst of the cycles of existence? The sixth and fifth centuries BC represent a profoundly significant moment,

---

[4] R. Parker, 'Greek Religion', in *Greece and the Hellenistic World* (ed. J. Boardman, J. Griffin and O. Murray; vol. 1 of *The Oxford History of the Classical World*; Oxford: Oxford University Press, 1988), 248–68 (248).

then, in human history, in which there emerged all over the ancient world new truth about reality beyond the truth of ancient myth.

It is this reality that led the German existentialist philosopher Karl Jaspers (1883–1969) to introduce to the world, in 1948, a thesis about the past that has become quite influential in some quarters. Jaspers proposed that the entire period from 800 until 200 BC (but especially the middle section of that timespan) could be conceived of as an 'axial age' – what he described as 'the most crucial turning point in history'.[5] It was the era during which the fundamental categories still employed in modern thinking were developed and in which 'world religions' began: rationality and practical experience were now set against myth, and religion became informed by ethics. Whatever the differences between the various revolts against 'old religion' during this 'axial age', the human condition was in the process transformed – there was an enlightenment. It is to this reality that modern cultures across the world (in China, India and the West) return again and again in order to renew themselves, recognizing as they do so that their fundamental concerns are the same. Indeed, this is precisely why Jaspers believes the 'axial age' to be so important, practically speaking, for modern people. It provides a basis for unity, for world peace – for a *new* 'axial age'.

I do not believe in Jaspers' 'axial age', for reasons I have articulated in a lengthy discourse elsewhere.[6] It is simply not possible to generalize, as Jaspers and indeed his followers and popularizers (like Karen Armstrong) have done, about 'the truth' underlying what are in fact the *very different* visions of reality being developed in the 'axial age'. All attempts to do so have only served to obscure the striking particularities of each vision, distorting each one in pursuit of an illusion. However, it cannot be denied that such visions (plural) were being developed; and this brings me to my proposal about how we should read Genesis against its ancient background.

As the elites among the Israelites sit in exile in Babylon in the first half of the sixth century, and as the Babylonian Empire is then taken over by the Persians (539–538 BC), and whether in Babylonia, or Persia, or back in Palestine, the Jewish people now sit in the vast Persian Empire throughout the remainder of sixth century and all the way through the fifth, it is the so-called 'axial age' in which they find themselves. The Persians themselves had already been grappling for some time in the preceding period with big questions about religion and society, and had arrived at their

---

[5] K. Jaspers, 'The Axial Age of Human History: A Base for the Unity of Mankind', *Commentary* 6 (1948): 430–5 (430).

[6] Provan, *Convenient Myths*, chs 1–3.

own 'axial age' solution, which we know as Zoroastrianism (named after its founding figure Zoroaster), which emerged out of eastern Iran in the centuries prior to its first appearance in recorded history in the mid-fifth-century BC work of the Greek historian Herodotus. Ultimately Zoroastrianism became the religion of the Persian Empire.

The best way in which to understand the book of Genesis, I propose, is to understand it as part of the distinctive 'axial age' response of Mosaic Yahwists to the kinds of questions we see arising in the sixth and fifth centuries all over the ancient world about 'old religion'. Specifically, it represents a response to such 'old religion' in its ancient Near Eastern forms (as we might well expect – it is not likely to be a direct response, e.g., to Hinduism!). This proposal does not imply that it is an entirely *fresh* response to ancient Near Eastern religion, out of line with the responses given by the ancestors of these final editors of Genesis. It is entirely reasonable to suppose that it represents, rather, the final development of a whole tradition of response by Mosaic Yahwists among the Israelites in the pre-exilic period – just as the Zoroastrianism of fifth-century Persia stands in continuity with a tradition that goes back at least three centuries beforehand.[7] Nevertheless, it is the sixth and fifth centuries that probably represent the historical, social and religious context for the final form of Genesis, as its authors wrestle with questions of faith and identity in a newly emerging world.

Mosaic Yahwism and the religion in the ancient Near East: a case study

How does this help us to read Genesis? Let us take the cosmology (a set of ideas about the nature of the cosmos) of Genesis 1 and 2 as an example, connecting with it in due course its anthropology. We all 'make something' of the world as we encounter it. How are we to understand the sun, for example? Is it a god? Are storms merely storms, or are we to see in them the activity of nature deities? The other peoples of the ancient Near East certainly 'made something' of the world. What did the authors of Genesis 1—2 believe?

They believed, first, that the 'heavens and the earth' (Genesis 1.1), that is, the cosmos, was *created* by *one personal* God. The other peoples of the

---

[7] For a helpful summary of the data relevant to the dating of Zoroastrianism, see S. Shaked, 'Zoroastrian Origins: Indian and Iranian connections', in *Axial Civilizations and World History* (JSRC 4; ed. J. P. Arnason, S. N. Eisenstadt and B. Wittrock; Leiden: Brill, 2005), 183–200 (183–9). Shaked himself opts for an eighth- or ninth-century date for Zoroaster.

ancient Near East certainly also believed that divinity was personal, but they believed in gods plural, rather than singular. And these gods did not create the cosmos, but came into being along *with* it, and embodied various aspects *of* it: the birth of the moon god coincides with the origin of the moon, for example. Divinity was made of the same 'stuff' as the remainder of the cosmos – there was continuity between divinity and nature – and played out its role in the cosmos *by way of* aspects of nature. In ancient Egypt, for example, the sky goddess Nut played out her role in the cosmos by *means* of the sky. In Genesis, however, *one personal* God *creates* the heavens, and everything in them (Gen. 1.1, 6–8, 14–19), and neither the heavens themselves nor anything in them is divine. In the same way God creates the *earth*, and all that is in it (Gen. 1.1, 9–13, 20–31), and nothing *there* is divine either.

Other peoples in the ancient world worshipped Hadad, the storm god known as 'Ba'al' in the OT, who was believed by Israel's close neighbours in the city of Ugarit in Syria to be the son of the high god El, and the consort of the goddess Anat. It was Hadad, they thought, who brought rain and thus fertility, enabling the agricultural cycle to continue. Genesis is also interested in nourishment for plants and animals; in growth, fertility and productivity; in water and agricultural cycles. But Genesis attributes all of these to one creator God, who creates the conditions in which life can arise, and who then oversees the functioning of the world to ensure that it flourishes. Genesis does not regard the earth itself as sharing in divinity.

The general way in which Genesis thus develops a cosmology that is very different from those of its neighbours clarifies particular aspects of the biblical text. In the ancient Near East, two of the objects in the sky – the sun and the moon – were especially significant. These were two of the most important gods in the pantheon, often named Shamash and Yarich respectively. The stars were widely held to control human destiny. In Genesis 1, significantly, the creation of these heavenly bodies is described at far greater length than anything else, except for the creation of human beings (Gen. 1.14–18). The authors spend time making clear that the heavenly bodies are merely 'lights' designed to be helpful to the creatures of the earth – and particularly to human beings, for whom they mark 'seasons and days and years' (Gen. 1.14). They even avoid the normal Hebrew words for sun and moon (*shemesh* and *yareach*), perhaps to make an especially clean break with the divine names Shamash and Yarich, which sound similar.

The word 'light', in turn, alerts us to another important aspect of the Genesis 1—2 creation account, for the Hebrew word used here is *ma'or*, most frequently used elsewhere in the Old Testament for the sanctuary light in the Tabernacle (the Israelites' portable temple prior to Solomon's time; e.g. Exod. 35.14, 28). This and other details of the text cumulatively make it clear that the cosmos is pictured in Genesis 1—2 as a temple – as sacred space. It may not be divine, but it *is* sacred. Temple-dedication ceremonies in the ancient Near East often lasted seven days; in Genesis 1 (along with the opening verses of Gen. 2) we have a six-day creative process completed by a seventh in which God comes to 'rest'. We are told of God's gathering of the waters into one place so that they could serve a useful purpose as seas (Gen. 1.9). This reflects the reality of the later Jerusalem Temple, within whose precincts there was a 'Sea of cast metal, circular in shape' (1 Kings 7.23–26). The garden in Eden in Genesis 2 – probably also a picture of the whole world, rather than a place within it – has its entrance on its east side (Gen. 3.24), just like the Jerusalem Temple. It is guarded by 'cherubim' – mysterious winged beings who appear elsewhere in the Old Testament only in connection with the Temple and the Tabernacle (e.g. Exod. 25.18–22; 26.1, 31; 1 Kings 6.23–28). And in Leviticus 26.11–12, we find God promising to walk among his people in the Tabernacle, just as Genesis 3.8 tells us he once walked among them in the garden. In sum, the Genesis creation account tells us that creation is God's temple-cosmos. Nothing created is divine, but creation *is* sacred space.

The cosmology then helps us to see more clearly the anthropology. What is a human being in Genesis 1—2? In the ancient Near East a deity's presence in his or her temple was typically marked by an 'image', in which the reality of the deity was thought to be embodied. Genesis 1.26–28 also knows of images of God in a temple, but they turn out to be human beings – all of them, male and female – who represent the one creator God in his temple-cosmos. Their vocation in Genesis 1 is to 'rule' and 'subdue' creation – language that echoes OT language elsewhere about kingship and military conquest. They are to exercise a kind of kingship over creation under God. The kingly care for the welfare of subjects and for justice for everyone that is also implied in these metaphors is mirrored, then, in the priestly language of Genesis 2, where the human vocation is defined in terms of 'earth-keeping'. Here the human being is placed in the garden by God 'to work it and take care of it' (Gen. 2.15) – the language of Numbers 3.7–8, when it describes the work of the priests in the Tabernacle.

The dominion given to human beings in Genesis 1—2, then, is not to be thought of in terms of *lording it over* the rest of creation, but in terms of just governance on behalf of the creator. The ruling king of Genesis 1 is at the same time the priestly servant of Genesis 2. Yet in this very transposition of the human being from being a servant of the image of God in a temple (the general ancient Near Eastern view) to *being* the image of God in *the* temple (i.e. the cosmos) something remarkable has happened in Israelite thinking when compared to the thinking of Israel's neighbours. Human beings are no longer fundamentally slave labour for the gods in a universe that operates fundamentally for the benefit of the gods. Humanity is not a cosmic afterthought designed to meet the needs of deity, including god-kings. Human beings are fundamentally the very images of God, all of them rulers and priests, placed in a cosmos fundamentally created *for them* and for the other creatures they are to look after.

Conclusion

There is much more that could be said about how the historical, social and religious context out of which Genesis emerged illuminates its cosmology and anthropology, as indeed every other aspect of the book; but this is not the place for that demonstration.[8] Enough has been said to make the point. If the literal sense of the text is of primary importance in under standing what the book of Genesis has to say, then that literal sense is intrinsically bound up with the historical, social and religious context in which the book first came to be, which I am taking to be the 'axial age' of the sixth and fifth centuries BC. This is 'the world of Genesis' that the text both implies and also addresses, with all its redactional perspective, rhetorical device and narrative art, as its authors offer a distinctive Mosaic Yahwist response to the 'old religion' of the ancient Near East, developing the very similar responses of their ancestors. It is the text of Genesis as literally understood in this context that can then be compared helpfully with other texts by way of structuralist reading strategies, further clarified by the insights of feminist and social scientific critics, and finally read in the context of the whole canon of Scripture and in relation to tradition by those who have either a scholarly interest, or a religious interest, or both, in doing so.

---

[8] Interested readers should read my book *Seriously Dangerous Religion: What the Old Testament Really Says and Why It Matters* (Waco: Baylor University Press, 2014). This book offers an OT theology that is organized around the big questions that religion and philosophy have always tried to answer, comparing and contrasting the OT answers (especially in Genesis) to those offered by 'old religion' and its successors, then by 'axial age' religions and their successors, and finally by more recent thinkers.

5

Creation: Genesis 1.1—2.25

In Chapters 1–4 we considered larger-scale questions about the interpretation of Genesis, both historically and in the present. In the remainder
of the book we shall give more focused attention to each of the 'Acts' of
the Genesis drama in turn, offering a close reading of the text, highlight-
ing key interpretative issues, and weaving in (selectively) consideration of
how that section of Genesis has been read historically. We begin with a
closer look at Genesis 1 and 2.

Two creation stories?

In the structure of Genesis as delineated by the *toledot* formulae described
in our Chapter 1, Genesis 1 and 2 are not part of the same section of the
book; Genesis 1.1—2.3 represent Act 1, and the remainder of Genesis 2
is part of Act 2. However, it makes good sense to think about Genesis 1 and
2 together, since both concern the creation of the world in general and of
humanity in particular, and the chapters' relationship to one another has
long been a matter of discussion. In the modern period it has become customary to refer to them as 'two creation accounts', a distinction reinforced
by the source-critical idea that Genesis 2.4b–25 originally came from the
source J and Genesis 1.1—2.4a originally from the source P. In justification
of this source division it is often said that the P account is different in
literary structure and style from J (P is liturgical in style, describing seven
days of orderly development, whereas J gives us a much more straightforward narrative); different in emphasis and indeed theology (P portrays
a transcendent God, one step removed from his creation and creating
through words, whereas in J God is 'hands on' in creation, fashioning much
like a potter, or a smith, or a farmer); and different in its choice of language
(P knows God as Elohim, and uses the verb *bara'* of God's creating; J knows
God as *Yahweh* Elohim, and uses different verbs like *yatsar*).

This division of sources in the middle of Genesis 2.4 builds on a more
ancient idea that verse 4a is more a postscript to what precedes than it is
a superscript to what follows. This ancient proposal is, however, implausible,
because all the other *toledot* formulae in Genesis *precede* the material to

which they refer. The source division is also implausible. It is forced on source critics, precisely because Genesis 2.4a employs *'elohim* and *bara'*, while Genesis 2.4b employs *yhwh 'elohim*. Therefore, the first part of the verse 'must' belong to P and the second 'must' belong to J. Yet the whole verse 'works' well as it stands, as a chiastic structure (in the Hebrew word order, heavens–earth–created/made–earth–heavens) picking up both the key verbs used earlier in Genesis 1 of God's creating (*bara'*, 'create', and *'asah*, 'make'). There is no 'problem' with Genesis 2.4, then, to which the source-critical theory is a necessary solution. The whole verse is a carefully and coherently crafted introduction to what follows in Genesis 2, consciously picking up the language of the preceding Genesis 1. This conclusion causes one in turn to question the source-critical approach to Genesis 1—2 more generally, because it suggests that language selection (especially with respect to names for God) is not a safe indicator of source division in these chapters. One author (it seems) can use both *yhwh 'elohim* and *'elohim*. This kind of variation in names for God by one author is indeed paralleled elsewhere in the OT. The book of Jonah is one good example (cf. Jonah 1.1, 3–4, 9–10, 14–15 with 3.5, 8–10; 4.2, 6–9).

Is there, perhaps, another way of accounting for the (remaining) differences between Genesis 1 and 2 than by positing the combination of originally separate written sources? What if a *single* author, wishing to emphasize God's transcendence before anything else, hit on the idea of a liturgical-style prologue to the whole book that described creation through God's words, before relaxing into a more typical narrative style and allowing God's creation (as it were) to be considered in more anthropomorphic terms? There is certainly no difficulty in imagining why an author writing against the historical, social and religious background described in our Chapter 4 should wish to proceed in this way. The peoples of the ancient Near East were familiar with personal, immanent gods. They were not familiar with a personal, transcendent One. That was what needed to be emphasized, first and foremost.

Whatever the truth of the process by which Genesis 1—2 came into their current form, they certainly do not sit on the page *now* as two creation stories. They exist now as one entity, albeit looking at creation from slightly differing perspectives. Genesis 1.1—2.3 describe creation as a sequence of steps that rise to an apex in the creation of humanity; everything else prepares the way for human beings. Genesis 2.4–25, on the other hand, describe creation as something that cannot function properly without human beings; it is only when there is a gardener, placed by God in the garden, that there can be such things (for example) as shrubs and plants. That is, in Genesis

2.4–25 all things wait for a human (*'adam*) to work the ground (*'adamah*); in Genesis 1.1—2.3, all things are made ready in advance *for* humanity.

One aspect of Genesis 1—2 that becomes clear at this point is that, although we are meant to read Genesis 2.4–25 in the light of Genesis 1.1—2.3, *within* each section chronology is evidently not an important concern of the author. The major concern is to emphasize the importance of human beings in relation to non-human creation, which is both 'there' for humanity, and yet non-functioning unless humanity is there. The order of 'events' in creation is *not* an important concern. This is why shrubs and plants 'precede' humanity in Genesis 1.11–12 (cf. 1.29–30), whereas in Genesis 2.4–7 there must be a gardener before there can be shrubs and plants. This is also why the animals in Genesis 2.19 are created after humanity (notwithstanding the ill-advised pluperfect of some English translations – 'the LORD God *had* formed out of the ground all the beasts of the field'), whereas in Genesis 1 they appear beforehand (1.24–25). Origen already noted long ago the difficulty of reading Genesis 1 in particular in strictly chronological terms: 'Who that has understanding', he asked, 'will suppose that the first, and second, and third day, and the evening and the morning, existed without a sun, and moon, and stars? And that the first day was, as it were, also without a sky?'[1] Neither Genesis 1 nor Genesis 2 is best read as if this kind of ordering of events were important.

The structure of the Prologue (Gen. 1.1—2.3)

If each section of Genesis, as demarcated by the *toledot* formulae, is somewhat like an act within a play, Act 1 functions somewhat like a prologue to the whole story, which we may break down structurally as involving six days of creation preceded by an introduction and followed by a conclusion:

Genesis 1.1–2	Introduction: the beginning of creation
Genesis 1.3–5	Day 1: the creation of light
Genesis 1.6–8	Day 2: the creation of heaven
Genesis 1.9–13	Day 3: the creation of earth and seas, and of vegetation, plants and trees
Genesis 1.14–19	Day 4: the creation of sun, moon and stars
Genesis 1.20–23	Day 5: the creation of sea creatures and birds
Genesis 1.24–31	Day 6: the creation of land creatures – cattle, creeping things and beasts, and also human beings
Genesis 2.1–2	Conclusion: the ending of creation

---

[1] Origen, *On First Principles* 4.1.16 (ANF 10:325).

Each of the first six days begins with God speaking, and together they form two parallel groups of three (days one to three and days four to six). The introduction that precedes these six days describes the state of the earth before creation as being *tohu wavohu*; that is, 'formless and empty'. During the first three days God deals with the first 'problem' (formlessness) by giving the cosmos a particular structure and shape, in which light is separated from darkness, the heavens from the earth, and the earth from the seas. The earth is also given the capacity to produce plants. In other words, it is made habitable. During the second set of three days, God deals with the second 'problem' (emptiness), providing inhabitants for each of the spheres he has created – luminaries for the heavens, birds and sea creatures for air and the seas, and land creatures for the earth. Each of the six days is replete with repeated phraseology: 'and God said', 'let there be', 'and so God made' and 'God saw that it was good'. It is this that gives Genesis 1.1—2.3 the liturgical 'feel' noted above. The days are not identical, however. Most notably, we find an increasing number of words being used as we move along through each set of three days, which makes it clear that the emphasis in giving 'form' to the cosmos lies on the creation of earth and seas (and of vegetation, plants and trees) on day three, and that the emphasis in 'filling' the cosmos lies on the creation of land creatures on day six (most especially human beings). As God 'speaks' creation into being in this way, so also his 'resting' involves cessation of speech; no words are spoken on the seventh day.

Selected issues of interpretation in the Prologue

Translations of the beginning to the Prologue often begin something like this: 'In the beginning God created the heavens and the earth. Now the earth . . .' (e.g. New International Version (NIV) of Gen. 1.1–2). It is possible, however, to translate in this alternative way: 'When God began to create the heavens and the earth, the earth . . .' (e.g. New Revised Standard Version (NRSV) footnote). At issue is the proper rendering of the first Hebrew word *bere'shit*, which gives us our most widely used Hebrew title for the book.[2] The syntax here is awkward, because the vowels provided to go along with the consonants do not furnish us with the definite article that we would expect in light of the following indicative verb *bara'* ('he created'). The larger interpretative question, whichever way we render *bere'shit bara'*,

---

[2] The English title of the book (Genesis) comes from the Latin transliteration of the word by which it was known to the Greek-speaking Jews of Alexandria.

is whether Genesis 1.2 already describes one of the creative acts of God introduced in verse 1, or whether it describes what was already there *before* God began. This is not best considered as a question about the ultimate origins of the cosmos – whether God, in the OT worldview, once created everything out of nothing (*ex nihilo*). The question is more focused than that. In the mind of the author, does Genesis 1.2 describe realities that existed (however they got there) before the creative acts of God that produced the inhabitable world as we know it? The answer to this question appears to be 'yes' (an answer already provided by pre-modern exegetes like Ibn Ezra).[3] Before God acted to change this reality, the world was a chaotic, uncivilized place. It was like a desolate, desert land (Hb. *tohu wavohu*), and it was like a dark, deep ocean (Hb. *tehom*), neither of which can sustain human life (or indeed various other kinds of life).[4] God is not said to create such entities in Genesis 1 – they are simply 'there', as the story of creation begins. The waters, in particular, sit there under the supervision of the Spirit of God that hovers like a bird overlooking the scene.

The contrast here is very great with ancient Near Eastern texts like the Mesopotamian *Enuma elish*, which tells of a great battle between the god Marduk and the dragon sea-goddess Tiamat prior to the emergence of our present reality.[5] There is no such battle in Genesis 1. The primal waters, sitting in darkness, simply wait in a docile manner to be organized into useful entities by God. This is what actually happens in Genesis 1.6–10. The waters become the rains and the oceans. The darkness, in verses 3–5, becomes night. The basic rhythms of time are in this way put in place.

The creation that thus begins to emerge is described as 'good' in Genesis 1 (Gen. 1.4, 9, 12, 18, 21, 25) and ultimately as 'very good' (1.31). This 'good' has sometimes been interpreted as 'perfect',[6] that is, as lacking in everything that we might think of as 'evil', including suffering.[7] This is, however, to read a considerable amount into the language of goodness, and it is almost certainly an error. In Genesis 1 itself we read that human

---

[3] He understood the biblical creation story as teaching 'the orderly transformation of preexistent matter into an environment suitable for human life'. N. Seidman, 'Translation', in *Reading Genesis: Ten Methods* (ed. R. Hendel; Cambridge: Cambridge University Press, 2010), 157–75 (165).

[4] Deut. 32.10; Isa. 34.11; Jer. 4.23; Ezek. 26.19–20; Job 6.18.

[5] See 'The Creation Epic', in *ANET*, 60–72.

[6] So, e.g., Wenham states that 'the refrain "And God saw that it was good" and the concluding statement "God saw all that he had made that it was really very good" bring out the perfection of creation.' G. J. Wenham, *Genesis 1–15* (WBC; Dallas: Word, 1987), 38.

[7] So, e.g., Calvin: 'For it appears that all the evils of the present life, which experience proves to be innumerable, have proceeded from the same fountain [i.e. the embrace of evil by human beings in the Fall]. The inclemency of the air, frost, thunders, unseasonable rains, drought, hail, and whatever is disorderly in the world, are the fruits of sin. Nor is there any other primary cause of diseases.' Calvin, *Genesis*, 1:177.

beings are tasked as God's image-bearers with ruling and subduing creation. This implies that there are already forces in God's good world that *require* being ruled and subdued. Goodness does not imply, then, a kind of static perfection such that there is no work to be done in the world – no effort or progress to be made. It does not necessarily imply, either, the absence of what modern people sometimes refer to as 'natural evil'.[8] We must be careful at this point not to fill biblical notions of 'good' with our own content, but rather to pay attention to what the biblical authors themselves meant and did not mean by such a term.

Human beings

Human beings, in this Prologue to the book of Genesis, are some of the land animals that God has made; they share the same day of creation. This commonality between humanity and the other creatures will be underlined in Genesis 2.18, where a search is made among the latter to see if any non-human creature is suitable as the kind of soulmate the human being requires. It is at least conceivable that this might be so, precisely because the other creatures are *like* humans in being 'living creatures' (*nefesh chayyah*, 2.7 and 2.19) who derive from the ground (*'adamah*, 2.7 and 2.19). At the same time, humans in both Genesis 1 and 2 are of a *different* order from God's other creatures. In Genesis 1, this is first intimated in the unparalleled language of verse 26, 'let us make man . . .' Whereas in verse 24 it is the earth itself that brings forth creatures, here it is specifically God, along with some 'others' who are not further identified. This has led to much speculation in the reading tradition, and to some concern, especially among ancient Jews concerned about the possible implication that divinity might be plural. Christians, more comfortable with notions of plurality in God, have seen the plural as a reference to Father and Son, or indeed to all three Persons of the Holy Trinity.[9] This is probably not what the original author meant, since there is no other explicit evidence of belief in a Trinity in OT times, nor in an eternal Son of God, but it is certainly a legitimate construal of the mysterious plural of Genesis 1.26 from the perspective of a Christian canonical reading, understanding the whole biblical story in the light of the way in which it concludes.

If we look within Genesis 1 itself for clues about the meaning of this plural, the most obvious 'other' in the 'us' is perhaps the Spirit of God

---

[8] For a more extensive discussion, see I. W. Provan, *Seriously Dangerous Religion: What the Old Testament Really Says and Why It Matters* (Waco: Baylor University Press, 2014), chs 5 and 9.

[9] So Augustine, *On the Trinity* 12.6.6, in *On the Trinity: Books 8–15* (CTHP; ed. G. B. Matthews; trans. S. McKenna; Cambridge: Cambridge University Press, 2002), 86.

mentioned in verse 2. Then again, Philo and many subsequent Jewish commentators consider the 'others' to be angels. God is addressing the members of his heavenly court (cf., e.g., Isa. 6.8; Job 1), deliberating with them as one might with a small child ('let's do this') rather than co-creating with them. Finally, some commentators have suggested that there are, really, no 'others', and that 'let us' is simply a conventional way of speaking that is analogous to 'the royal we' – a plural of majesty or even of self-encouragement (cf. Gen. 11.7, 'let us go down'), just as a human being might 'address' his or her soul (cf. Ps. 116.7).[10]

The image and likeness of God

The special status of human beings is further indicated in Genesis 1 by the fact that they are said to be created in the 'image' (*tselem*) and 'likeness' (*demut*) of God. They are made to resemble God in certain ways, and they are also created to represent God in certain ways – as described in Genesis 1.26 and 28, where they are to 'rule' (*radah*) and 'subdue' (*kavash*) creation. Both the ontological and functional aspects of the metaphor have been much discussed throughout the history of biblical interpretation. Ontologically, ancient Christian exegesis from Irenaeus onwards (*c.* AD 180) tended to interpret the image and the likeness as two distinct aspects of humanness. The image referred to natural qualities like reason, and the likeness to supernatural graces.[11] This approach, however, requires us to depart from the old Jewish wisdom about the Bible being literature that has been written in 'normal' language, because it seems clear that 'according to our likeness' is in fact an explanatory gloss on 'in our image', and that both are ways of saying the same thing. Much effort has then been invested in proposals about specific human qualities to which image and likeness together are meant to refer – aspects of personhood that humans share with the creator (and perhaps with the angels), but not with the rest of creation. Reason, personality, free will, self-consciousness and intelligence have all been suggested (among other possibilities), with the first of these being the most popular,[12] although some interpreters of Genesis 1 have avoided discussion of the image entirely out of religious

---

[10] This is the kind of explanation preferred, e.g., by S. R. Driver, who thinks of the plural as referring to 'the fullness of attributes and powers conceived as united within the Godhead' (cited in Wenham, *Genesis 1–15*, 28).

[11] Note, e.g., Origen, *On First Principles* 3.6.1 (*ANF* 10:262–3).

[12] E.g. Maimonides, *The Guide for the Perplexed* 1.2 (trans. M. Friedlander; 2nd ed.; New York: Dover, 1904), 15 (similarly to Philo), takes Adam as created 'in the image of God' as referring to the creation of the human intellect, through the development of which one can achieve communion with God.

sensibility. Josephus falls into this latter category; he 'omits the reference to the *imago dei* because he regards nothing created as capable of being the direct image of God'.[13]

As to the question of *function*, it has often been noted that the language of 'ruling' and 'subduing' is that of kingship in the OT and, further, that this language suggests fairly aggressive behaviour by the king. In modern times, in fact, the notion of aggressive human dominion over nature that arises out of the Genesis text has been much blamed for human depredations in respect of the rest of creation. This critique is in some respects justified; Genesis 1 has indeed been read by some as justifying a rapacious approach to the world in which we live.[14] At the same time, however, it should be remembered that among the duties of kings in the ancient Near East was that of looking after the welfare of their subjects – a theme that comes out very clearly in the OT itself (e.g. in Ps. 72) – and that certainly in the OT, in particular, human kingship is always understood as rightly exercised only under God who is King. Properly exercised royal power in the OT is not absolute and unfettered power that can be deployed just in any way that the king desires. The function of the human image-bearers of God in Genesis 1, likewise, is not to exercise autonomous dominion over other creatures, but to exercise this dominion under God and as representatives of God.

Genesis 2 will shortly develop the understanding of the human vocation in terms of a priestly care for God's garden, and Genesis 6—9 will portray the righteous Noah as the first great conservationist of history. The wording of Genesis 2.15 is particularly significant in this context: 'The LORD God took the man and put him in the Garden of Eden to work it and take care of it' – literally, to 'serve it and keep/guard it' (Hb. *'avad* and *shamar*). This is religious language, which underlines the importance and sacred nature of the task. We should note here in particular Numbers 3.7–8, where the same vocabulary is used of the priests performing duties (*shamar*) and doing the work (*'avad*) in the Tabernacle (see further our Chapter 4 above).

---

[13] J. R. Levison, *Portraits of Adam in Early Judaism: From Sirach to 2 Baruch* (JSPSup 1; Sheffield: University of Sheffield Press, 1988), 147. There has also been significant modern criticism of the tendency 'to identify the image of God with that which separates human beings from other forms.' T. W. Jennings, 'Theological Anthropology and the Human Genome Project', in *Adam, Eve, and the Genome* (TSC; ed. S. B. Thistlethwaite; Minneapolis: Fortress, 2003), 93–111 (109).

[14] E.g. L. White, 'The Historical Roots of Our Ecologic Crisis', *Science* 155 (1967): 1203–7. This essay is reproduced in *Western Man and Environmental Ethics* (ed. I. G. Barbour; Reading: Addison-Wesley, 1973), 18–30. For a response, see I. W. Provan, 'The Land Is Mine and You Are Only Tenants: Earth-Keeping and People-Keeping in the Old Testament', in *Many Heavens, One Earth: Readings on Religion and the Environment* (ed. C. C. Cain; Lanham, MD: Lexington, 2012), 33–50.

The completion of creation

Finally, the seventh day in the Prologue is especially interesting, because we are told here that God 'blesses' it and makes it 'holy'. What does it mean to bless a day? The implication, in the light of the blessing language in Genesis 1.22, 28 (where blessing is closely tied to fruitfulness and multiplication) is that the seventh day is designed to be productive in its own way, independent of human effort. Those who observe the Sabbath day as 'holy' (and thus as separate from the other six days) will enjoy divine blessing in their lives, simply in the act of observing it.

The ordered, very good creation of God is celebrated already in other biblical texts like Psalms 8 and 104, and celebration of creation has remained an important theme in the interpretative tradition down through the ages, not least at the time of the Reformation, when sermons about creation abounded, marvellous natural phenomena were much depicted, and natural histories much published:

> Not only did the splendor and beauty of the natural world give evidence of their divine creator but also every natural object, from heavenly bodies to animals to plants, had multiple moral and symbolic meanings attached to it. The book of nature, like Scripture, had emanated from the word of God.[15]

It was indeed such convictions about divinely ordained order in the cosmos that created the conditions in which modern Western science arose and flourished,[16] such that an early scientist like Johannes Kepler could make his famous comment, 'I was merely thinking God's thoughts after him.' The scientific developments of the succeeding centuries have, of course, caused significant reflection among biblical interpreters as to how far Genesis 1.1—2.3 should itself be read as science,[17] with the great majority concluding along with John Calvin (cf. our Chapter 3 above) that it should not – that it speaks to philosophical matters such as the nature of God, the world and the human person, rather than to the matters of physics, chemistry and biology that so interest modern scientists.

---

[15] K. M. Crowther, *Adam and Eve in the Protestant Reformation* (Cambridge: Cambridge University Press, 2010), 8. She cites as one example H. H. Frey's *Biblical Animal Book* (1595): 'For each animal, Frey assembles passages from the Bible and from various theological writings that refer to the particular creature' (212).

[16] M. B. Foster, 'The Christian Doctrine of Creation and the Rise of Modern Natural Science', *Mind* 43 (1934): 446–68.

[17] For one 'snapshot' of the progress of the conversation, see J. H. Brooke, 'Samuel Wilberforce, Thomas Huxley, and Genesis', in *The Oxford Handbook of Reception History of the Bible* (ed. M. Lieb, E. Mason, J. Roberts and C. Rowland; Oxford: Oxford University Press, 2011), 397–412.

Selected issues of interpretation in Genesis 2.4–25

If Genesis 1.1—2.3 describe creation as a sequence of steps that rise to an apex in the creation of humanity, Genesis 2.4–25 now describe it from a different point of view: human beings represent the indispensable centre point of creation, without which it cannot properly function. Here shrubs and plants cannot exist because (among other things) there is not yet a 'man to work the ground' (2.5), and other animals cannot exist because there is no human being to name them, thereby giving them functions and indeed causing them to 'be' (2.19–20). The remainder of creation comes into existence, then, with a proto-human already crucially function-ing at its centre. I say proto-human, because before we get to Genesis 2.22–25 we do not even have a male and a female, which together make up the image of God in Genesis 1. Before that point, we have not yet arrived at the blessed state of 'very good' that Genesis 1.31 describes. Genesis 2.18 is explicit about this: 'It is *not good* for the man to be alone.' The creation of humanity is not yet complete. And this raises our first issue of interpretation in Genesis 2.4–25. What exactly *is* the being that God forms from the dust of the ground in Genesis 2.7?

In the Hebrew it is *ha'adam*, the creature that comes from the ground (*ha'adamah*). In many translations (such as the NIV) this is translated as 'man', but this translation has the potential to mislead, for it might be read as implying 'male'. Since it is only with Genesis 2.25 that we have gender differentiation and that it even becomes possible to refer to 'a man' (*'adam*) and 'his wife', it seems wiser to avoid the word 'man' until that point and to translate *'adam* earlier in the chapter as 'earthling' (capturing the play on *'adam* and *'adamah* in the Hb.). It is only with the naming of the woman as 'Eve' in Genesis 3.20 that it becomes sensible then to go further and to translate *'adam* as a personal name, Adam. English translations actually display quite a bit of variation on this point, as they struggle with the dif-ferent senses of *'adam* throughout Genesis 2 and 3. The NIV begins to use 'Adam' in Genesis 2.20 when the *animals* are first named, but strangely does not employ it again until Genesis 3.17 and then in Genesis 3.20. The NRSV, on the other hand, does not use Adam at all until Genesis 4.25. The old King James Version (KJV) uses it in Genesis 2.19–21, 23; 3.8–9, 17.[18]

As in Genesis 1.2, so in Genesis 2.4–7 the primeval waters are already in existence as God's creative acts get going; they water 'the whole surface

---

[18] I am indebted here to P. Trible in *God and the Rhetoric of Sexuality* (OBT 2; Philadelphia: Fortress, 1978), ch. 4.

of the ground'. Without human beings to organize irrigation, however – and without rain – nothing more can happen.[19] The cycles of nature, therefore, are delayed here until the crucial figure is in place who can make *use* of both rain and groundwater in order to grow the garden and to keep it orderly and under control. The earthling who is then created, it should be noted, is a 'living being' (*nefesh chayyah*, Gen. 2.7) – not a soul placed in a body, but a body-with-a-soul. Hebrew anthropology comes at human beings from various perspectives: it can speak of the *ruach* (spirit), when thinking of psychic life; the *nefesh* (soul), when thinking of life more generally, or about desire; the *lev* (heart), when thinking of the intellect; and entities like the kidneys or bowels, when describing deep emotion. However, the human being is not viewed as a collection of parts. The whole person is seen in the part described, considered from that particular point of view.[20]

The garden in Eden

The garden in which this human gardener is placed, located in 'Eden', is described in Genesis 2.8–14. It is said to be 'in the east', which implies initially that it is geographically located in Mesopotamia (from an Israelite point of view). However, as one reads the Genesis story we discover that human beings only end up in Mesopotamia as the result of eastward migration from their starting point (Gen. 3.24; 4.16; 11.2). If Eden is in the east, then it certainly appears to be further west than Babylon. Many have speculated about its location, and some have set out in search of it. Basil of Caesarea used it to account for the fact that ancient Christians prayed facing towards the east.[21] But is it really a specific place in the world at all? Reading Genesis 1 and 2 together certainly raises that question in the reader's mind.

Genesis 1 outlines a human vocation that involves dominion over the whole earth, and already describes the creation of trees in that global context (1.11–12, 29), as well as the creation of beasts and birds and indeed

---

[19] This mirrors the reality in ancient Mesopotamia, where the annual floodwaters of the Tigris and Euphrates rivers were not necessarily helpful and indeed could be destructive unless they could be 'managed' (i.e. 'ruled' and 'subdued') by humans.

[20] H. W. Wolff, *Anthropology of the Old Testament* (London: SCM, 2011).

[21] Basil, *On the Holy Spirit* 27.66 (trans. D. Anderson; Crestwood, NY: St Vladimir's Seminary Press, 1980), 100. Already 'during the Renaissance . . . Paradise had become a geographical reality . . . [a]nd its location became in principle discoverable.' P. C. Almond, *Adam and Eve in Seventeenth-Century Thought* (Cambridge: Cambridge University Press, 1999), 70. In the seventeenth century, some still held to an earlier view, articulated by Tertullian, that Eden was to be found in the Antipodes or beneath the equator (Almond, *Adam and Eve*, 72).

of female humans as well as male humans. Genesis 2 repeats all of this in the context of the garden. A natural implication of this is that the garden is actually co-extensive with the whole earth. In fact, if the garden is not the whole earth, it is unclear in the story how the whole earth will ever be populated and governed by human beings in line with the instruction in Genesis 1.28, unless they embrace evil; for the human pair only actually leave the garden in Genesis 3.23 as a *result* of their embrace of evil. Is their sin, then, a prerequisite for the fulfilling of the creation mandate? This does not appear to be a very plausible interpretation of the story. More probably, the garden in Eden is not so much a particular *place* in the world, but a *state of being* in the world.[22] Eden represents the world as it is when there is harmony between God and his creatures. This is in line with the comments in our Chapter 4 above concerning the garden as an archetypal sanctuary.

Many of the motifs of Eden in the book of Genesis are in fact those of the divine dwelling described in Mesopotamian and Canaanite myth, including the source of subterranean life-giving waters that supply the whole earth, abundant fertility, and trees possessing supernatural qualities and great beauty. Consider, for example, the trees on 'the cedar mountain, the dwelling of the gods' mentioned in the Gilgamesh Epic, which are said to be luxuriant. No mortal is intended to enter there. The land of Dilmun, the most celebrated example of the garden of the gods in Mesopotamian literature, is described in the Sumerian myth called *Enki and Ninhursag*. That land is watered by 'waters of abundance' from the earth, which gush forth to fertilize it. In Ugaritic myth, the high god El dwells 'at the source of the double river, midst the upspringings of the deeps'. The divine council meets in this place, and decrees of cosmic importance are issued there. It is to this place that Yamm sends messengers demanding the surrender of Ba'al. Also, both Anat and Asherah go to El's dwelling to seek permission for the building of a temple for Ba'al. It is in this divine garden, variously conceived, that the sexual union of the deities occurs; the marriage of Enki and Ninhursag takes place in Dilmun, and in the Ugaritic Ba'al cycle El anticipates some sexual activity on the occasion of a visit from his consort Asherah, only to discover that she has come for other reasons.[23]

---

[22] Such an understanding is already implied in the Vulgate translation of Gen. 2.8, which does not mention 'the east', but only 'a paradise of pleasure from the beginning', and it is represented throughout the subsequent interpretative tradition. E.g. 'Oliver Cromwell's chaplain, Peter Sterry . . . believed that Paradise had been in the midst of man and had not so much been lost or ruined as hid beneath the besmirched image of God.' Almond, *Adam and Eve*, 66.

[23] For access to these various ancient Near Eastern texts, see 'The Epic of Gilgamesh' (*ANET*, 27–98), 'Enki and Ninhursag: A Paradise Myth' (*ANET*, 37–41), and 'The Balu Myth' (*COS* 1.86:242–83).

The description of the garden in Eden in Genesis 2.4–25, and on into chapter 3, contains many of these same motifs, although the story is a distinctively biblical story. Thus mortal beings are not only *allowed* in the Genesis garden but are *intrinsic* to the place, and sexual union is restricted to the *images* of the deity, and does not take place *within the divine* itself. Yet it is also the fact that we have a distinctive Israelite version of an older story that underlines the probability that Eden is 'the world', since the dwelling of God in biblical thinking is not a single country or temple. It is the entire world.[24]

Eden lost and found

The beauty of the world as first created by God, and in particular the beauty of its first human beings, is much commented upon in the interpretative tradition. Philo holds Adam to have been a perfect creature, and other strands of Jewish tradition agree, stating that it was only with his later sin that he lost some of his splendour, each subsequent generation losing still more.[25] This same emphasis on the original beauty of the human form is developed in much later art in the West. Adam and Eve have been represented by such notables as Michelangelo (*The Creation of Adam*, 1511), Titian (*Fall*, 1570), and Dürer, whose fascination with the perfect human form is patent in his *Adam and Eve* (1504), in which the primal couple appear in nearly symmetrical, idealized poses. Dürer has in fact left us written reflections on his artistic theory relating to such matters: his *Underweysung der Messung* (*Manual of Measurement*, 1525), and *Vier Bücher von menschlichen Proportion* (*Four Books of Human Proportion*, 1528).[26] Adam and Eve have also been represented by other Flemish, Dutch and German masters, including the brothers Van Eyck and Lucas Cranach, as well as by Blake, Chagall, Rodin and Epstein.

Beyond the human figures that live within it, Eden has haunted Western literature and thought throughout the generations, inspiring music, art

---

[24] The idea that Eden is the whole world already shows up in such early authors as Philo, Clement of Alexandria and Hugh of St Victor, as well as in Luther's *Table Talk* (Almond, *Adam and Eve*, 74–5).

[25] Philo, *On the Creation*, 47.136–41; *Gen. Rab.* 11.2, 12.6, in *Midrash Rabbah* (ed. M. Simon; trans. H. Freedman; 3rd ed.; 10 vols; London: Soncino, 1983), 1:81, 91–2; *b. Bat.* 58a, in *The Babylonian Talmud* (ed. I. Epstein; 18 vols; London: Soncino, 1935–48), 11:233.

[26] 'Sixteenth-century artists and writers displayed considerable interest in the physical nature of the first human beings and how their bodies were changed by the Fall. They saw the body as both a real physical entity and a symbol of the spiritual state' (Crowther, *Adam and Eve*, 6, with various examples following throughout Chapter 2, as she examines 'representations of the creation and fall of Adam and Eve in paintings and printed images, sermons, plays, poems, and medical and anatomical texts').

and literature that wistfully notes its loss and (or) advocates its retrieval –
whether in the present or in future time. In Joni Mitchell's famous song
about Woodstock (1970), it is a place we've got to get back to, because
that is where we really belong. In Dante's *Divine Comedy*, however, it may
only be found atop Mount Purgatory.[27] Its loss is alluded to in Shakespeare's
Hamlet, where it is choked by weeds and governed by the serpent Claudius,
who has taken his father's crown;[28] in many of the poets of the First World
War period;[29] and in Golding's *Lord of the Flies*, where paradise is spoiled by
young but corrupt humans.[30] Its retrieval is anticipated in the early modern
notion that the development of the sciences would 'restore that which had
been damaged in the Fall, and . . . return the earth to its primevally perfect
state'.[31] Francis Bacon (1561–1626), for example,

> shared the hope of alchemists and magical writers, that the abundance of
> Eden might be recreated on earth, in Bacon's case by experiment, mechan-
> ical skill, and intense cooperative effort . . . Labour, the curse of fallen man,
> might be the means whereby he would rise again.[32]

'In modern Europe', writes Efraim Sicher, 'the city was projected as the model
of a new Eden.'[33] This idea has then become a foil for much modern literature that portrays the city as, in reality, a 'corrupt prison-paradise ruled
by a Benefactor who takes charge of the human soul'.[34] This rejection of
Eden-as-contemporary-utopia can then be allied, in the midst and aftermath of the industrial revolution, with the search for Eden back behind
modernity, perhaps in a romantically imagined golden age populated

[27] Dante, *Purgatorio*, 28–33. See further P. Boitani, 'Dante and the Bible: A Sketch', in Lieb, *Reception History*, 281–93.
[28] W. Shakespeare, *Hamlet*, 1.2.133–7 (ed. H. Jenkins; London: Thomson Learning, 2003), 188.
[29] J. Potter argues that a 'paradise lost' motif figures in many of these poets (e.g. David Jones and Wilfred Owen): 'The Great War Poets', *The Blackwell Companion to the Bible in English Literature* (ed. R. Lemon et al.; Oxford: Wiley-Blackwell, 2009), 681–95 (683–4). 'Everything would have been different, for it would have been another world', writes Edward Thomas, in 'As the Team's Head Brass', in which a felled elm tree emphasizes the lost possibilities.
[30] W. Golding, *Lord of the Flies* (London: Penguin, 1999).
[31] Almond, *Adam and Eve*, 35.
[32] C. Hill, *The World Turned Upside Down: Radical Ideas during the English Revolution* (New York: Viking, 1972), 131.
[33] E. Sicher, 'Hard Times in Paradise: An Example of an Inverted Biblical Pattern', in *Biblical Patterns in Modern Literature* (BJS 77; ed. D. H. Hirsch and N. Aschkenasy; Chico, CA: Scholars, 1984), 165–72 (165).
[34] E.g. Sicher, 'Hard Times' mentions Y. Zamyatin's fantasy *We* (1921; English trans. New York: E. P. Dutton, 1924), in which the 'closed contours of the urban false Eden provide a metaphor . . . for a refuta-tion of the premise that the needs of man are reducible simple equations and square roots' (168). Zamyatin's work responds to 'the utopias of his literary master, H. G. Wells', and inspired G. Orwell's *1984* (170).

by our happy Palaeolithic ancestors that is said to have existed before the rise of human civilization that corrupted it.[35] The influence of such ideas is sometimes discovered in surprising places, such as Huxley's *Brave New World*, in which we encounter 'a Jesus figure in the guise of a modern noble savage'.[36] This romantically construed 'Eden' does not necessarily have much to do with the biblical Eden, however, which is often represented negatively in Romantic literature.[37] For Lawrence, for example, Eden is a repressive place, and human beings only find freedom (and especially sexual freedom) when they depart from it.[38] This rejection of the biblical idea of the original creation as a good and beautiful Edenic space is also found in Blake's *The Book of Urizen*, where creation is 'a series of violent ruptures and divisions . . . a tearing apart of an original dynamic unity'.[39]

The two trees

The garden in Genesis 2 has two trees that are of particular importance in the biblical story, and both have attracted a great deal of interest from biblical interpreters over the course of the centuries. One is the tree of life. There is no evidence in the story that the human beings have ever eaten from this tree, even though in Genesis 2.16–17 they are not explicitly forbidden from doing so; in fact, Genesis 3.22 implies clearly that they have *not* yet done so. This suggests that the authors of Genesis 2.4–25 consider it to have been the *destiny* of human beings in God's creation, though mortal, to achieve immortality, but that they did not in fact achieve this before being expelled from the garden.[40]

---

[35] See I. W. Provan, *Convenient Myths: The Axial Age, Dark Green Religion, and the World That Never Was* (Waco: Baylor University Press, 2013), chs 4–6.

[36] Sicher, 'Hard Times', 170.

[37] Romantic writers in general, from the late eighteenth century onwards, have tended to rework biblical themes in strikingly radical ways, often seeking to subvert the religious tradition. On the other hand, Hirst argues that even where the Romantic poets (in particular) 'retold story from Scripture in order to alter or reverse Scriptural doctrine, the traditional standpoint retained some of its authority and tended to reaffirm itself'. W. Z. Hirst, 'The Reassertion of Biblical Views in European Romanticism', in Hirsch and Aschkenasy, *Biblical Patterns*, 73–83 (73).

[38] E.g. in his poem 'Figs', 'a number of sexually mature and liberated women mock their creator's narrow morality; while in *Lady Chatterley's Lover*, Mellors and Constance are 'descendants of Adam and Eve rediscovering paradise'. T. R. Wright, 'D. H. Lawrence', in Lemon et al., *Bible in English Literature*, 654–66 (657, 660). Wright interestingly traces some of the influences upon Lawrence as he came to abandon a traditional Christian interpretation of Genesis.

[39] J. Roberts and C. Rowland, 'William Blake', in Lemon et al., *Bible in English Literature*, 373–82 (374).

[40] Ben Sira is one of the earliest interpreters to raise this question as to whether death is already a reality in the world before Adam and Eve transgress: 'death [for Ben Sira] is part of God's ordering of the cosmos . . . not a later aberration in the cosmos' (Levison, *Portraits of Adam*, 43). For the author of *2 Baruch*, it was not death as such that resulted from Adam's sin, but *untimely* death (Levison, *Portraits of Adam*, 139, and more generally on early Judaism, 156–9).

The second tree is the tree of the knowledge of good and evil, and the question has often been asked: which kind of knowledge is in view? Various ideas have been advanced. First, some have considered it to be sexual knowledge.[41] This appears to have been the ancient view of *2 Baruch* 56.6–10.[42] Philo understands the matter more broadly in terms of physical pleasures: Adam yielded to his physical passions, and because of this he lost a higher level of knowledge and descended to a lower.[43] For John Milton, in *Paradise Lost*, Adam's rationality is overcome by his love for Eve; he follows her willingly to her doom, more desirous of possessing her than of obeying God.[44] And the idea that the tree, the fruit and the serpent are all connected with sex remains very popular among modern advertisers.[45] Against this idea, we may note that Genesis 1 presents sexuality as part of the created order already ('be fruitful and multiply'), and the sexual impulse is connected there with being made in the image of God.[46]

Second, some have thought that the forbidden knowledge is cultural knowledge of the kind described in Genesis 4. A contemporary writer who holds this view is Karen Armstrong, in *A Short History of Myth*.[47] However, it seems from Genesis 1—2 that human beings are already given a vocation by God, and that co-operation with God in subduing the earth is intrinsic to the creation mandate. What would be the point of forbidding cultural knowledge in this context? Moreover, Genesis does not itself make this kind of connection anywhere.

Third, some have considered the reference to be to moral insight.[48] Human beings are presented with the opportunity to discriminate between

---

41 R. Gordis, 'The Knowledge of Good and Evil in the Old Testament and the Qumran Scrolls', *JBL* 76 (1957): 123–38 (130–6).

42 Levison, *Portraits of Adam*, 141.

43 Philo, *On the Creation*, 52.150—53.152.

44 J. Milton, *Paradise Lost*, 9.990–9, in *Paradise Lost by John Milton: Parallel Prose Edition* (ed. D. Danielson; Vancouver: Regent College Publishing, 2008), 412. See further on Milton, M. Lieb, 'John Milton', in Lemon et al., *Bible in English Literature*, 269–85.

45 See K. B. Edwards, *Admen and Eve: The Bible in Contemporary Advertising* (BMW 48; Sheffield: Sheffield Phoenix, 2012), chs 3–4; and L. S. Schearing and V. H. Ziegler, *Enticed by Eden: How Western Culture Uses, Confuses, (and Sometimes Abuses) Adam and Eve* (Waco: Baylor University Press, 2013), ch. 5. The persistently sneering tone of the latter book, and its lack of discrimination in its choice of targets, unfortunately lessens its impact in those areas where it really does have something important to say.

46 Here Milton (*Paradise Lost*, 4.309–10) has it right against the majority of his contemporaries, who held that Adam and Eve could not have had sex in Eden: 'And by her yielded, by him best receivd, / Yielded with coy submission, modest pride, / And sweet reluctant amorous delay.' See also D. Danielson, 'Eve', in D. L. Jeffrey, *A Dictionary of Biblical Tradition in English Literature* (Grand Rapids: Eerdmans, 1992), 251–4 (253); and Almond, *Adam and Eve*, 165.

47 K. Armstrong, *A Short History of Myth* (Toronto: Knopf, 2005), 60. So also J. Zerzan, *Twilight of the Machines* (Port Townsend, WA: Feral House, 2008).

48 Gordis, 'Knowledge', 124–5.

right and wrong. Before eating from the tree, they are in such close communion with God that moral discrimination is not necessary. However, a moral sense is already implied in Genesis 1 in the image-of-God language and in the commission to govern the world properly. It is also clearly the case in Genesis 3 that God holds the human couple accountable for their actions, implying a moral sense prior to the eating of the fruit rather than only afterwards.

Faced with these various difficulties, finally, some see the fundamental 'problem' in the human actions in this chapter, not as eating from the tree in itself (since its very existence implies that eventually its fruit might be consumed), but as doing so prematurely. In the same way that a child grows up and becomes an adult, 'knowing good and evil' and having wisdom or insight, human beings were scheduled one day to 'know good and evil'. The emphasis in Genesis 3 lies on the *grasping* after knowledge, in independence of God, prior to the right time. This does indeed seem to be the best option for understanding what the original authors were trying to say.

Male and female

Finally in this chapter, we must give some attention to the division of humanity into male and female that is described in Genesis 2.18–25. First of all, many biblical interpreters through the ages have understood the positioning of this account towards the end of Genesis 2 to be hermeneutically significant. They have found in it, in fact, the foundations for a particular view of male–female relations that is hierarchical in nature: woman comes 'after' man, therefore man has authority over woman.[49] However, even assuming for a moment that the earthling in Genesis 2 is a man, we surely cannot draw any conclusions about the nature of male–female relationships simply from the fact that the woman apparently comes 'after' the man. The 'man' himself comes last in the chain of creation in Genesis 1, and he is formed out of the ground in Genesis 2; yet he is not said on that basis to be less important than the rest of creation, or indeed to be subordinate to it. If one thinks that the 'order' of events in Genesis 1—2 is necessarily significant – and this has already been questioned above – one could in fact just as easily interpret the evidence in the opposite manner, holding that what comes last is pre-eminent. This is, indeed, how *Genesis Rabbah* interprets it: Adam (and Eve) were 'created after everything

---

[49] So, e.g., P. Charron (1608): 'the woman then the last in good and in generation, and by occasion the first in evil and the occasion thereof, is justly subject unto man, the first in good and the last in evil' (Almond, *Adam and Eve*, 150).

in order to rule over everything', and they are indeed urged, 'make haste and eat before He creates other worlds which will rule over you.'[50]

Then, second, if we are reading Genesis 2 along with Genesis 1, we have already been told in Genesis 1.27 that the *'adam* created in the image of God and given dominion over creation is both male and female. It is precisely *joint* identity as image of God and *joint* authority over creation that is in view in Genesis 1. Augustine is surely mistaken, then, when he differentiates between woman and man in terms of the divine image, asserting that when the woman is considered in herself 'she is not the image of God', whereas the man 'is by himself alone the image of God as fully and completely as when he and the woman are joined together as one'.[51] He has rightly been criticized for such a view, along with those later scholastics with their Aristotelian biology who regarded women as comprising a 'secondary biological species' with a 'defective capacity for humanity'.[52]

Basil of Caesarea already takes a different view back in the fourth century, insisting that 'woman is also in the image of God and that the male and female natures are equal in virtue', and Bede (AD 672–735) adopts the same idea: 'woman is really created in the image of God in that she possesses a rational mind.'[53] Later, Lutherans also insisted that Eve 'was not an imperfect version of the male, as Aristotle had asserted, but a perfect creation in her own right' and they also 'elevated her into a role model rather than the embodiment of all that was wrong with the female sex'.[54] This general statement about the image of God as male and female having been made in Genesis 1.27, it is particularly difficult then to think that we are meant to draw any theological conclusion simply from the order

---

[50] *Gen. Rab.* 19.4; cf. *Num. Rab.* 12.4 (in M. Simon, ed., *Midrash Rabbah*, 5:458), where we are told that 'after all the rest of the work of creation was accomplished He created Adam and Eve to rule over all.' Jewish tradition could also hold, however, that Adam was created last so that 'he should not grow proud. For they can say to him, "The mosquito came before you in the works of creation."' *Tosef. Sanh.* 8.8 in *The Tosefta* (trans. Jacob Neusner; 2 vols; Peabody, MA: Hendrickson, 2002), 2:1174. The high view of human beings that is apparent in all such biblically influenced perspectives stands in stark contrast to the opinion of Nietzsche, as expressed in his retelling of Genesis 1—2 in *The Anti-Christ* 'in which God creates man out of sheer boredom' (Wright, 'Lawrence', 656).

[51] Augustine, *On the Trinity*, 12.7.10. This not entirely consistent, however, with another view expressed in *The Literal Meaning of Genesis*, 3.22.34: 'women are not excluded from this grace of renewal and this reformation of the image of God, although on the physical side their sexual characteristics may suggest otherwise, namely, that man alone is said to be the image and glory of God. By the same token, in the original creation of man, inasmuch as woman was a human being, she certainly had a mind, and a rational mind, and therefore she also was made to the image of God.'

[52] R. R. Ruether, 'The Western Tradition and Violence against Women in the Home', in *Christianity, Patriarchy, and Abuse: A Feminist Critique* (ed. J. C. Brown and C. R. Bohn; New York: Pilgrim, 1989), 31–41 (32).

[53] J. Flood, *Representations of Eve in Antiquity and the English Middle Ages* (RSMRC 9; New York: Routledge, 2011), 21–2.

[54] Crowther, *Adam and Eve*, 104, 138.

of events as described in Genesis 2. Here it is easier to agree with ancient writers like John Chrysostom than with some others: '[God speaking to the woman after the Fall:] In the beginning I created you equal in esteem to your husband, and my intention was that in everything you would share with him as an equal.'[55] Likewise Peter Lombard (1100–60), who emphasizes that the woman was created from the man's side

> so that it should be shown that she was created for the partnership of love, lest, if perhaps she had been made from his head, she should be perceived as set over man in domination; or if from his feet, as if subject to him in servitude.[56]

Third, on this matter of order, it is by no means clear in any case (as I have pointed out above) that we should think of *'adam* in Genesis 2.7–21 as a man in our gendered sense at all. We are not dealing here with a 'man' who then produces a woman, but with an earthling that is then sexually differentiated and produces a man and a woman. This idea that Adam was first created as a hermaphrodite and only later gendered is already found in early Jewish tradition, and it turns up later in both heterodox and orthodox Christian contexts. For example, we find it in certain Gnostic texts from Nag Hammadi, and also in the writings of seventeenth-century authors like John Cleveland, in his poem 'Upon an Hermophrodite', where 'Adam, till his rib was lost, had both sexes thus engrossed'.[57]

Division into two

What is the purpose of the division of one into two? The problem to be overcome in Genesis 2 is that there is no 'helper suitable for' the earthling (*'ezer keneghdo*). This word 'helper' (*'ezer*) is used most often in the OT of divine assistance provided to human beings (e.g. in Hos. 13.9). It speaks, then, of a strength in the 'earthling' that is insufficient by itself for the tasks that have been given to it. These tasks are, in the language of Genesis 1, to subdue and to rule over creation (1.26, 28); in the language of Genesis 2, they are to work the garden and take care of it (2.15). The human vocation in the cosmos, we learn in both chapters, can only be fulfilled in community, not individually. Augustine crucially misses the point here:

---

[55] Chrysostom, *Homilies on Genesis*, 17.36, in *Saint John Chrysostom: Homilies on Genesis 1–17* (FC 74; ed. T. P. Halton; trans. R. C. Hill; Washington, DC: Catholic University of America Press, 1985), 240.

[56] Quoted in Flood, *Representations of Eve*, 66. For a similar line of argument in Luther, see Ruether, 'Western Tradition', 33: 'According to Luther, Eve was not inferior to Adam in the original creation.'

[57] In Jewish tradition, note, e.g., *'Erub.* 18a, in *The Babylonian Talmud* (ed. I. Epstein; 18 vols; London: Soncino, 1935–48), 3:123–5; *Gen. Rab.* 8.1; cf. also *Jub.* 2.14 and 3.18 in 'Book of Jubilees', in *The Apocrypha and Pseudepigrapha of the Old Testament* (ed. and trans. R. H. Charles; 2 vols; Oxford: Clarendon, 1976), 2:14, 16. For the rest, see further I. Dunderberg, 'Gnostic Interpretations of Genesis', in Lieb, *Reception History*, 383–96; and Almond, *Adam and Eve*, 3–8.

Now, if the woman was not made for the man to be his helper in begetting children, in what was she to help him? She was not to till the earth with him, for there was not yet any toil to make help necessary. If there were any such need, a male helper would be better, and the same could be said of the comfort of another's presence if Adam were perhaps weary of solitude. How much more agreeably could two male friends, rather than a man and a woman, enjoy companionship and conversation in a life shared together . . . Consequently, I do not see in what sense the woman was made as a helper for the man if not for the sake of bearing children.[58]

Women, Augustine asserts, are really not of any help to men at all except in producing children! It seems most unlikely that this is what our Genesis authors believed. A human being needs strong and 'suitable' help, they claim – help that is literally (but awkwardly) in Hebrew 'like opposite him' (*keneghdo*). That is: the help must be both similar to the earthling ('like' him) and yet also different from him ('opposite, over against, at a distance from him'). No other creature, it turns out, can function in such a way; none is 'like opposite him' to a sufficient degree. And so the earthling is divided, and it becomes male and female.

Much interpretative tradition speaks of the raw material out of which the woman is thus made in terms of a 'rib' that is taken from Adam. Some of this tradition is very specific: *Targum Pseudo-Jonathan* to Genesis 2.21 identifies the thirteenth rib on Adam's right side.[59] This interpretation was already widely accepted by the time of the earliest English translations (including the KJV), but it is probably not the best understanding of the Hebrew. More probably the idea is that Adam is cut in half, so that there come into existence two 'sides'.[60] One becomes male and the other female. These are now separate beings, who nonetheless exist in the closest possible relationship; she is, as the male affirms, 'bone of my bones and flesh of my flesh' (2.23). Elsewhere in the OT, this combination of 'bone' and 'flesh' refers to a member of one's family (e.g. Gen. 29.14). In Genesis 2 the language has an even more intimate significance, for the male and the female are destined to become again 'one flesh' in marriage (Genesis 2.24) – to 'return', as it were, to their original condition as the inhabitants of one body.

---

[58] Augustine, *Literal Meaning of Genesis*, 9.5.9.

[59] J. Bowker, *The Targums and Rabbinic Literature: An Introduction to Jewish Interpretations of Literature* (Cambridge: Cambridge University Press, 1969), 112.

[60] The Hb. *tsela'* typically refers elsewhere in the OT to one side of something over against the other, and the earliest translations in Aramaic, Greek and Latin all choose words to translate *tsela'* that allow for this interpretation (while also allowing for 'rib').

6

The entrance of evil: Genesis 3.1–24

The story of the 'descendants' of the heavens and the earth (Act 2 of the drama of Genesis) continues in Genesis 3 with an account of the entry of moral evil into the world of human experience. It is a story of temptation, wrongdoing and discovery; and then, of consequences.

Temptation, wrongdoing and discovery (Gen. 3.1–13)

At the heart of the story lies one 'of the wild animals the LORD God had made', who is first introduced using the Hebrew adjective *'arum* (Gen. 3.1). This word captures well the dilemma that faces the human pair in dealing with the creature, for it occurs in both positive and negative contexts in the wisdom literature of the OT, and it can connote either 'prudent' or 'crafty' depending on the context. So, is this a creature that possesses a virtue that the truly wise should cultivate, or a vice that they should avoid? The people who must make this judgement have themselves just been described, in the previous verse (2.25), as *'arummim*, 'naked' (from the Hb. *'arom*). This looks like a deliberate play on words, and such play will continue throughout this story. Shortly the serpent will tempt the naked (innocent) couple to eat some fruit because it will make them knowledgeable, but in fact they will discover instead that they are naked (*'erummim*, Gen. 3.7; *'erom*, 3.10–11), and they will need to be clothed.

The serpent and the origin of evil

What is this serpent that unexpectedly talks? The popular assumption since antiquity has been that it is a manifestation of Satan, the devil. There is in fact nothing in the OT in favour of such a view,[1] which is first reflected only in later apocryphal and pseudepigraphical texts like the Wisdom of Solomon, which suggests that death entered the world 'through the devil's envy' (2.24), and *2 Enoch*, which claims that Satan 'entered and seduced' Eve (*2 En.* 31.5).[2] All that can be said about the serpent in Genesis

---

[1] There is very little in the NT either. Rom. 16.20, 'The God of peace will soon crush Satan under your feet', perhaps alludes to Gen. 3.15.

[2] See Charles, *Apocrypha and Pseudepigrapha*, 1:538; 2:450.

itself is that it is an agent of the dark side of things. It is a vehicle for the powers of chaos; a creature of God that has gone bad. Jewish tradition later developed the idea of seduction, postulating that the serpent wished to lead Eve into sin because it desired her.[3] This led in later times to extravagant theories about the line of Cain that allegedly arose from this union.[4] The 1966 film *The Bible . . . In the Beginning* appears to play with this sexual theme: 'The serpent seems to have an almost human shape, including its face, but is also reptilian looking. Eve seems to experience almost a moment of sexual ecstasy as she bites the fruit.'[5]

Where did this evil come from in the first place? The book of Genesis does not answer this question. It is not interested in the ultimate origins of evil, but only in how evil first entered into this particular world in which human beings live. Insofar as that is the question, the answer of Genesis is that 'in the beginning' there was no evil in this world, but simply one omnipotent, transcendent, creator God who is wholly good (Gen. 1—2). The good in the world comes from this good God, but the evil in it comes from God's creatures, who turn away from what is good – first the serpent, and then the human beings.

The temptation

The subtlety of the serpent is quickly revealed in his clever words. His initial question already has a note of scepticism in it ('Did God really say?'), and it reframes the divine command of Genesis 2 in an entirely misleading way. In Genesis 2.16 God says, 'You are free to eat from any [= every] tree in the garden' (Hb. *mikkol 'ets-haggan 'akol to'kel*), and he then exempts only one tree. His vocabulary, that is, suggests mainly freedom. In Genesis 3.1, however, the serpent's ploy is to suggest to the woman that she is dealing with a God of unreasonable prohibition: 'You must not eat from any [= every] tree in the garden' (*lo' to'kelu mikkol 'ets-haggan*). The focus falls now, not on God's generosity in what he allows, but on the one thing that God has disallowed. In the ungenerous and suspicious attitude to God that the serpent thus inculcates in the human pair, we see their first step away from a right relationship with God, which biblically speak-ing is one of implicit trust and obedience. We may contrast Abraham's later faith and obedience to God's command, in one testing instance in

[3] So *Sotah* 9a–b, in *The Babylonian Talmud* (ed. I. Epstein; 18 vols; London: Soncino, 1935–48), 8:40.
[4] P. C. Almond, *Adam and Eve in Seventeenth-Century Thought* (Cambridge: Cambridge University Press, 1999), 173–7.
[5] J. S. Lang, *The Bible on the Big Screen: A Guide from Silent Films to Today's Movies* (Grand Rapids: Baker Books, 2007), 187.

Genesis 22, with the human failure in Genesis 3, in the midst of their own test, to put the prohibition in the larger context of God's blessing.

The woman happens to be the one who replies to the serpent (cf. 2 Cor. 11.3; 1 Tim. 2.14), but we should not imagine that the man is elsewhere and uninvolved.[6] His presence is explicitly indicated in Genesis 3.6, where his wife gives some of the fruit of the forbidden tree to her husband, 'who was with her'. These words have not been given sufficient weight by many readers throughout the ages, with the consequence that the woman has tended, at different times and in different places, to attract much more blame than the man for the human revolt against God. In the earliest period, for example, Tertullian's writings typically blame both parties for the debacle, but in his *Apparel of Women* he certainly focuses on the woman.[7] In such a way of reading Genesis 3, Eve easily becomes, not just the occasion of Adam's sin, but the cause of it – she is the temptress who leads her husband astray, and even bullies him into eating.[8]

All sorts of reasons are then developed for why the serpent chose to approach the woman and *not* the man. Perhaps she was weaker and more frail than he – an idea that became well entrenched by the fifteenth century, when *The Triumph of Women* by Juan Rodríguez del Padrón (*c.*1398–1450) attacks it by suggesting that 'the serpent approaches the woman before Adam, not because of her supposed frailty, but because he was jealous of her glory and marvelous beauty'.[9] In the Middle Ages the theme of Eve's *credulity*, in particular, was often 'repeated in the temptation scenes of the mystery plays'.[10] All such reading depends on the explicit or implicit assumption that the woman is alone with the serpent; but the story does not suggest that this is so. It only suggests that the woman

---

[6] This line of interpretation has been popular, however; note, e.g., *Gen. Rab.* 19.3, which suggests either that Adam was asleep or that he was away with God on a journey. A. L. Lerner, *Eternally Eve: Images of Eve in the Hebrew Bible, Midrash, and Modern Jewish Poetry* (HBISJW; Waltham, MA: Brandeis University Press, 2007), 96.

[7] Tertullian, *The Apparel of Women*, 1.1.1–2, in *Tertullian: Disciplinary, Moral and Ascetical Works* (FC 10; trans. R. Arbesmann, E. J. Daly and E. A. Quain; Washington, DC: Catholic University of America Press, 1959), 117–18.

[8] E.g. Ambrose, *Paradise*, 6.33, in *Saint Ambrose: Hexameron, Paradise, and Cain and Abel* (FC 42; trans. J. J. Savage; Washington, DC: Catholic University of America Press, 1961), 311; *Gen. Rab.* 19.5. See further J. Flood, *Representations of Eve in Antiquity and the English Middle Ages* (RSMRC 9; New York: Routledge, 2011), ch. 1; Lerner, *Eternally Eve*, 100; and K. B. Edwards, *Admen and Eve: The Bible in Contemporary Advertising* (BMW 48; Sheffield: Sheffield Phoenix, 2012) (11, and all of ch. 3, 'Bad Girls Sell Well'), who shows how modern advertisers 'use images of Eve as temptress in order to sell to women the ideal of female heterosexual sexuality as a means to obtain power'.

[9] Flood, *Representations of Eve*, 85–6.

[10] D. Danielson, 'Eve', in D. L. Jeffrey, *A Dictionary of Biblical Tradition in English Literature* (Grand Rapids: Eerdmans, 1992), 253.

carried on the conversation with the serpent, and that the man was a silent partner in it.

What does the human reply to the serpent suggest? It suggests that they are already moving in the serpent's direction. 'We may eat fruit from the trees in the garden' (*mipperi 'ets-haggan no'kel*, Gen. 3.2). These words are a poor representation of God's generosity as expressed in Genesis 2.16 ('You are free to eat from any [every] tree in the garden', *mikkol 'ets-haggan 'akol to'kel*). They do not stress that the fruit is indeed to be eaten (the infinitive absolute form, *'akol*, which lies behind the English 'free', is omitted), nor that the humans may eat from *any* tree. What is more, the woman *adds* to the divine prohibition in respect of the *one* forbidden tree, asserting that they are not even to 'touch' it. The God of prohibition is looming larger. The serpent's response to the woman's reply then takes the whole matter further: 'You will not surely die.' This is now a direct contradiction to God's words in Genesis 2.17, 'you will surely die.' An alternative scenario is presented: 'your eyes will be opened, and you will be like God, knowing good and evil.' Humanity, claims the serpent, will achieve wisdom, independently of God. The human pair believe the serpent's words, set the tree of the knowledge of good and evil on the same level as all the other trees (they see that 'the fruit of the tree was good for food and pleasing to the eye'; cf. Gen. 2.9), and eat.

What happens next is surprising, for things work out (apparently) just as the serpent had said. The human pair do not die; their eyes *are* opened; and they do become like God. God himself will explicitly acknowledge the last of these realities in Genesis 3.22: they 'become like one of us, knowing good and evil'. It seems for a moment, then, that it is God who has not been telling the truth in this story, and that it is the serpent who is the truth-teller. Yet there is already an indication in Genesis 3.6–7 that the 'advance' made by the human pair is problematic. The wisdom that they have acquired appears to bring with it a desire to hide from each other. A disruption of some kind has occurred, relationally; and as we read on, we discover its full dimensions, which were not known in advance, but were themselves 'hidden' in the simple consequence, 'you die'. The man and the woman were created to be one flesh, naked but not ashamed (2.24–25); now they are concealed from each other (3.7, by the fig leaves). Something has come between them, and nakedness is no longer un-problematic in the midst of unity and innocence; it has become something shameful. This hiding from each other in due course leads on to hiding from God as well, when they hear him 'walking in the garden in the cool of the day' (i.e. in the afternoon, when the sun's heat is not so oppressive).

This is turn leads to a painful conversation in which blame for the disaster is shifted from person to person, and from creature to creature. The man blames the woman, but also God: 'The woman *you* put here with me – she gave me some fruit.' The woman blames the serpent, recognizing that she has been deceived.

Consequences (Gen. 3.14–24)

Hitherto in the Genesis story God has been resolutely a God of blessing. Now we discover the antithesis – that God can also curse. First the serpent is 'Cursed . . . above all the livestock and all the wild animals', and the soil will later be cursed as well (Gen. 3.17). The *serpent* thus faces the consequences of his actions, but it also seems that in some degree *all* animals are affected by his actions (since the wording implies that they are caught up in the curse). What does the curse mean for the serpent in particular? He will 'crawl on his belly and eat dust'. This is not to be taken literalistically to imply that normal snakes at one time did *not* crawl on their bellies; this snake is, after all, far from being a normal snake. The idea is this: that just as normal snakes do crawl along the ground, so this 'serpent' who thought himself so wise and exalted – and who represents the forces of darkness arrayed against God and against human beings – will be brought low and (metaphorically) will 'crawl on his belly and eat dust'. He will be humiliated. Indeed, where kinship between humans and animals was the hallmark of the creation story in Genesis 1 and 2, enmity will be the keynote of this snake's world from this point on, as he strikes at human heels and, in turn, human feet seek to destroy him. The long-term, biblical battle between humans and the forces of chaos and darkness that seek to destroy them has now begun.

In Christian tradition, beginning in the NT, this battle will not come to an end until Jesus Christ returns at the end of time to lead his armies to victory over all the dark powers – having entered history once already as 'the last Adam' who saves his people from their sins (Rom. 5.12–20; 1 Cor. 15.12–58). It is this twofold victory of Christ over evil that is already read into Genesis 3.15 itself by several of the early Church Fathers.[11] It

---

[11] So, e.g., Irenaeus: 'Christ completely renewed all things, both taking up the battle against our enemy and crushing him who at the beginning had led us captive in Adam, trampling on his head, as you find in Genesis that God said to the serpent, "I will put enmity between you and the woman, and between you and the seed of the woman." From then on it was proclaimed that he who was to be born of a virgin, after the likeness of Adam, would be on the watch for the serpent's head.' Irenaeus, *Against Heresies*, 5.21.1 (ACCS 1:90–1).

is referenced again and again in later Western literature, beginning with the twelfth-century Anglo-Norman *Jeu d'Adam* ('one of the oldest and best examples of the transitional or semi-liturgical drama'),[12] and other medieval mystery plays from England, France and Spain. One of the most famous examples is *Paradise Lost* by the English Puritan writer John Milton (1667), in which Jesus offers himself as a sacrifice to pay for the sins of humankind so that God the Father can be both just and merciful, anticipating that once the debt is paid,

> Thou wilt not leave me in the loathsom grave
> His prey, nor suffer my unspotted Soule,
> For ever with corruption there to dwell;
> But I shall rise Victorious, and subdue
> My Vanquisher.[13]

Paradise Lost was shortly afterwards dramatized by John Dryden in his *The State of Innocence and Fall of Man* (1677), transforming Milton's blank verse into rhyming couplets of the kind that Milton himself greatly disliked and that certain commentators of the time greatly criticized.[14]

The same approach to the question of evil is evidenced in Christian art right from *its* beginnings. For example, the oldest extant church building in the world at Dura Europos (third century AD) contains pictorial representations of Adam and Eve, standing on each side of the tree of knowledge, and above them

> the Good Shepherd of St. Luke's Gospel, bearing a huge ram on his shoulders ...
> The candidate for baptism might well reflect that Adam's transgression calls
> for the Saviour's arrival to seek and to save that which was lost.[15]

The sacrificial victim in other early Christian art is often a lamb; for example, on Vatican Sarcophagus 104 (fourth century AD) we find the serpent coiling its way up the tree of knowledge while, 'as if to show that there are grounds for hope, a lamb stands on its hind legs in front of Eve'.[16] Later, we find Masaccio's moving *Expulsion of Adam and Eve from Eden* (*c.*1424–7) juxtaposed in the Brancacci Chapel of Santa Maria del Carmine

---

[12] P. Studer (ed.), *Le Mystère d'Adam: An Anglo-Norman Drama of the Twelfth Century* (Manchester: Manchester University Press, 1928), xxi.

[13] J. Milton, *Paradise Lost*, 3.246–51.

[14] J. Haydn's oratorio *The Creation* was also greatly influenced by *Paradise Lost*. M. Stern, *Bible and Music: Influences of the Old Testament on Western Music* (Jersey City, NJ: Ktav, 2011), 1–14.

[15] R. Milburn, *Early Christian Art and Architecture* (Los Angeles: University of California Press, 1988), 12.

[16] Milburn, *Early Christian Art*, 68.

in Florence with his *Tribute Money* (1425), in which St Peter plays a prominent role, suggesting a connection between the fall of humankind and subsequent salvation in Christ.[17]

As the hold of the Christian tradition on Western life then begins to loosen in the modern period, and as prevailing opinion about the true nature of the human 'problem' therefore begins to alter, the emphasis of artistic and literary interpretation inevitably begins to change. Thus George Bernard Shaw's *Back to Methuselah* (1921) uses the Adam and Eve story, not to speak about moral evil and the human need for victory through Christ, but as the starting point for a narrative that envisages a benevolent 'force' directing evolution towards a future perfection.[18] Archibald MacLeish's poetic drama *Nobodaddy* (1926) uses it to ponder the condition of human self-consciousness in an indifferent universe,[19] and in his *Songs for Eve* (1954) he 'glorifies Eve's sin as a kind of Byronic rebellion, seeing the unfallen state as tedious and insipid and, hence, disobedience to God as an act of transcendence'.[20] For Marcel Proust, 'the creation of woman according to the Bible is [itself] the story of the first crime, perceived as the foundation of all crimes powering the imagination and psychology of the culture of the West.'[21] The problem lies not with the entrance of evil into the world, but with the taking of the rib from Adam in the first place, which compels man

> to set out on a search in order to restore the loss, which for the narrator [of Proust's *La Prisonnière*, 1923] is the 'restoration of stolen property'. Proceeding to the bitter end, that sometimes ends in the death of the woman.[22]

What happens to the woman?

The woman also suffers consequences in Genesis 3, although they do not yet involve death. These consequences have often been understood in much the way that the NIV suggests in its translation of Genesis 3.16 (for similar translations see for example NRSV, the English Standard Version (ESV), *The Message* and the New American Standard Bible (NASB)): 'I will greatly increase your pains in childbearing; with pain you will give birth to children. Your desire will be for your husband, and he will rule over you.'

---

[17] The same juxtaposition is already found on the Junius Bassus sarcophagus (fourth century AD), one of the most famous pieces of early Christian relief sculpture. Milburn, *Early Christian Art*, 74.

[18] G. B. Shaw, *Back to Methuselah* (London: Constable: 1921).

[19] A. MacLeish, *Nobodaddy* (Cambridge, MA: Dunster House, 1926).

[20] Danielson, 'Eve', 254.

[21] J. Hassine, 'The Creation of Eve in the Writings of Marcel Proust', in *Biblical Patterns in Modern Literature* (BJS 77; ed. D. H. Hirsch and N. Aschkenasy; Chico, CA: Scholars, 1984), 95–104 (102).

[22] Hassine, 'Creation of Eve', 102.

The second part of this verse is relatively unproblematic, although there has been much discussion over the centuries about the precise nature of the woman's 'desire'. The near context makes it all but certain, however, that we are reading about a desire to dominate and to conquer; Genesis 4.7 uses exactly the same rare Hebrew word, *teshuqah*, to refer to sin's desire to gobble up Cain. In all probability, then, Genesis 3.16 refers to a female desire to control, even to consume, her husband. Intended for partnership in Genesis 1, the human pair will no longer pursue it. She will try to dominate him, and he will seek to 'rule' her (Hb. *mashal*). This word *mashal* also appears in Genesis 4.7, '[Sin] desires to have you, but you must *master* it.' Another important instance is found in Psalm 8.6–8,

> You made them *rulers* over the works of your hands; you put everything under their feet: all flocks and herds, and the animals of the wild, the birds in the sky, and the fish in the sea, all that swim the paths of the seas.

So in Genesis 3.16, infected now by evil, the man will relate to the woman as if she were a *part* of the creation over which humans are given dominion, rather than co-ruler *over* creation along with the man.

This reading implies, of course, the prior reading of Genesis 1 and 2 offered in my Chapter 5 above. Some have argued differently, claiming that female subordination to the male is already envisaged in Genesis 1 and 2. Therefore, the argument goes, Genesis 3 is not speaking about the *beginning* of subordination; it is just that, once evil enters the human heart, male headship becomes harsh and exploitative instead of caring and nurturing.[23] I follow the lead, however, of John Chrysostom, when he paraphrases Genesis 3.16 in this way:

> In the beginning I created you equal in esteem to your husband, and my intention was that in everything you would share with him as an equal, and as I entrusted control of everything to your husband, so did I to you; but you abused your equality of status. Hence I subject you to your husband.[24]

The first part of Genesis 3.16 is more problematic. It has often been understood as a reference to childbirth: the 'pains' in question are labour pains.[25] However, a review of other OT uses of the rare Hebrew terms *'itstsavon*

---

[23] Thus, e.g., Wenham: 'Evidently [the author] does not regard female subordination to be a judgment on her sin. In that (*sic*) the woman was made from man to be his helper and is twice named by man . . . indicates his authority over her.' G. J. Wenham, *Genesis 1–15* (WBC; Dallas: Word, 1987), 81.

[24] Chrysostom, *Homilies on Genesis*, 17.36.

[25] Again, Chrysostom: 'I [God] will greatly aggravate the pain of your labor . . . each time without fail you will personally have a reminder, through the distress and pain of each birth, of the magnitude of this sin of disobedience.' Chrysostom, *Homilies on Genesis*, 17.30–1.

and *'etsev* that lie behind NIV's 'pains' and 'pain', along with their related forms, inspires no confidence in this interpretation.[26] The verbal root *'tsb* is never used elsewhere in the OT of birth pangs, with one possible exception in 1 Chronicles 4.9; and this turns out on closer inspection not to be an exception at all.[27] Conversely, there is a well-established vocabulary for birth pangs in the OT that comprises quite different words (verbal roots like *tsrr* and *chul*, and nouns like *chevel*). Moreover, NIV's 'childbearing' is a very strange translation of the Hebrew term *herayon*, for elsewhere in the OT *herayon* clearly refers to conception or pregnancy, and not to childbirth.[28] It is quite unlikely, then, that labour pains are in view in Genesis 3.16. It is much more likely that the 'pain' envisaged is bound up with the difficult *circumstances* into which the woman will now bring children as they are born: 'I will greatly increase your pain and your conception; in painful circumstances you will give birth to children.' The old KJV is similar to this ('I will greatly multiply thy sorrow and thy conception ... in sorrow ...'), and it is interesting that already back in ancient times the Greek Septuagint (LXX) translation of Genesis 3.16 also read the line as referring to generalized pain – it makes no reference to childbearing.

Whence might come this generalized pain? The context in Genesis 3 suggests that it is most immediately connected with the change that occurs in the woman's relationship with her husband. She now finds herself embroiled with him in a struggle for dominance; she will therefore experience family in the context of pain. This same reality of marital dysfunction may indeed also explain the reference to the increase in the number of her conceptions. Possibly the idea is that sex will become detached from sensible, responsible dominion of the world, which should involve among other things a commitment to the well-being of all human beings (including all women).

It is worth noting that the woman is not envisaged in Genesis 3 as only *beginning* to experience pain after evil enters the world. Suffering does not *begin* at this point in the biblical story; it only *increases*. Suffering as such, in the course of bringing children into the world and raising them, is not considered incompatible in Genesis with life in God's good creation before the serpent appears. Nor for that matter is pain in general. God's good

---

[26] See Gen. 3.17; 5.29; Prov. 5.8–10; 10.22; 14.23; 15.1; Ps. 127.2; 1 Chron. 4.9.

[27] See further I. W. Provan, 'Pain in Childbirth? Further Thoughts on "An Attractive Fragment" (1 Chronicles 4:9–10)', in *Let Us Go Up to Zion: Essays in Honour of H. G. M. Williamson on the Occasion of His Sixty-Fifth Birthday* (ed. I. Provan and M. Boda; Leiden: Brill), 285–96.

[28] Hos. 9.11; Ruth 4.13.

world is not envisaged in Genesis as lacking in challenges and problems that human beings must overcome in order to live a blessed life in it, and to bring blessing to creation itself. This is already implied in the language of 'ruling and subduing' in Genesis 1. There is work to be done in the world; it needs to be controlled and shaped in various ways. The human relationship with the remainder of creation, therefore, is inevitably marked from the beginning by struggle. The embrace of evil simply makes the struggle more intense.[29]

What happens to the man?

If the immediate context for understanding Genesis 3.16a is provided by Genesis 3.16b, then certainly the slightly broader context is provided by Genesis 3.17. The woman suffers pain (*'itstsavon*) in the home, it now turns out, not only because she is in conflict with the man, but also because the man is in conflict with the earth, and the entire community suffers as a result: 'Cursed is the ground because of you; in pain (*'itstsavon*) you will eat of it all the days of your life.' Food production becomes more challenging. It is not that there is work, now, where there was none before – work is part of the human vocation as it is described in Genesis 1—2. In biblical faith, human beings are created (as we have seen) to 'serve the garden and keep/guard it' (2.15); they are created to rule and subdue the earth, which (as we have seen) implies that the earth requires ruling and subduing in the aftermath of divine creating. Effort would always have been required, whether in agriculture or in the raising of children.

So work is already part of the human vocation; but now it will involve more pain than hitherto, for the ground has been cursed by God. It will still provide food, claims Genesis 3, but only at greater cost – that is the implication of verse 18, where 'thorns and thistles' suggests a rather desolate place (as in Hos. 10.8) in the midst of which it might yet be possible to grow 'green plants' (Hb. *'esev hassadeh*, lit. 'plants of the field') that are good to eat. These thorns and thistles are themselves not newly created after evil enters human experience. They are already part of the vegetation of the earth, assuredly coming under the heading of Hb. *siach*, the inedible plants noted in Genesis 2.5 (NIV's 'shrubs'). Both edible and inedible plants already exist, as we get to Genesis 3 (note the *'esev mazriya' zera'* and *'esev zorea' zera'*, 'seed-bearing plants', in Genesis 1.11–12, 29), and both will continue to grow as we look ahead *from* Genesis 3. However,

---

[29] For modern perspectives on the curse on Eve in popular culture, see T. Sanders, *Approaching Eden: Adam and Eve in Popular Culture* (Lanham, MD: Rowman and Littlefield, 2009), 113–27.

much harder work will now be required to grow enough of the former to survive.

In sum, a change will come about in the circumstances of both the man and the woman, in respect of core aspects of their vocation. The man's creation calling involved working the land; the woman's, conceiving, birthing and raising children. Both callings are now marked by greater pain (*'itstsavon* in Gen. 3.16 and 3.17) – which includes the pain of living with each other.

What happens to both of them?

Beyond pain there is death. We have been awaiting a reference to death since Genesis 3.6 ('When you eat of it you will surely die'), but we do not encounter one until Genesis 3.19. Even here, it is not a report of death, but only a promise of it. The tree of life had offered the possibility of a different ending to the human story. But now, the normal processes of life will be allowed to play themselves out, and instead of eating the fruit of the tree that God had provided, and knowing life, human beings will eat food only until they 'return to the ground'. The human destination is *not* now different from the human origin: 'for dust you are and to dust you will return.' Human beings will return to the dust with which they have spent their whole working life struggling. They are set on this pathway, as Genesis 3 closes, by way of banishment from the place where the tree of life grows (3.22–24). They no longer live, as it were, within God's sanctuary, but outside it.[30] That is the implication of the note about the 'cherubim', pictures of which are said elsewhere to adorn the Tabernacle and Temple (Exod. 26.31; 1 Kings 6.29); two of which form the throne of God on top of the ark of the covenant (Exod. 25.18–22); and two of which guard the inner sanctuary of the Temple (1 Kings 6.23–28). However we may construe the symbolism of those cherubim in Tabernacle and Temple, there is no ambiguity about the intention in Genesis 3. The cherubim *here* are intended to keep humans out of the divine sphere, rather than to welcome them into it. They exist to guard the way to the tree of life, rather than allow access to it. That is also the function of the mysterious 'flaming sword flashing back and forth'.[31]

---

[30] Some modern scholars interpret this punishment as evidence of God's injustice; so A. M. Dershowitz, *The Genesis of Justice: Ten Stories of Biblical Injustice That Led to the Ten Commandments and Modern Law* (New York: Warner Books, 2000), 30–44. There is no evidence that this is how the biblical writers understood it.

[31] For modern perspectives on 'death' in Genesis 3 in popular culture, see Sanders, *Approaching Eden*, 91–112.

Before we get to the banishment, however, we encounter a new name and new clothes (Gen. 3.20–21). To understand the significance of the former we must first understand something about the meaning of Genesis 2.23. Many have read this verse as involving a 'naming' of the female by the male that indicates his claim to *authority* over her – because, it is claimed, authority is what the act of naming typically signifies in the OT.[32] However, although the 'naming' of people *is* often carried out in the OT by those who have authority over them (e.g. parents in respect of children), it cannot be demonstrated that the act of naming people in itself *involves* an assertion of authority. A strong example that points in the opposite direction is Hagar's naming of God in Genesis 16.13. So in general, there is no strong reason to thinking of naming as 'taking authority'. And in Genesis 2.23 itself, the naming *certainly* carries no connotation of any claim to authority.

Note, first of all, that in spite of how this verse is often characterized, the man names, not only the woman (Hb. *'ishshah*), but also himself (Hb. *'ish*). Does this imply that the male is taking authority over *himself*? Surely this is not what is intended. Second, the names that the male chooses indicate the *mutuality* that exists between the two persons who were just beforehand one being; they do not imply any kind of hierarchy. He is *'ish*, and she is *'ishshah*. These nouns are, linguistically, in the closest possible relationship with each other; consonantally, only an 'h' separates them. And finally, the naming in Genesis 2.23 must be read against the background of the earlier naming of the non-human creatures in Genesis 2.19–20. That naming is certainly not about taking 'authority' either. Throughout the ancient Near East, 'naming' was simply part of the process by which something came into existence and was assigned a function.[33] Thus an Egyptian text, the *Ritual of Amun*, tells us that prior to creation 'no god had come into being and no name had been invented for anything'. The Mesopotamian text *Enuma elish* likewise speaks of the period when 'no gods whatever had been brought into being, uncalled by name, their destinies undetermined'.[34] In this ancient worldview, the birth of the gods is intrinsically bound up with the assigning of their functions and roles in the cosmos; more generally, to create something is to name it, and to give it a function within an ordered world.

---

[32] So e.g. Wenham, *Genesis 1–15*, 70: 'Though they are equal in nature, that man names woman (cf. 3:20) indicates that she is expected to be subordinate to him . . .'

[33] J. H. Walton, *Ancient Near Eastern Thought and the Old Testament: Introducing the Conceptual World of the Hebrew Bible* (Grand Rapids: Baker Academic, 2006), 87–92, 188–90.

[34] *ANET*, 61.

With this background in mind we quickly come to understand that, in naming the creatures in Genesis 2, the human being is joining with God in *creating the world*, not least by assigning these creatures *roles* in the world. Their names speak not so much of what they *are* as of where they *fit* in the cosmos. In Genesis 2.23, likewise, the newly created human beings who find themselves in the closest possible relationship to each other assign themselves a place in the cosmos. They do so as the two aspects of the *'adam* that is to rule the whole creation (Gen. 1.26–28). This is where men and women 'fit' in the cosmos – together with each other, and ruling over the kingdom they have been given to govern. Just two chapters further on in Genesis, Eve will name Cain; and again, the naming is not about taking *authority*. It is about where Cain 'fits' in the story (4.1).

This intimacy of *'ish* and *'ishshah* in Genesis 2 is symbolized in the fact that they are 'naked, and they felt no shame' (Gen. 2.25); and this reality brings us back to Genesis 3. With the entry of evil into the world, we are told here, comes shame – precisely because of nakedness. This leads initially to hasty and ill-thought-out attempts at clothing (*chagorot*, loincloths made of fig leaves, 3.7), so that nakedness may be avoided. Now, in Genesis 3.21, God accommodates himself to this new reality of human shame. If there must be clothing, at least it shall be proper clothing (*kotnot*, 'tunics', made of animal skin).[35]

At the same time, *'ishshah* becomes *chawwah*, 'Eve' (v. 20). The name is ambiguous. Its choice is connected explicitly by the author to the fact that *chawwah* becomes the mother of all the living (*cha*). This might be seen as reflecting something positive: God's blessing of fertility continues in the midst even of the problems that the human actions have created. On the other hand, the name *chawwah*, along with the statement that 'the man named his wife', reminds the reader very much of Genesis 2.19–20, where God brings every 'living creature' (*chayyah*) to the earth creature and *yiqra' ha'adam shemot* – 'the adam-creature called names' for them all. It is when the earthling finds what it is looking for that *'ishshah*, 'woman', is announced (Gen. 2.23, *not* using the Hb. verb *qara'*, 'called', which we find in Gen. 2.19–20 regarding the *animals*). This first naming of the female in Genesis 2 signifies, then, that the female is *one* with the *'ish* who is speaking (she is *'ishshah*), rather than distanced from him. In the second naming in Genesis 3, on the other hand, the man 'names' his

---

[35] The singular is *kuttonet*, which refers to the main ordinary garment of a person – a long shirt reaching to the knees or ankles. Augustine presses beyond the text in claiming that these tunics represent in themselves divine punishment for pride: 'since the likeness to God is his honor, the likeness to the beasts is his disgrace.' Augustine, *On the Trinity*, 12.11.16.

wife (Hb. *qara'*) as he has previously named the animals (Hb. *qara'*); and he names her with a name (*chawwah*) that *reminds* us of the animals (*chayyah*). This is a naming that speaks of a *distancing* between male and female (now known as *'adam* and *chawwah*), just as *'ish* and *'ishshah* spoke of their closeness.

Therefore: God's ongoing blessing is certainly evidenced in the name 'Eve', but so too is the disordered nature of the world in which God's blessing will now work out. Indeed, the woman is essentially defined in Genesis 3, even as the chapter reminds us of God's blessing, in terms of *one aspect* of her vocation in the world (motherhood), rather than in terms of her *entire* vocation, which is to rule over creation alongside the man. *'Adam*, male and female (Gen. 1.26), has now become *'adam*, male, and *chawwah*, female.

It seems clear that our Genesis authors do not understand this new form of existence outside the garden in positive terms. Yet there has always been a line of interpretation that finds the glass to be at least half full – that finds the first sin to be a *felix culpa* (a happy fault). Ancient Christian perspectives on this idea, going back as far as Ambrose and Augustine, are micely illustrated by Milton's Adam, who wonders whether he should repent of his sin or rejoice in it, given that greater good and more glory for God will eventually result from it.[36] Here the emphasis lies on the great salvation that ultimately arises from the transgression. Contemporary writing tends to focus not so much on ultimate as on present benefits, however mixed they may be. For example, in her poem 'The Expulsion', Katha Pollitt pictures Adam as happy, now, that in Eve he has 'someone to blame' for all the things that later occur in human history, while Eve is also content that from this point onwards Adam will always need her.

Reflections on 'The Fall'

Genesis 3 has commonly been read as referring to a 'Fall' from the originally perfect condition in which human beings found the world, and the consequences of this 'Fall' have often been considered to be the 'givens' of current human experience. On this view, we live in a world bequeathed to us by our first ancestors, and there is little or nothing that can be done about it. Indeed, to seek to overcome the God-ordained 'givens' of life is to rebel against God. This view of Genesis 3 has in turn produced a particular view of human life. In this worldview, passive suffering has often been commended, hierarchy in male–female relations mandated, slavery

---

[36] Milton, *Paradise Lost*, 12.469–78.

promoted and technology resisted.[37] Human beings sit under the ongoing judgement of God, and we can only endure it until we die. To seek to change the world is to be impious.

It is important to recognize that the remainder of the OT does not interpret Genesis 3 in such a manner. First of all, it does not view the events of Genesis 3 as having significantly affected the nature of creation as God's *good* creation – a place blessed by God and entirely wonderful in its nature. As we read the great creation psalms of the OT, for example, we find them describing creation in exactly the same way as Genesis 1—2 – and this is the creation that the psalmists are currently *experiencing*, even after moral evil has entered the picture. It is a place in which the goodness of God is everywhere to be seen and experienced. Second, the remainder of the OT specifically does not view the events of Genesis 3 as inevitably leading to ongoing relational problems between God and human beings. In subsequent chapters of Genesis itself, Abel has a good relationship with God, and both Enoch (5.24) and Noah 'walked with God' (6.9). Even Cain is clearly presented with a choice in Genesis 4 – submit to sin or master it (4.7). There is nothing inevitable about his submission. Even after his murder of Abel, Cain is described as living in God's presence and talking with God (see esp. 4.14, 16, which speak of him *then* leaving God's presence). So the expulsion of the human beings from the garden does not mean that they cannot commune with and walk with God.[38]

Further (and predictably, if disharmony between God and humans is not biblically inevitable), the remainder of the OT does not regard the *other consequences* of the sin of Adam and Eve as inevitable either. Increased pain is associated with pregnancy and children in Genesis 3.16; but the predominant note struck by the OT when mothers and children are

---

[37] Consider, e.g., that J. S. Murray's important 1790 essay on the equality of the sexes was published in a context in which 'for her opponent, and to a large extent most of American society, the Scriptures contained only one meaning, in the case of Gen. 3:16 one that justified woman's subordination to man'. H. J. Marsman, *Women in Ugarit and Israel: Their Social and Religious Position in the Context of the Ancient Near East* (Leiden: Brill, 2003), 4. Consider also the resistance of his fellow countrymen in Scotland when about 50 years later, in 1847, J. Simpson advocated the use of anaesthetics in childbirth. To use chloroform for the purpose of relieving a woman's birth pangs, they argued, was to evade one aspect of the Genesis curse on woman.

[38] Some Jewish tradition, indeed, has Adam himself repenting of sin, learning from the example of Cain (e.g. *Gen. Rab.* 22.13). The opposite opinion is found in Ephrem the Syrian: the reason God began by cursing the serpent was so that 'when justice appeased its anger on this creature, Adam and Eve should grow afraid and repent so that there might be a possibility for grace to preserve them from the curses of justice. But when the serpent had been cursed and Adam and Eve had still made no supplication, God came to them with punishment.' *Commentary on Genesis*, 2.30.1 (ACCS 1:92).

described is joy, and not pain (e.g. Pss. 113.4–9; 127.3). In part this may be because there is nothing biblically inevitable, either, about the cursing of the ground. To the extent that female 'pain' concerns economic circumstances, then, it is not inevitably increased (note Ps. 128; Deut. 33.13–16). The OT as a whole continues to know God as a God of blessing in these respects – one who blesses the land, and one who blesses the family. Specifically in our opening chapters of Genesis, Noah is regarded as overcoming the curse on the ground in Genesis 9.20, where as 'a man of the soil' (a farmer) he is the first to plant a vineyard. In this way he fulfils his father's hope that he would give human beings relief in respect of 'the labour and painful toil of our hands caused by the ground the LORD has cursed' (Gen. 5.29). As to the struggle for supremacy in relationships that Genesis 3.16 envisages, again this is by no means seen as inevitable. For example, the woman who in Genesis 3.1–6 takes the initiative and introduces alienation into the relationship with her man becomes in the Song of Songs the woman who, in taking initiative, draws the man into intimacy.

In sum, the remainder of the OT does not view the events of Genesis 3 as *cataclysmic* events that somehow inevitably change everything about the world in which we live. Indeed, the rest of the OT does not ever again even refer *back* to the events of Genesis 3 as important for human beings in the present, when it comes to understanding the world in which we live, or how we should live in relation to God and the rest of creation. It does know that sin, chaos and darkness are threats to creation, and have been so ever since the beginning. It knows, further, that human beings can and do embrace sin, chaos and darkness, and become implicated in it – indeed, that they are catapulted into the midst of it, and touched by it, simply by virtue of being born (the notion of original sin).[39] But the OT does not regard it as inevitable that we must live in the world of Genesis 3, and indeed it urges us *not* to do so, but in turning to God to know a different world. There are two pathways upon which we can walk in life, Genesis claims. One involves obedience and blessing, the other disobedience (autonomy) and cursing (e.g. Deut. 30.15–20). We should choose life.

---

[39] Interpretations as to the 'how' of sin in human beings have of course been deeply influenced over the course of the centuries by changing scientific paradigms, as partially documented by S. B. Thistlethwaite, 'A Gene for Violence? Genetic Determinism and Sin', in *Adam, Eve, and the Genome* (TSC; ed. S. B. Thistlethwaite; Minneapolis: Fortress, 2003), 145–60.

7

From Cain to the great flood:
Genesis 4.1—6.8

We turn in this chapter to the conclusion of Act 2 of the Genesis drama (the story as it unfolds from Cain and Abel down to Seth in Gen. 4.1–26), and then to Act 3 (Gen. 5.1–6.8), where we encounter the family history of Adam down to Noah, prior to the great flood. The first set of issues we need to address concerns sequencing.

Reading Genesis 1—11 sequentially: some issues

The reader of Genesis 2—3 naturally assumes, on the first read-through, that insofar as the story concerns human beings, he or she is reading about the origins of all humanity. Adam and Eve are the first humans, the latter being explicitly 'mother of all the living' (Gen. 3.20); all further humans are their descendants. When we get to the story of the great flood, a similar narrative movement appears to be implied. Adam's descendant Noah enters the boat he has built along with his immediate family members and representatives of all the other creatures who cannot otherwise survive the loss of *terra firma*. The flood, it seems, covers the whole earth, wiping out all life except what is preserved with Noah in the ark (e.g. Gen. 6.7, 18–20); only Noah and the other family members in the ark provide human continuity between the period before the flood and the period after it. As one might expect under these circumstances, all humans speak one language in the immediate aftermath of the flood (Gen. 11.1), as the descendants of Noah's sons Shem, Ham and Japheth spread out over the whole earth and become the people groups known in the remainder of the biblical story (Gen. 10). Within this context, the story of Cain and Abel is then most naturally read as describing the immediate sequel to the story of human sin in the garden, describing the spread of the 'infection' of evil out from Adam and Eve to their children, with the immediately subsequent chapters describing the 'pandemic' that follows.

Curiously, however, various aspects of Genesis 1—11 resist this straightforward reading of these chapters. In Genesis 4, for example (as Walter

Moberly points out), 'internal details are in significant ways at odds with its present context at the outset of human life upon earth'.[1] The most obvious case is also the most famous: whence came Cain's wife (Gen. 4.17)? Did he marry a sister who is not otherwise mentioned? This is only one aspect of a larger issue, however, since throughout Genesis 4 it is presupposed that the earth outside the garden is already populated even as the family of Adam and Eve encounter it. Abel is said to be a keeper of sheep, and Cain a tiller of the ground (Gen. 4.2), which implies a wider population with familiar tasks already assigned to different groups; Abel is one of the people in *this* category and Cain is one of those in *that* category. When Cain and Abel go into the open countryside, moreover, the point is that they are leaving other people behind them, for murder is best committed without an audience (4.8); the story implies a distinction between populated and unpopulated spheres. Later, we find that Cain is afraid of exile from his home precisely because he will be moving among people who are not his kin, and he will be vulnerable to attack (4.13–14). However, if we are really to conceive of the world at this point in the Genesis story as inhabited only by a few offspring of Adam and Eve, they would occupy a very limited space. The more Cain were to wander, the further away from other people he would be. Later on, finally, there is reference to the building of a city (4.17), which once again presupposes population density.

In sum, Genesis 4 appears to presuppose an already-populated earth; yet readers of Genesis 1—3 are *apparently* required, at this point in the story, to believe in an almost entirely *unpopulated* earth. So *is it* the intention of Genesis 2 and 3, after all, to describe the very first human pair from whom all others are descended? Or do we perhaps have in Genesis 2—4 only the story of one particular family, told in such a way as to make them representative of human beings more generally, and thus to illustrate the human condition?

We face similar issues later in Genesis when we transition from the story of Cain and Abel to the story of the great flood. The flood appears to be envisaged as universal in nature, wiping out all life on earth except what is preserved with Noah in the ark. Yet in Genesis 6.4 we read about 'the Nephilim', who are said to live both before the flood and after it (Gen. 6.4). And indeed, we meet them again in Numbers 13.33, where the majority of the spies sent by Joshua to spy out Canaan report giants

---

[1] R. W. L. Moberly, *The Theology of the Book of Genesis* (OTT; Cambridge: Cambridge University Press, 2009), 23.

whom they call by this name, and who are designated as the sons of Anak. The Anakim are themselves associated elsewhere in the OT with the Rephaim (e.g. Deut. 2.10–11), who appear in Genesis 14.5 and 15.18–21 and have an entire land named after them in Deuteronomy 2.20, albeit that in this text they are already a declining force. Deuteronomy 3.11 also alerts us to this decline, referencing King Og of Bashan as the only one remaining 'of the remnant of the Rephaim'. Very probably Goliath is regarded in the OT as one of the last of these people (1 Sam. 17.1–58; cf. 2 Sam. 21.15–21). These stories probably give us some insight into the significance of the term Nephilim, which means 'fallen ones'. They have all fallen in battle by the time the story is being told – they are indeed 'heroes of old', even though they are 'men of renown' (Gen. 6.4).

A universal flood is also problematic when it comes to the account of Cain's descendants in Genesis 4.17–24. Some of these descendants are said to be the 'fathers' of those engaged in well-known lines of work *now* (i.e. in the time of the author): for example, Jabal is 'the father of those who live in tents and raise livestock' *now* (4.20), and Jubal is 'the father of all who play the harp and the flute' *now* (4.21). Such sentiments imply a lack of awareness of any great flood that wiped out everyone apart from Noah's family; continuity of culture, at least, is implied, even if strict family descent is not (since 'father' does not need to imply biological descent). So *is it* the intention of the flood narrative, after all, to describe a global cataclysm that once destroyed all non-marine life outside the ark? And if it is, how do we account for the 'problematic' texts? Is it possible that a much more localized story of a significant flood has been given 'cosmic' dimensions, and thus come to serve the purpose of the Genesis authors in writing about God's ongoing relationship with the whole world?

Such features in the narrative of Genesis 1—11 have long attracted interpretative attention, leading to all sorts of moves designed to solve the 'sequencing problem'. For example, *Genesis Rabbah* proposes that we read Genesis 4.1–2 as involving the birth, not just of Cain and Abel, but also of three female children: 'Only two entered the bed, but seven left it: Cain and his twin sister, Abel and his two twin sisters.'[2] The problem of Cain's wife is thus resolved, with females to spare.[3] With respect to the Nephilim,

---

[2] *Gen. Rab.* 22.2.

[3] Augustine and others also adopted the sister-marriage idea: 'As, therefore, the human race, subsequently to the first marriage of the man who was made of dust, and his wife who was made out of his side, required the union of males and females in order that it might multiply, and as there were no human beings except those who had been born of these two, men took their sisters for wives.' Augustine, *City of God*, 15.16.1–2 (FC 14; trans. G. G. Walsh and G. Monahan; Washington DC: Catholic University of America Press, 1952), 450–1.

some Jewish tradition speculated that one of the Nephilim hitched a ride on the roof of the ark, surviving the flood along with Noah and his family.[4] However, such solutions do violence to the plain sense of the text, and they fail to convince. We must adjust our expectations, it seems, about the kind of narrative we are reading. It is not, in our modern terms, a straightforward narrative, in which 'sequence' functions in a normal manner, one 'event' simply following another. Rather, as Walter Moberly puts it,

> A story whose narrative assumptions apparently originate from the world familiar to the time of the biblical narrator has been set in a context long antecedent to that world – the very beginnings of life upon earth. From this it follows, *not* that one should not take the narrative sequence from Adam and Eve to Cain and Abel with imaginative seriousness as part of the developing storyline, but that in analytical terms one should recognize that the narrative is, in a very real and important sense, artificial . . . The purpose of the literary construction would appear to be so to juxtapose certain archetypal portrayals of life under God that an interpretative lens is provided for reading God's call of Abraham and Israel that follows.[5]

From this it follows that the reader must accept certain constraints on the kinds of questions (s)he asks of the text, recognizing which ones it was probably designed to answer and which ones not. It may even be that (s)he will feel compelled to revisit some of what is said in Genesis 1—3 and reflect on the true intention of some of the statements that are made there. For example, it is in fact not necessary to understand the phrase 'mother of all the living' (Gen. 3.20) as a reference to biological descent, any more than we must understand Jabal as 'the father of those who live in tents and raise livestock' in such biological terms (Gen. 4.20). Perhaps it is the significance of Eve in introducing evil into human experience rather than responding to the call of God that is more the focus of this language: she brings to birth (as it were) the world as we know it, now entirely infected by evil. 'All the living' are touched by it.[6]

---

[4] *Pirqe R. El.* 22, in *Pirke de Rabbi Eliezer* (trans. G. Friedlander; 4th ed.; New York: Sepher-Hermon, 1981), 158–73 (167): 'Noah only was left, and they that were with him in the ark . . . except Og, king of Bashan, who sat down on a piece of wood under the gutter of the ark. He swore to Noah and to his sons that he would be their servant forever. What did Noah do? He bored an aperture in the ark, and he put through it his food daily for him, and he also was left.'

[5] Moberly, *Theology of the Book of Genesis*, 27–8.

[6] I am following the lead here of J. H. Walton, *The Lost World of Adam and Eve: Genesis 2–3 and the Human Origins Debate* (Downers Grove: IVP Academic, forthcoming, 2015), who in general cautions his readers against reading modern concerns about material origins into ancient literature like Genesis 1—3 that probably had no such interests in mind.

Cain, Abel and Seth (Gen. 4.1–26)

As Genesis 4 opens, and despite the sin of chapter 3, we find a world still operating under God's blessing. A child is born, whose name *qayin* (Cain) sounds somewhat similar to the verb *qanah*, which lies behind NIV's translation 'I have brought forth'. In the Hebrew, however, the meaning of Eve's words about the birth is not quite so clear. Technically, the possibilities are: 'I have bought a man with Yahweh'; 'I have created a man with Yahweh'; and 'I have bought/created a man – Yahweh!' The last of these makes little sense, however. The first is not much better, and it involves taking the Hebrew particle *'et* ('with'), unusually, as a substitute for *me'et* ('from'). So although the verb *qanah*, 'to create', is rarer than the verb *qanah*, 'to buy', it is probably the best option in Genesis 4.1 (cf. Genesis 14.19, 22, 'God Most High, Creator of heaven and earth'). If so, Eve is claiming to have created Cain, with God's help. In the context of the story so far, and especially in the light of what Genesis 3.22 tells us about Eve's newfound 'godlikeness', it is not difficult to find a particular significance in this claim. The name Cain, then, speaks of the human tendency towards self-divinization. The name Abel (*hebel*) certainly speaks, conversely, of the reality of human existence as mortal. *Hebel* means 'breath' or 'breeze' (e.g. Isa. 57.13), and thus, by extension, things that are insubstantial or fleeting, or actions that are in vain or to no purpose.[7] In particular, human life itself is said to be ephemeral or fleeting in the OT (Pss. 39.4; 144.4). So Abel's name predicts his life, which is short.

Anger and murder

The immediate cause of the problem between the brothers is identified in Genesis 4.3–5, where we discover that 'The LORD looked with favour on Abel and his offering, but on Cain and his offering he did not look with favour'. The reason for the disfavour is not explicitly clear, but it is likely that it is because Cain brings to God only '*some of the fruits* of the soil', while Abel brings '*fat portions* from some of the firstborn of his flock'. In other words, Abel is careful to bring his very best to God, while Cain fails do to so.[8] Cain's resulting anger brings him to a crossroads in his relationship with God, very much like his parents before him. If he does what is right, God tells him, he will be 'lifted up' (NIV's 'accepted', 4.7), both

---

[7] See BDB, 210–11.
[8] This view is already found in Ephrem the Syrian: 'Abel was very discerning in his choice of offerings, whereas Cain showed no such discernment. Abel selected and offered the choicest of his firstborn and of his fat ones, while Cain either offered young grains or certain fruits that are found at the same time as the young grains.' Ephrem, *Commentary on Genesis*, 3.2.1 (ACCS 1:104).

metaphorically (in the sense of acceptance with God) and physically (in terms of his 'fallen' face, Hb. *nafal*). However, if Cain fails to master sin, pictured as a wild animal waiting to pounce and needing to be 'ruled' just like an animal (Hb. *mashal*), then trouble will follow. As it turns out, sin prevails, and Cain murders his brother.[9] This following in his parents' footsteps is indicated in the pattern of the conversation between Cain and God, which follows that of chapter 3. The sin is followed by a question from God ('Where is your brother Abel?', 4.9), which is followed in turn by a lie, and by an evasion of responsibility. The evasion of responsibility ('Am I my brother's keeper?') is then followed by a divine curse (4.11), which is structurally similar to Genesis 3.14:

3.14   Cursed are you above all the livestock (*'arur 'attah
                mikkol-habbehemah*)
4.11 (NRSV)   You are cursed from the ground (*'arur 'attah min-
                ha'adamah*)

This suggests that the sense of Genesis 4.11 is perhaps: 'you are *more* cursed than the land.' The greater sin of Genesis 4 is met with a greater punishment, because the land has been polluted by Abel's blood (cf. Num. 35.33; 2 Sam. 21.1–14; Hos. 4.2–3).

To this point this new chapter in the story of Genesis is not particularly difficult to follow. Two ways have opened up before Cain, just as they opened up before his parents, and he has fallen into wickedness just like them, murdering the innocent Abel in the process. Later books in the Bible develop this same idea, presenting Abel as a prototype of the righteous and Cain as a prototype of the wicked. For example, in Hebrews 11.4, 'By faith Abel offered God a better sacrifice than Cain did.' In 1 John 3.12, the reader is urged, 'Do not be like Cain, who belonged to the evil one and murdered his brother. And why did he murder him? Because his own actions were evil and his brother's were righteous.' Early Jewish tradition follows the same line. Philo regards Cain as representing an evil tendency in human beings to turn away from God and towards the self, while Josephus 'highlights Cain's rapacity and his passion for order and security'.[10]

---

[9] *Gen. Rab.* reflects a tradition that Abel actually overcame Cain in the struggle, but released his hold on him after he begged for mercy, whereupon Cain killed Abel (22.8).

[10] Philo, *On the Birth of Abel and the Sacrifices Offered by Him and His Brother* 1.2, in *The Works of Philo* (trans. C. D. Yonge; Peabody, MA: Hendrickson, 1993), 94–111 (94); Josephus, *Ant.* 1.2.2 (trans. H. St. J. Thackeray et al.; 10 vols; LCL; Cambridge: Harvard University Press, 1926–65). For the quote, see J. M. Dean, 'Cain', in D. L. Jeffrey, *A Dictionary of Biblical Tradition in English Literature* (Grand Rapids: Eerdmans, 1992), 120–2 (121). See further on early interpretation of Cain and Abel, J. Byron, 'Cain and Abel in Second Temple Literature and Beyond', in *The Book of Genesis: Composition, Reception, and Interpretation* (VTSup 152; ed. C. A. Evans, J. N. Lohr and D. L. Petersen; Leiden: Brill, 2012), 331–51.

In the early Christian tradition, Augustine's *City of God* invites its readers to consider that 'the conflict between Cain and Abel displayed the hostility between . . . two cities . . . the city of God and the city of men' – an ongoing conflict between the redeemed and the unredeemed, 'who love this world as their home and find their happiness in the worldly felicity of the earthly city', that would span the entirety of time.[11] In this Christian tradition Abel, the innocent shepherd who died yet made an acceptable sacrifice to God, was inevitably understood (with the help of Matt. 23.25 and Heb. 12.24) as a prefiguration of Jesus Christ and also of the Christian martyrs.[12] This same idea appears again in a much later context in Byron's *Cain*, where Abel dies uttering Christ's words on the cross, asking God to forgive his killer.[13]

Crime and punishment

However, if the story of Genesis 4 thus far is fairly straightforward, what happens next is initially surprising. The cursed human being, we discover, is sent into exile (Gen. 4.11–12). This is surprising, because, typically in the OT, blood is 'removed' in respect of illicit killing in three ways: by monetary compensation, by execution or by exile. The first is not common in the OT (note Exod. 21.29–30; 2 Sam. 21.1–9; Prov. 13.8), and the third appears only as a temporary solution in the case of accidental homicide (note Exod. 21.12–14; Num. 35.9–34; Deut. 19.1–6). In cases of premeditated homicide, neither exile nor monetary compensation is regarded elsewhere in the OT as a sufficient remedy (note Num. 35.31–34; Deut. 19.11–13). Genesis 9.6 will shortly say the same thing, and give a reason for it: 'Whoever sheds the blood of man, by man shall his blood be shed; for in the image of God has God made man.' Human life is precious, and its loss must be marked by another loss. So in cases of pre-meditated murder, the murderer should be handed over to 'the avenger of blood' (as Deuteronomy calls him) – a near relative of the victim, who can avenge his death.

---

[11] Augustine, *City of God*, 15.5, 15.

[12] This identification of Abel with Jesus then made it easy, unfortunately, for Cain to be associated with the 'Christ-killers', the Jews. Consider the words of Ambrose, e.g.: 'In Cain we perceive the parricidal people of the Jews, who were stained with the blood of their Lord, their Creator, and, as a result of the child-bearing of the Virgin Mary, their Brother, also. By Abel we understand the Christian who cleaves to God.' Ambrose, *Cain and Abel*, 1.2.5, in *Saint Ambrose: Hexameron, Paradise, and Cain and Abel* (FC 42; trans. J. J. Savage; Washington, DC: Catholic University of America Press, 1961), 362. This view is later reflected in medieval art, in which Cain is sometimes portrayed wearing the pointed hat (*Judenhut*) that was forced on the Jews during the Middle Ages.

[13] Byron, *Cain: A Mystery*, 3.318–20, in *Dramatic Works of Lord Byron* (New York: A. V. Blake, 1840), 205–63 (257).

Yet revenge might not be desired by the wronged family – especially if the perpetrator were a family member. We do find one other narrative example where such a case is described: the case of David's son Absalom, who murders his brother Amnon (2 Sam. 13.34—14.33). This is a fascinating case, because when the wise woman of Tekoa comes to David at Joab's behest to address David about Absalom, who is living away from the royal court, she uses a story about an avenger of blood to make her point. She tells a tale about her two imaginary sons, one of whom kills the other in a fight and is pursued by the broader family, who want to put him to death. She asks David to intervene on her behalf, to prevent the avenger of blood from adding to the destruction, and David agrees to do this. Then the Tekoan woman asks the king why it is that he has not likewise brought Absalom back to court, when it is in his power to do so. We are reminded by her question precisely that neither David himself, nor anyone else, pursued Absalom for killing Amnon. Exile was essentially chosen as the appropriate punishment for murder in this case, rather than execution (Absalom is, one supposes, 'dead' to David by being in exile). It is also made clear in this story that this 'death' need not last forever, if the family simply decides in favour of reconciliation. Indeed, the woman refers to God's ways of dealing with human beings as her chosen template for the action that she would like David to take (2 Sam. 14.14): 'Like water spilled on the ground, which cannot be recovered, so we must die. But God does not take away life; instead, he devises ways so that a banished person may not remain estranged from him.'

It is against this background that we should understand Genesis 4. A murder has occurred, and that is a serious matter that needs to be addressed. In this case, though, there is no evidence of any desire on the part of Adam to exact vengeance on Cain. One cannot easily imagine that such a desire would typically have been found within Israelite families when it came to one of their own (as the case of David and Absalom also indicates). Exile is therefore chosen as the punishment.[14] Cain is driven away from the land and becomes 'a restless wanderer on the earth' – a rootless person, cut off from family ties and family protection, and without any family member

---

[14] Some Jewish tradition, apparently reflecting concern about the way in which the punishment in Gen. 4 does not fit the crime, introduces the idea that Cain repented of his sin, thereby escaping the punishment he deserved. So *Gen. Rab.* 22.13, where Adam goes on to lament the fact that he himself had not realized how powerful repentance could be. This view is disputed by Ephrem the Syrian, who addresses Cain thus: 'Did [Justice] not delay so that you might repent? Did Justice not distance itself from its own knowledge and ask you as if it did not know, so that you might confess?' Ephrem, *Commentary on Genesis*, 3.7.1 (ACCS 1:107).

available even to avenge *his* death should it occur ('whoever finds me will kill me', 4.14). The expulsion (Hb. *giresh*, 3.24) of Adam and Eve from the garden had not disrupted human relationships in this radical manner – they remained a functioning family. The expulsion (Hb. *giresh*, 4.14) of Cain from the land is far more severe. It represents a disruption not only of the *family* relationships but also of the *divine–human* relationship – and this also more severely than before. Hitherto human beings have still been living in God's 'presence' (4.14 and 4.16), but now Cain will need to leave this 'presence'. Murder is a serious matter, and if it does not result in death, at least it leads to severe punishment.

Cain in exile

Yet even in this severe punishment, the blessing of God first introduced in Genesis 1 is still to be seen in Genesis 4. Cain fears that to be sent into exile is virtually to *be* sentenced to death, since he may be killed in exile without fear of retribution (4.13). This punishment, he feels, is more than he can bear. But God promises that he himself will be Cain's avenger of blood (4.15): 'if anyone kills Cain, he will suffer vengeance seven times over'; that is, suffer the full measure of vengeance (cf. Ps. 79.12, 'Pay back into the laps of our neighbours seven times the reproach they have hurled at you, O Lord!'). Furthermore, God puts a 'mark' on Cain to warn others away[15] – a 'sign' (Hb. *'ot*) that indicates, in the context of the book of Genesis, God's blessing and goodwill towards people (cf. Gen. 1.14; 9.13; 17.11).[16] A murderer who deserves to die is instead only exiled, and in his exile he is treated by God as part of his own family – someone whose blood God will avenge.

This continued blessing on Cain is immediately seen in Genesis 4.17–18, in that he produces a family line responsible for many wonderful aspects of human culture (4.20–22) – the development of livestock farming, music and metalworking. We also see here, however, the continuation of Cain's violent tendencies, as well as the introduction of other aspects of human culture that are not quite so positive from the biblical point of view. The seventh generation after Cain – represented by Lamech and representing

---

[15] *Gen. Rab.* nevertheless holds that the sign of Cain was not protective, but rather a sign of shame and an example for murderers (22.12).

[16] The 'mark' is traditionally a letter or a name on Cain's forehead or arm: *Tg. Ps.-J.* to Gen. 4.37 (trans. M. Maher; Collegeville, MN: Liturgical Press, 1987), 34; *Pirqe R. El.* 21. However, other ideas have been mooted: an involuntary shaking of the head, a psychological condition or even a black skin. See further R. Mellinkoff, *The Mark of Cain* (Berkeley: University of California Press, 1981).

the 'fullness' or 'perfection' of Cain's line – is particularly problematic. Lamech kills a man for wounding (Hb. *petsaʿ*) and injuring him (Hb. *chabburah*, Gen. 4.23). His violence is neither legal nor just, as Exodus 21.23–25 implies: 'you are to take life for life . . . wound for wound (Hb. *petsaʿ*), bruise for bruise (Hb. *chabburah*).' There is in fact something quite perverse about referring back to God's promise to Cain in such a context, precisely because Lamech has not been killed, and he is not being avenged. An act of divine grace has been twisted into something dark, and then celebrated in a poem (Gen. 4.23–24). And so the alienation of human from human in the Genesis story becomes even more pronounced as we reach Lamech. Here we encounter the breakdown, not just of sibling relationships, but of broader community relationships. Shortly the whole human community will slide into complete chaos and anarchy, as violence fills the earth (6.11–13).

This is a view of human culture that is very different from the one we find in Mesopotamian counterparts to the book of Genesis. Like the biblical tradition, Mesopotamian tradition roots arts and crafts in primeval times, telling us of seven superhuman sages who arose from the sea before the flood and taught humanity civilizational skills (writing, agriculture and city-building). The oldest of these sages is Adapa, associated with the city of Eridu (generally regarded in Mesopotamian tradition as the first city to be founded). In this way of thinking, civilization is made possible by the gods, and it is directly rooted in the divine will; human progress is blessed by the gods. The book of Genesis takes a more nuanced view: there *is* cultural progress in God's good world, but it is accompanied by the inexorable advance of darkness, and the gods are certainly not behind it all. Cultural advancement is a much more ambiguous entity here. It occurs in the midst of assertions of autonomy from God, acts of defiance against God, and barbarism.

Cain and Abel interpreted

The story of Cain and Abel has inspired a considerable amount of Western art and music. Early representations of Abel's sacrifice appear on a first-century sarcophagus from Rome, and Byzantine mosaics of the sixth and seventh centuries from Ravenna connect it with the later Abraham story. Later, Ghiberti included the story on the fifteenth-century bronze doors of the Baptistery in Florence, and it is the subject of famous paintings by Titian, Tintoretto, Rubens, and others. Scarlatti set it to music in 1706 (*Cain, ovvero il primo omicidio*), Thomas Arne in 1744 (*The Death of Abel*), Conradin Kreutzer in 1810 (*La Mort d'Abel*) and Max Zenger in 1867

(*Cain*), to name but a few.[17] It was turned into a ballet by Marc Blitzstein in 1930, and into a narration with orchestra by Darius Milhaud in 1945.[18]

The story has also inspired a considerable amount of Western literature, with varying assessments of the two main human protagonists being offered, as well as some commentary on God himself. Much interpretation follows the line already articulated in the Bible, in which Cain is plainly wicked and Abel righteous. This is true of the medieval mystery plays, for example, 'which uniformly contrast Abel's humble righteousness with Cain's proud rebelliousness, and . . . stress that Abel makes offering willingly and gives his best lamb, while Cain grudgingly sacrifices his worst'.[19] Abel's innocent blood is evoked in similar vein in three of Shakespeare's plays (*Hamlet*, *Richard II* and *Henry VI*), in Milton's *Paradise Lost*, and in Shelley's drama *Hellas* (1822) where the fallen cry out for vengeance just like the blood of Abel from the dust.[20] Cain's crime haunts the story of *Beowulf*, and in Dante's *Inferno* it stands behind the naming of the part of hell (Caina) where people are punished for treachery to kin.[21] For Dryden, 'Cain is the archetype of violence and murder, a spirit "latent" in Adam's seed which would lead ultimately to the religious divisions of Dryden's times'.[22] He is, for Coleridge in his unfinished 'The Wanderings of Cain' (1828) a perpetually cursed man, pursued by a relentless God who will not leave him be.[23]

But what does this say about God? This is a question developed by Byron in his epic poem *Cain: A Mystery* (1821), which was widely condemned at the time as blasphemous because of its challenge to the idea of divine benevolence. Here the murderer becomes 'an iconoclast questioning divine justice who possibly holds God responsible for the murder because

---

[17] N. M. Sarna et al., 'Cain', *EncJud* 4:340–2.

[18] Sarna, 'Cain'; M. Stern, *Bible and Music: Influences of the Old Testament on Western Music* (Jersey City, NJ: Ktav, 2011), 15–27.

[19] J. S. Hill, 'Abel', in Jeffrey, *Biblical Tradition*, 4–6 (5).

[20] W. Shakespeare, *Hamlet*, 3.3.36–8; *Richard II*, 1.1.104–6; *Henry VI*, 1.3.38–40; J. Milton, *Paradise Lost*, 11.429–47; P. B. Shelley, *Hellas*, in *The Complete Poetical Works of Shelley* (ed. T. Hutchinson; Oxford: Clarendon, 1904; repr. Cambridge: Chadwyck-Healey, 1994), 493–523 (505). See Hill, 'Abel', 5–6, for these and other examples.

[21] R. D. Fulk, ed. and trans., *The Beowulf Manuscript: Complete Texts and the Fight at Finnsburg*, 99–114 (DOML 3; Cambridge, MA: Harvard University Press, 2010), 92–3; Dante Alighieri, *Inferno*, 5.107; 32.58 (vol. 1 of *The Divine Comedy*; trans. H. W. Longfellow; Boston: Ticknor and Fields, 1867), 31, 200, 236 n. 107.

[22] Dryden, *The Hind and the Panther*, 1.279 (London: Jacob Tonson, 1687), 16. See Dean, 'Cain', 122.

[23] 'And Cain lifted up his voice and cried bitterly, and said, "The Mighty One that persecuteth me is on this side and on that; he pursueth my soul like the wind, like the sand-blast he passeth through me; he is around me even as the air! O that I might be utterly no more! I desire to die."' S. T. Coleridge, 'The Wanderings of Cain', 2:31–3, in *The Works of Samuel Taylor Coleridge* (WPL; Hertfordshire: Wordsworth Editions, 1994), 288–92.

He created Cain and failed as Keeper of Abel'.[24] Despite Blake's response to Byron along traditional lines in *The Ghost of Abel* (1822) – in which the ghost cries out for vengeance in respect of the murdering brother – it is the Byronic romanticizing of Cain that has marked the modern period. He provides a template for all sorts of characters in modern narrative, from Twain's *Adventures of Huckleberry Finn* (1884), through Melville's *Moby Dick* (1851) and Steinbeck's *East of Eden* (1952), and on to García Márquez's *One Hundred Years of Solitude* (1967).[25] The optimism of the third of these is particularly striking when compared to some earlier treatments of Cain as 'cursed man'. Steinbeck's world is certainly one that is marked by dysfunction, including that which is brought about by poor decisions. Yet in this world 'east of Eden' there is also much good to be found, and to remain stuck in negative cycles of anger, revenge and guilt is not inevitable. Nor is it inevitable that sons and daughters will follow the example of their own parents. The Chinese cook Lee's own studies of Genesis 4, we learn, have led him to see that God neither promises Cain that in time he will master sin, nor commands him to do so, but rather tells him that he *may* (Hb. *timshol*, from the verb *mashal*). And the novel ends with this word of hope, addressed by Adam to his son Caleb: 'You may master.' It is possible to move ahead.

The line of Seth

Having followed the line of Cain through several generations, Genesis 4 finally returns to the primal couple of Act 2 (Adam and Eve) in order to describe the different line of descent that begins with Seth. It may be significant, now that we have read Cain's story, that Eve does not here repeat

---

[24] W. Z. Hirst, 'George Gordon Byron', in *The Blackwell Companion to the Bible in English Literature* (ed. R. Lemon et al.; Oxford: Wiley-Blackwell, 2009), 438–50 (449). See further W. Z. Hirst, 'Reassertion', in Lemon et al., *Bible in English Literature*, 75: 'Byron . . . projected his own yearning for lost Eden and his obsession with the temptation of man, mortality, heightened consciousness, and "fury against the inadequacy of his state to his conceptions" into Cain . . .'

[25] M. Twain, *Adventures of Huckleberry Finn* (NCE 34; ed. S. Bradley, R. C. Beatty and E. H. Long; New York: W. W. Norton and Co., 1962); J. Steinbeck, *East of Eden* (New York: Viking, 1952; repr. London: Penguin, 2000); H. Melville, *Moby Dick* (ed. H. Parker and H. Hayford; 2nd ed.; New York: W. W. Norton and Co., 2002); G. García Márquez, *One Hundred Years of Solitude* (New York: Harper and Row, 1970). The account of the Buendía family in the last of these four works displays marked similarity 'to the Biblical account of the history of man from Genesis to Apocalypse', and its main character, José Arcadio Buendía, certainly begins by reminding us of Cain, 'killing a friend who has offended him' and setting off eastwards, 'away from the coast that is civilization, in order to resettle elsewhere with his wife and some of his neighbors'. The new Eden that José founds is subsequently devastated by an apocalyptic hurricane. M. Morello-Frosch, 'One Hundred Years of Solitude by Gabriel Marquez, or Genesis Re-Written', in *Biblical Patterns in Modern Literature* (BJS 77; ed. D. H. Hirsch and N. Aschkenasy; Chico, CA: Scholars, 1984), 155–63 (155–6).

her claim to co-creation, but simply says, 'God has granted me another child in place of Abel' (Gen. 4.25). This seemingly more humble approach to procreation[26] is certainly consistent with the brighter note upon which the whole account of the 'descendants of the heavens and the earth' ends. 'At that time men [= people] began to call on the name of the LORD' (4.26); that is, they began to worship Yahweh.[27] Since this cannot refer to the beginning of worship of Yahweh as such, because that was already happening before (e.g. in the sacrifices of Cain and Abel), we must assume that it is a reference to the beginning of *widespread* worship of Yahweh, just as the earlier verses mark other significant beginnings in human cultural development. After the digression represented by the disobedient Cain, and after his expulsion from the territory near the garden, there is a restoration of worship in the land, connected with the birth of Seth.

The line of Seth has proved to be an object of fascination for some interpreters through the ages, not least those of Gnostic persuasion, who have indulged in fantastic speculations about it and were much criticized for this by Church Fathers such as Irenaeus.[28] An early story about an imagined Sethian journey to Paradise, first found in the first-century AD *Apocalypse of Moses*, later came to be linked to Christian traditions that traced the wood of Christ's cross back to Paradise, and this is reflected in medieval mystery plays.[29] In the Reformation Seth plays a more humble role, representing (in a story told by Philip Melanchthon in 1539) the righteous Christian who knows his doctrine and who can be trusted to guard the public peace and promote true religion. Cain's doctrine, by contrast, is far from Reformed. This same story was later much retold, often in the form of dialogues and plays, such as Hans Sachs' *The Unequal Children of Adam and Eve* (1558). In such literature Cain was routinely represented as a Roman Catholic: 'Most Lutheran authors used the figure of Cain to stigmatize Catholic beliefs.'[30]

---

[26] 'Unlike the wonder and joy expressed at that other birth, this statement is one of resignation.' K. R. R. Gros Louis, 'Genesis 3–11', in *Literary Interpretations of Biblical Narratives* (2 vols; Nashville: Abingdon, 1982), 2:44. Also A. L. Lerner, *Eternally Eve: Images of Eve in the Hebrew Bible, Midrash, and Modern Jewish Poetry* (HBISJW; Waltham, MA: Brandeis University Press, 2007), 155: 'Eve emerges from this chapter somewhat chastened, but wiser than she was at the beginning . . . She has suffered the consequences of her hubristic stance at the beginning of the chapter and has learned from them.'

[27] Cf. Gen. 12.8; 13.4; 21.33; 26.25.

[28] I. Dunderberg, 'Gnostic Interpretations of Genesis', in *The Oxford Handbook of Reception History of the Bible* (ed. M. Lieb, E. Mason, J. Roberts and C. Rowland; Oxford: Oxford University Press, 2011), 390–2.

[29] E. C. Quinn, 'Seth', in Jeffrey, *Biblical Tradition*, 695–6.

[30] K. M. Crowther, *Adam and Eve in the Protestant Reformation* (Cambridge: Cambridge University Press, 2010), 226–57 (250).

An interesting interpretative footnote to the story in Genesis 4 concerns Eve, who is still alive as the chapter ends and is never said subsequently to die (unlike her husband Adam, Gen. 5.5). This has led to several imaginative modern construals of Eve's life after Genesis 4, including one operatic production (*Lilith*, 2000) in which Eve is joined by Lilith at Adam's funeral.[31] In Jewish tradition, Lilith is a seductive demon whose liaisons with Adam after he parts from Eve in the aftermath of the curses of Genesis 3 produce male and female demon-offspring, who now fill the world. Lilith can also be seen in this tradition as a 'first Eve', created from the earth at the same time as Adam but later leaving him as the result of a dispute about equality.[32] After an inauspicious literary career during the pre-modern Christian era, Lilith eventually made it big in the Romantic period and afterwards, appearing for example in Goethe's *Faust* (Part 1, 1808); in Browning's 'Adam, Lilith, and Eve' (1883); in MacDonald's *Lilith* (1895); in Shaw's *Back to Methuselah* (1921); in Joyce's *Ulysses* (1922); and even in Lewis's *The Lion, the Witch, and the Wardrobe* (1950), where the White Witch is said to be one of Lilith's offspring.[33] She also turns up in the work of another 'Inkling', Charles Williams, when in *Descent into Hell* (1937) Lily Sammile, who promises the heroine Pauline utter happiness, turns out in the end to be Lilith, 'who was the wife of Adam before Eve, and for salvation from whom Eve was devised after the mist had covered the land of Eden'.[34] It is this same Lilith who turns up at the funeral in the 2000 opera just mentioned, at which point (with a nice modern twist) Eve is left to explain her presence there to her son and daughter.

The descendants of Adam (Gen. 5.1—6.8)

In a sense we could paraphrase most of the next section of Genesis (Act 3) in this way: 'a long time passed.' In Genesis 5 the author moves from the story of Genesis 2—4 to the story of Genesis 6—9 as quickly as possible, using the most abbreviated form of story that he can – the genealogy.

---

[31] Lerner, *Eternally Eve*, 158.

[32] *Erub.* 18b; *Gen. Rab.* 20.11; *Zohar* 3.19a, in *The Zohar: Pritzker Edition* (trans. D. C. Matt; 7 vols; Stanford, CA: Stanford University Press, 2012), 7:117–20. See further G. Scholem, 'Lilith', *EncJud* 13:17–20.

[33] J. W. von Goethe, *Faust: Part One and Part Two*, 4196–223 (LOLA; trans. C. E. Passage; Indianapolis: Bobbs-Merrill, 1965), 144; R. Browning, 'Adam, Lilith, and Eve', in *The Complete Poetical Works of Robert Browning* (ed. A. Birrell; New York: Macmillan, 1915), 1200; G. MacDonald, *Lilith: A Duplex* (London: Chatto & Windus, 1895; repr. Whitehorn, CA: Johannesen, 1994); G. B. Shaw, *Back to Methuselah* (London: Constable, 1921); J. Joyce, *Ulysses* (Harmondsworth, Middlesex: Penguin, 1954); C. S. Lewis, *The Lion, The Witch, and the Wardrobe* (New York: HarperCollins, 2000). For other literature, see R. Schell, 'Lilith', in Jeffrey, *Biblical Tradition*, 454–5.

[34] C. Williams, *Descent into Hell* (Grand Rapids: Eerdmans, 1966), 207.

The Sumerian Flood Story mentions seven to ten kings who reigned before the flood (the numbers vary in different versions of the story), all of them for an exceptionally long time. The last of these is called Ziusudra, the Sumerian name for the survivor of the flood. Here in Genesis 5 we read of nine descendants of Adam, all of whom also live for an exceptionally long time. The last of these is Noah, the survivor of the flood. Of course, the biblical tradition concerns human beings in general, not the first king and his descendants, and this is consistent with the democratization of kingship already noted in Genesis 1. All human beings 'rule' in Genesis – not just kings. Among all the characters mentioned in this genealogy, Enoch and (a second) Lamech are of particular interest.

Enoch (Gen. 5.21–24) is the seventh in line from Adam – the 'full flowering' of Adam's line as it passes through Seth, just like the earlier Lamech in the case of the line of Cain. Widespread formalized worship of Yahweh began around the time of Seth's birth; later, we are told, Enoch 'walked with God'. The phrase reminds us of God walking in the garden in communion with the first humans, and it anticipates what is said of later righteous Israelites (e.g. Noah, Gen. 6.9; Abraham, 17.1). It is later generalized of all the righteous by the prophet Micah (Mic. 6.8): 'And what does the LORD require of you? To act justly and to love mercy and to walk humbly with your God.' So we see in Enoch and Noah, but perhaps also in this whole line of Seth (in view of Gen. 4.26) something of a restoration of the relationship with God once lost in the garden. In the case of Enoch in particular, we apparently read of a complete reversal of the consequences of the sin in the garden, since Enoch lived and then 'he was no more, because God took him away' (Gen. 5.24). Apparently Enoch is granted access to the tree of life, and does not die. Elijah will later experience the same thing (2 Kings 2).

The Lamech mentioned in Genesis 5.28–31 reminds us, of course, of the Lamech of Genesis 4, and serves to underline the differences between the lines of Cain and Seth. He is no boastful murderer, but simply the father of Noah (Hb. *noach*), whom he hopes will bring him what the NIV describes as 'comfort' (the Hb. verb *nacham*) 'in the labour and painful toil of our hands' (5.29). This is best understood, however, not as consolation *in the midst of* ongoing labour and painful toil, but as *relief* from it (so NRSV).[35] It is an active 'comforting' that is in mind, involving a change in circumstances. It is this rest from labour and toil that the name 'Noah' itself implies, for it derives from the verb *nuach*, which means 'to rest' (Exod.

---

[35] This is how the Piel of the verb *nacham* is used in passages like Isa. 51.3; Jer. 31.13–14; Zech. 1.17; Pss. 71.20; 86.17; 119.81–84.

20.11; 23.12; Deut. 5.14) – to cease from work. The use of *noach* and *nacham* together imply that Lamech is not merely anticipating *comfort* in the midst of painful toil, then, but looking for *relief* from the cursing of the ground mentioned in Genesis 3.17. The fulfilment of this hope is found after the flood when Noah becomes the first person to plant a vineyard. Successful agriculture is instituted, just as animal husbandry, music and metalworking have previously been so (Gen. 4.20–22).

Before we get to that happy outcome, however, the reader must endure with the rest of creation the flood itself, the background to which is first provided in Genesis 6.1–8. Here we encounter first a curious account concerning certain 'sons of God' who marry 'daughters of men'. Most likely the sons of God in this context are angelic beings (as in Job 1.6), conceived of here as intermarrying with human females in much the way that we commonly find in ancient Near Eastern texts, including those from Mesopotamia and Egypt. Less plausible options include the ideas that the 'sons of God' are human beings of the line of Seth,[36] or that they are human kings.[37] As we look at how 'sons of God' is used elsewhere in the OT, the first idea is simply not credible. In the second case, 'son of God' is indeed used elsewhere in the OT of the human king (e.g. Pss. 2.7; 82). However, it is important to note the precise way in which Genesis 6.2 is written, and what it reminds us of. It is written so as to imply a *contrast* between the human and the divine ('sons of *God* ... daughters of *'adam'*), and to remind us of an earlier, important infringement of the *boundary* between the human and the divine:

> Genesis 3.6   The woman saw (Hb. *ra'ah*) that the tree was good (Hb. *tov*) ... and she took (Hb. *laqach*)
>
> Genesis 6.2   The sons of God (Hb. *ra'ah*) saw the daughters of *'adam*, that they were beautiful (Hb. *tov*), and they married them (Hb. *laqach*)

When we recall, in addition, the emphasis in the creation story that everything in creation should reproduce 'according to its kind', and the later prohibitions in Torah concerning various kinds of 'mixing' of different things, especially in the sexual realm – the crossing of set boundaries with respect to intercourse with animals or with human beings of the same gender (Lev 20.13, 16) – it seems clear that here in Genesis 6 a different boundary is described as having been crossed. It is the boundary between the heavens

---

[36] This was argued, e.g., by Augustine (*City of God*, 15.23). See also Aquinas, *Summa Theologiae*, 1.52.1.
[37] E.g. M. Kline, 'Divine Kingship and Genesis 6:1–4', *WTJ* 24 (1962): 187–204.

and the earth. It is Genesis 3 all over again, and most likely we are to think that from the human side, the motivation is just the same as in that earlier chapter: these people want immortality. The daughters of *'adam* therefore willingly intermarry with divine beings, in order to produce offspring who will attain eternal life. The similar consequence itself indicates the similar motivation. And just as the human grasping after divinity in Genesis 3 leads to death (eventually), the involvement of human beings in these marriages also brings death (Gen. 6.3): 'my Spirit will not contend with humans for ever, for they are mortal; their days will be a hundred and twenty years.' God's Spirit (Hb. *ruach*) is probably to be understood here as the breath of life (*ruach*) mentioned in Genesis 2.17 (and also in the upcoming 6.17 and 7.15). This breath will not 'abide' or 'remain' with *'adam* forever (NRSV, better than NIV's 'contend'); lifetimes will now be shorter.[38] It must be made unequivocally clear to human beings that they are mortal.

The ultimate background against which this biblical objection to the conjoining of sex and religion in pursuit of immortality is to be understood is probably that of ancient Near Eastern sacred marriage rituals, which had the purpose of ensuring control over fertility. Already back in the ancient Sumerian period (*c.*2700–1800 BC) we encounter a sacred marriage rite involving the goddess Inanna (the personification of Venus) and her divine spouse Dumuzi, once a priest-king of ancient Uruk. All the kings of the Third Dynasty of Ur and of the Isin Dynasty impersonated Dumuzi, now deified, in this sacred marriage rite, which was believed to fertilize nature and society alike for the coming year, and thus to ensure plenty and abundance for the land.[39] It is this same notion of marriage between a god and a mortal that then appears in mythological form in the later Akkadian *Epic of Gilgamesh*, where Ishtar tries to seduce the hero Gilgamesh.[40] Gilgamesh himself is said in the *Epic* to be a product of sexual intercourse between his human father Lugalbanda and his goddess mother Ninsun, and to be partly divine on that account. It is precisely the view of the world that is implied in such a ritual that is rejected by the Hebrew authors of Genesis, who do not understand the 'gods' as being truly gods, do not see the true God as being continuous with creation and capable of manipulation through fertility rites, and who do not understand

---

[38] This is a strange thing to say, when it is clear that *'adam* had already been fated to die in Gen. 3. However, the Hb. *'olam* does not necessarily mean literally 'forever'. It often refers simply to a long period of time.

[39] S. N. Kramer, 'Cuneiform Studies and History of Literature', *APSP* 107 (1963): 485–527 (489–90).

[40] J. B. Pritchard (ed.), *Ancient Near Eastern Texts Relating to the Old Testament* (3rd ed. with suppl.; Princeton: Princeton University Press, 1969), 83.

kings as gods or demi-gods, capable of intercourse with divinity. Genesis 6.1–4 tells us, in fact, that ancient fertility religion has always been an affront to the true and living God – part of the wrong-headed human campaign to grasp hold of immortality. Far from ensuring the fertility of the earth, Genesis claims, such religion leads to its undoing.

The undoing is first introduced in Genesis 6.5–8. If God's first response to the terrible state of the world – symbolized by societal engagement in fertility religion – is to reassert his control over life and death, it is soon overwhelmed by a second response. Wickedness is now rampant on the earth – that is what the Lord 'sees' when he looks at it (6.5). The significance of the wording becomes clear as we set Genesis 6.5 alongside Genesis 3.6 and 6.2 and read them all in the light of Genesis 1:

Genesis 1.10   God saw (Hb. *ra'ah*) that it was good (Hb. *tov*)

Genesis 3.6   The woman saw (Hb. *ra'ah*) that the tree was good (Hb. *tov*) . . . and she took (Hb. *laqach*)

Genesis 6.2   The sons of God (Hb. *ra'ah*) saw the daughters of *'adam*, that they were beautiful (Hb. *tov*), and they married them (Hb. *laqach*)

Genesis 6.5   The Lord saw (Hb. *ra'ah*) how great the wickedness (Hb. *ra'ah*) of the human race had become on the earth

The language suggests a direct connection between the current state of affairs that God 'sees', on the one hand, and the actions of Genesis 6.1–2, on the other – just as 6.1–2 is connected with 3.6 by the nature of the wrong action. The world has descended into chaos, because its fundamental ordering in terms of heavens and earth has been undermined. As so often in Hebrew literature, the wordplay underlines the point that is being made. The wickedness that now exists in the world encompasses everything, from the 'inclinations of the thoughts of the human heart' outwards (a general statement, which is obviously not to be taken too absolutely, since Noah was not like this). Consequently, a catastrophe is announced that will involve the destruction of humans 'and animals, and creatures that move along the ground, and birds of the air' (6.7) – an 'uncreation' so far as animal life is concerned. This underlines the way in which the whole of the created order is conceived of in Genesis as an organic unity. The fate of creation is bound up with the fate of the human creatures who have been created to look after it. Among those creatures, happily, there is one person who finds 'favour in the eyes of the Lord' (6.8). So this ending to the account of 'the descendants of Adam' carries hope for a future beyond the catastrophe, in the family of the person to whose account we now turn.

8

From Noah to the tower of Babel: Genesis 6.9—11.26

In this chapter we shall cover the ground occupied by Acts 4, 5 and 6 of the Genesis drama. Act 4 (Gen. 6.9–9.29) tells the story of the descendants of Noah, whose family survives the flood, down as far as Shem, Ham and Japheth. Act 5 (Gen. 10.1—11.9) recounts the family history of Shem, Ham and Japheth, describing the origins of the nations after the flood, including the account of the scattering at Babel. Act 6 (Gen. 11.10–26) briefly describes the family history of Shem, leading us into the story of Abraham that occupies the central part of the book.

The history of the flood narrative (Gen. 6.9—9.29)

Act 4 of the book of Genesis has often been regarded by modern scholars as providing some of the best evidence available for the Documentary Hypothesis concerning the Pentateuch that was described in our Chapter 3 above. As John Barton once put it, even while acknowledging some of the problems that arise from extensive source-critical theorizing, 'No-one, to my way of thinking, has yet shown that the flood narrative of Genesis 6—9 forms a coherent unit, according to any literary conventions that can plausibly be reconstructed even if one is looking for them.'[1] Yet serious questions arise when the proposed documentary sources in Genesis 6—9 are scrutinized.[2]

For example, the J source turns out to be a story in which Noah is instructed to go into an ark (7.1–5) that has not previously been built or even mentioned. It is also a story that provides us with no account of

---

[1] J. Barton, *Reading the Old Testament: Method in Biblical Study* (Philadelphia: Westminster, 1984), 28. So also R. S. Kawashima, 'Sources and Redaction', in *Reading Genesis: Ten Methods* (ed. R. Hendel; Cambridge: Cambridge University Press, 2010), ch. 3, for whom the Genesis flood story, 'having rather clear source divisions, provides a relatively simple test case' (69).

[2] A typical breakdown of the 'source' P in the flood story is provided by S. R. Driver, *The Book of Genesis* (2nd ed.; London: Methuen, 1904), iv–v: Gen. 6.9–22; 7.6, 11, 13–16a, 17a, 18–21, 24; 8.1–2a, 3b–5, 13a, 14–19; 9.1–17, 28–29. The source J comprises Gen. 7.1–5, 7–10, 12, 16b, 17b, 22–23; 8.2b–3a, 6–12, 13b, 20–22; 9.18–27.

Noah leaving this mysteriously appearing ark. In one moment he is float-
ing around, sending doves out in search of land (8.6–12), and discovering
that 'the surface of the ground was dry' (8.13b); in the very next, he is
building an altar and sacrificing (8.20–22). This is a somewhat terse 'source',
to say the least, and most source critics feel compelled to argue that we
no longer possess all of it. The editor who put the biblical flood story
together used only what was useful to him, omitting parts of J that he did
not need, because he already possessed parts of P that could do the job.
But if he was prepared to *omit* parts of J for this reason, why did he *include*
other parts of J that are allegedly either duplicates of, or in conflict, with
material in P? It is such ill-fitting passages that provide source critics with
evidence that J and P are combined in the flood story in the first place.
Why are *these* sections of J 'useful' enough to be included? There is no
clearly satisfactory answer to this question.

Then we must also note that, if *indeed* the two sources are to be distinguished from each other on the basis of passages that cover the same
ground (the so-called 'doublet' passages), their separation does not always
lead to consistency with respect to another criterion used by source critics
to distinguish them, namely the employment of different names for God
('Yahweh' and 'Elohim'; see further our Chapter 5 above). If Genesis 7.13–15
belong to P, then the doublet passage in Genesis 7.7–10 must surely belong
to J; but the latter passage very inconveniently refers to God as 'Elohim'
in verse 9, which is a 'P-usage'. The implausibility of the ways in which
source critics attempt to get around such problems in their analysis of the
book of Genesis is well illustrated by these words from E. A. Speiser:

> There are many sections in Genesis . . . which do not mention the Deity.
> Nor is the mere occurrence of Elohim decisive in itself, since the term can
> also be used . . . not only for alien gods and idols but also in the broader
> sense of our Providence, Heaven, Fate, and is actually so attested in the
> J source, among others. The evidence remains significant, but one-sided:
> Elohim could well appear in any document, as is only natural in the circum-
> stances; on the other hand, Yahweh is in Genesis the exclusive companion
> of J (barring occasional lapses in the composite text under the influence of
> an adjacent passage from another source).[3]

It would not be unfair, I think, to summarize Speiser's comments here
as follows: 'Yahweh' and 'Elohim' appear in passages assigned by source
critic to both J and P, but we shall explain away all the occurrences that
are inconvenient to the source theory. This is not very convincing logic.

---

[3] E. A. Speiser, *Genesis* (AB; Garden City, NY: Doubleday, 1964), xxiii.

Already in the flood narrative it fails to convince.[4] By the time we get to the closing chapters of Genesis (Gen. 37—50), it fails to command any kind of assent. Here 'Elohim' is *invariably* used in allegedly J-contexts, and 'Yahweh' is almost entirely restricted to a cluster of verses in Genesis 39 (39.2–3, 5, 21, 23; the one exception is found in Gen. 49.18). Walter Moberly's theory about the divine names here certainly seems much more likely than Wellhausen's to be correct: a narrator selectively added references to 'Yahweh', where it seemed important to do so, to a section of the Genesis story that originally referred to God throughout as 'Elohim'.[5]

What kind of story is the flood narrative?

However (precisely) the biblical flood story was once composed, as we turn to the text that we now have before us we find that Act 4 of Genesis begins by briefly recapitulating what the end of Act 3 tells us about the background to the flood. We are reminded here, in particular, about the righteousness of Noah. This righteousness is asserted rather than described, prompting early questions about it among Jewish interpreters,[6] and some enterprising answers: that Noah introduced new technologies, thus bringing relief in the midst of work (as his father had foreseen, Gen. 5.29); that he waited a long time before building the ark in the hope that people would repent (and that he urged people to repent);[7] or that he took great care of the animals in the ark.[8]

The divine plan to save creation even in the midst of God's judgement is next introduced, involving a large boat in which Noah, his extended family and animal-creation-in-miniature will ride out the watery chaos soon to descend upon the earth (Gen. 6.14–22). This boat is unsurprisingly read in later Christian tradition as analogous to the Church, by way of a

---

[4] As to what the deployment of other source-critical 'criteria' achieves in this narrative, see R. N. Whybray, *The Making of the Pentateuch: A Methodological Study* (JSOTSup 53; Sheffield: Sheffield Academic, 1987), 83 (on 'repetition'), 89 ('contradiction'). It is worth quoting a line from the latter, in view of my comments above about the 'terseness' of J: 'The contradictions in the story of the Flood . . . do not, by themselves, justify a documentary analysis which can only be made to work by means of the assumption of the omission by a redactor of important elements in one of the two postulated documents.'

[5] R. W. L. Moberly, *The Old Testament of the Old Testament: Patriarchal Narratives and Mosaic Yahwism* (OBT; Minneapolis: Fortress, 1992), 70–1. See further Whybray, *Making of the Pentateuch*, 63–72.

[6] E.g. Philo, *Allegorical Interpretation* 3.77, in *The Works of Philo* (trans. C. D. Yonge; Peabody, MA: Hendrickson, 1993), 50–79 (58).

[7] *Tanh. Gen.* 11; *Tanh. Noah* 5; Josephus, *Ant.*, 1.74. See also in the NT, 2 Pet. 2.5 and its reference to 'Noah, a preacher of righteousness'. This idea is picked up later by, among others, Milton in *Paradise Lost*, 11.719–27.

[8] *Sanh.* 108b; *Tanh. B.* 58.2.

passage like 1 Peter 3.20–21, 'God waited patiently in the days of Noah while the ark was being built. In it only a few people, eight in all, were saved through water, and this water symbolises baptism that now saves you also.' In such Christian reading, Noah is seen as prefiguring Christ himself. These links having been made between Noah and Christ, ark and Church, we find the Noah story being evoked in the art of the early Christian catacombs in Rome (e.g. the catacomb of Priscilla), in the medieval mystery plays, in the carvings of Gothic cathedrals like Wells and Salisbury, and perhaps most famously, by Michelangelo, in the Sistine Chapel in the Vatican. The flood also finds its way into music (for example, the 1876 oratorio *Le Déluge* by Saint-Saëns, and Britten's 1957 children's opera, *Noye's Fludde*),[9] and modern film: John Huston's *The Bible . . . In the Beginning* (1966) and Darren Aronofsky's *Noah* (2014).[10]

The arrival of the watery chaos is announced in Genesis 7.11–12. Waters pour in from below and above, with the ultimate consequence that

> Every living thing on the face of the earth was wiped out; men and animals and the creatures that move along the ground and the birds were wiped from the earth. Only Noah was left, and those with him in the ark.
>
> (Gen. 7.23)

The turning point in the narrative (well illustrated in Wenham's structural analysis reproduced in our Chapter 1) comes in Genesis 8.1, when 'God remembered Noah and all the wild animals and the livestock that were with him in the ark'. This remembrance brings redemption, as it does later in Israel's story in Exodus 2.24. Having risen to their highest point just prior to Genesis 8.1, the waters now begin to recede, until the boat comes to rest in mountains in the area of Ararat (ancient Urartu, modern Armenia, Gen. 8.4). Dry land continues to appear out of the midst of water, as it does also in Genesis 1; creation is being reborn. The earth becomes once again habitable, producing vegetation (of which the 'olive leaf' in Gen. 8.11 is the first sign).[11] The creatures in the ark emerge, as

---

[9] D. Young, E. E. Halevy and H. Z. Hirschberg, 'Noah', *EncJud* 15:287–90 (289–90); M. Stern, *Bible and Music: Influences of the Old Testament on Western Music* (Jersey City, NJ: Ktav, 2011), 29–40.

[10] For the rewriting of Noah in modern times as scientist, revolutionary, utopian, church-builder and survivor of nuclear war (to mention but a few possibilities), see further P. Goetsch, 'Noah', in D. L. Jeffrey, *A Dictionary of Biblical Tradition in English Literature* (Grand Rapids: Eerdmans, 1992), 551–2 (552).

[11] The birds that Noah sends out from the ark are an important feature of medieval art respecting the flood. The dove represents the Holy Spirit, while the raven 'signifies the mouth and jaws of hell . . . through which biting and mastication punish numberless victims and feed an insatiable appetite.' A. C. Labriola, 'The Bible and Iconography', in *The Oxford Handbook of Reception History of the Bible* (ed. M. Lieb, E. Mason, J. Roberts and C. Rowland; Oxford: Oxford University Press, 2011), 175–99 (184).

in Genesis 1, to 'multiply on the earth and be fruitful and increase in number upon it' (8.17). These include Noah's wife who, according to an early Gnostic version of the flood story, was reluctant to embark in the first place, attempting to prevent the building of the ark and eventually to burn it.[12]

It seems clear as we read this story taken by itself that a universal flood is in view. It seems equally clear, as we saw in our Chapter 7, that aspects of the surrounding context in Genesis 1—11 raise questions about precisely this idea: the survival of 'the Nephilim' who are said to live both before the flood and after it (Gen. 6.4), and of the descendants of Cain who carry on various lines of work initiated by their forebears (Gen. 4.17–24). This should already prompt the reader to enquire about the kind of story we are reading here, and about which kinds of questions an interpreter may sensibly ask of it. If indeed Moberly is correct that 'the purpose of the literary construction . . . [is] to juxtapose certain archetypal portrayals of life under God' prior to Abraham's time,[13] rather than (say) provide a modern-sounding journalistic account of the ancient past, then this fact matters for interpretation.

It is important to ponder this, because of the tendency of many interpreters throughout history and right down to the present day to press the text into answering questions of a scientific and historical kind that it was very probably never intended to answer. At its most extreme, this approach results in a highly literalistic reading of the flood story that leads us into very problematic areas when it comes to squaring its perceived truth-claims with what is otherwise known (especially nowadays) about reality.[14] Where did all the water come from, and where did it go afterwards? If the sea level rose all over the earth as high as the peak of Mount Ararat (c.16,946 feet), the oceans would have had to triple in volume in the course of 150 days and then speedily return to normal. Whither did this vast amount of water then drain? Certainly it did not evaporate, because if it had, our

---

[12] Goetsch, 'Noah', 552, who notes the continuing prominence of Noah's wife in later medieval mystery plays.

[13] R. W. L. Moberly, *The Theology of the Book of Genesis* (OTT; Cambridge: Cambridge University Press, 2009), 28.

[14] I have in mind the kind of reading represented by J. C. Whitcomb, Jr and H. M. Morris, *The Genesis Flood: The Biblical Record and Its Scientific Implications* (Philadelphia: Presbyterian and Reformed, 1961); and N. M. Meyer, *Noah's Ark: Pitched and Parked* (Winona Lake: BMH Books, 1977). Such readings necessitate the production of a new 'science' ('creation science') that replaces modern science, and is promoted in school curricula as well as in various museums in different parts of the world. See further 'Creation Museums', accessed 26 October 2012, <http://nwcreation.net/museums.html>; and T. Sanders, *Approaching Eden: Adam and Eve in Popular Culture* (Lanham, MD: Rowman and Littlefield, 2009), 129–53.

atmosphere would not be compatible with life as we know it (and we would not, in fact, know it, because we would be dead). Then again, how can there still be freshwater lakes and seas if salt water mixed with all the other water-bodies across the earth, and how did fish accustomed to each environment survive? How are we to understand the logistics of animal-care in the ark – eight people caring for an estimated 42,000 animals?[15] What did they do with the huge amounts of excrement and urine, and how did they replenish the lost fluids?

And after the floodwaters receded, how did the dove fly down the mountain to find an olive tree (only found at low elevations) and then back up again to the top of the mountain, given that doves are not physic-ally equipped to fly at such altitudes? How did Noah, his family members and the animals make the trek down such a formidable mountain, and how did the animals make their way over mountains and across deserts to return to their native habitats? How would animals today found only in Australia (for example) have managed to get to that continent? And what did the carnivores eat while their prey populations were growing in number once again (see further below)?[16] Plausible answers to such questions are very difficult to come by, and this may further suggest that we are not really tracking with the fundamental concerns of the Genesis authors when we ask them.

It is these fundamental concerns that I introduced in our Chapter 4 above, where I suggested that the best way in which to approach the book of Genesis is to understand it as part of the distinctive 'axial age' response of Mosaic Yahwists to the kinds of questions we see arising all over the ancient world in the sixth and fifth centuries BC about 'old religion', as its authors wrestled with questions of faith and identity in a newly emerging world. That is to say: *their* questions, not ours. In that chapter I illustrated the value of this approach specifically with reference to matters of cosmology and anthropology. That exercise suggests that we shall gain deeper insight into what the Genesis flood story is really about if we reflect on the ancient cultural context in which it was composed.

Stories of a great flood are known from cultures all around the world – by one count, 68 people groups have flood stories – and these include the account in the Mesopotamian *Epic of Gilgamesh*, dating originally from early in the second millennium BC and found in its latest and fullest form in a

---

[15] This issue already surfaces in early Jewish reflection, which tells us that the human care-givers put in 24-hour shifts throughout the sojourn in the ark (*Sanh.* 108b; *Tanh. B.* 58.2).

[16] For these and other questions, see J. H. Walton, *Genesis* (NIVAC; Grand Rapids: Zondervan, 2001), 316–32.

version from the neo-Assyrian period (*c.*650 BC).[17] The part of the story that concerns a flood appears to have been adapted from an older account told in the *Atrahasis Epic*, in which the god Enlil tries to exterminate humanity only to be foiled by Enki, who advises his faithful worshipper Atrahasis to build a vessel in which he can survive the deluge.[18] The storm rages for seven days and nights, Atrahasis survives, and afterwards he sacrifices. A furious Enlil convenes a divine assembly where a post-flood compromise is reached among the gods to limit the expanding human population. In the neo-Assyrian version of the story, the hero is named Ut-napishtim, and he is warned of the flood by the god Ea, who tells him to load into the boat 'the seed of life of all kinds', his family, relations and skilled craft workers, as well as animals. The party rides out a mighty seven-day storm until the vessel eventually comes to rest on Mount Nisir. Seven days later Ut-napishtim sends out a dove, a swallow and a raven; the raven does not return. Ut-napishtim offers a sacrifice around which the gods, 'having smelled the sweet odour', gather 'like flies'. Enki scolds Enlil for sending a destructive flood instead of a less severe punishment to 'diminish humankind', and in response Enlil makes Ut-napishtim immortal, along with his wife. It is this story that is related by Ut-napishtim to Gilgamesh while he is on his own quest for immortality.

The similarities between these two Mesopotamian accounts of a great flood and our biblical account are striking; Gordon Wenham notes 17 specific points of similarity specifically between the Genesis narrative and the *Epic of Gilgamesh*.[19] The differences are equally striking. In Genesis, there is one God and not a pantheon of gods. This one God, who is *for* his creation, causes the flood as a one-time, not-be-repeated response to human wickedness, precisely because humanity is *ruining* creation. The flood is not part of a divine crusade against humanity arising merely out of divine irritation with the expanding human population. God in the book of Genesis in fact delights in the multiplication of humanity and of the rest of his creatures – he commands it, and he ensures its continuance throughout Genesis. After the flood, we are specifically told that everything else that God says must be understood in the context of the blessing of fertility (Gen. 9.1, 7). There is no divine council, here in Genesis, to decide on ongoing population control; the death and destruction that the flood brings are understood in the context of a God who is *for* creation and *for* life.

---

[17] 'Gilgamesh', trans. B. R. Foster (*COS* 1.132:458–60).

[18] 'Atra-Hasis', trans. B. R. Foster (*COS* 1.130:450–2).

[19] G. J. Wenham, 'The Coherence of the Flood Narrative', *VT* 28 (1978): 346–7.

Finally, the immortality theme of the *Epic of Gilgamesh* is also missing in Genesis. The God of whom Genesis knows does not do deals with human beings about immortality (even though he is capable of granting it, as in the case of Enoch, Gen. 5.24). Therefore Noah, although he is righteous, still dies; he is not Ut-napishtim. Indeed, his very name suggests the distinction. Ut-napishtim means 'I have found life', and it speaks of something that happened to him personally. Noah's name is associated in Genesis with the relief from God's curse on the ground for which his father Lamech yearns in Genesis 5.29. This relief becomes something of a reality in Genesis 8.21 (God promises never again to curse the ground) and in Genesis 9.20 (where Noah is a 'man of the ground', and successful agriculture is instituted, to join the animal husbandry, music and metalworking of Gen. 4.20–22). Noah's name, in other words, speaks of the ongoing blessing of God on *all* of humanity after the flood, not just on one person.

So what do we have in Genesis 6.9—9.29? It seems likely that we have a very particular and very Hebrew version of something that already existed in the Mesopotamian literary tradition – an OT retelling of an ancient story, designed to reframe what was already known about the distant past so that it conformed to what the ancient Hebrews believed to be true about God, the world, human beings and human society. What Genesis wants to say about all of this is that human beings, as they once emerged into the light of God, embracing it and rejecting it (as we saw in Gen. 2—4), then developing society and culture (as we saw in Gen. 4), continued to grasp after immortality and to fall into darkness (Gen. 6). In response to this darkness came God's judgement in the form of natural disaster. But the judgement came from a God who is good, and who works in his world to redeem the righteous, along with the rest of his creation. More than that, as we shall see, this God has made everlasting commitments, not just to the righteous, but to all of creation, which has been reborn.

War on creation

If indeed creation has been reborn, however, this does not mean that in the aftermath of the great flood we have simply returned to the beginning. Genesis 9.1–7 makes this clear. In Eden (as in the ark) human creation and animal creation found themselves in a harmonious relationship. Now, however,

> The fear and dread of you will fall upon all the beasts of the earth and all the birds of the air, upon every creature that moves along the ground, and upon all the fish of the sea; they are given into your hands.   (Gen. 9.2)

The animals (or at least some of them) now look upon their human counter-parts not simply as subjects look upon their king (Gen. 1), but as residents of a land look upon a conquering army; that is what this language of 'fear and dread' implies (cf. Deut. 11.25). In turn, this implies that human beings in the post-flood era will abandon their God-given responsibility to exercise just and appropriate dominion over the rest of creation. War will be declared on animal creation.

As a divine concession, it seems, to this new reality, 'Everything that lives and moves will be food for you. Just as I gave you the green plants, I now give you everything' (9.3). Biblical interpreters have sometimes understood these words as divine permission to move from a vegetarian state (Gen. 1.29) to a carnivorous state, and the NIV translations of this verse and the preceding ones do perhaps give this same impression. On this view, the original creation as described in Genesis 1 is a vegetarian place, unmarked by predation.[20] Meat-eating only becomes a facet of life on earth, whether in the human or in the non-human world, after human beings embrace evil, and specifically, only after the flood. However, this represents an implausible reading of Genesis 1—9.

To understand that this is so, we must return to Genesis 1, where the non-human land animals that ultimately appear on the sixth day are subdivided into three groups, described in the NIV as wild animals, livestock and all the creatures that move along the ground (Gen. 1.24–25). The distinction between livestock and wild animals is obvious enough – it is the dis-tinction between the domestic and non-domestic spheres. The distinction between these two groups and the third (Hb. *remes*) is not so clear. Certainly a distinction within the class of *wild* animals is intended – in Genesis 1—11, *remes* can itself refer to wild animals as an *entire* class. The NIV appears to suggest by its translation ('all the creatures that move along the ground') a distinction between *larger* and *smaller* wild animals. There is, however, little reason to believe that size is what differentiates the two groups. This proposal appears to represent little more than a guess arising out of the alleged nuance of the verb *ramas* itself ('to creep, move lightly'). However, Psalm 104.20 tells us that 'all the animals of the forest prowl' (or 'creep', *ramas*). It is evidently not only of small animals that the verb can be used in the OT. Much more plausible is the idea that our Genesis authors intend,

---

[20] So, e.g., V. P. Hamilton, *Genesis 1–17* (Grand Rapids: Eerdmans, 1990), 313: 'The opening chapter of Genesis was quite explicit that in the beginning man and the animals were vegetarian.' The view is much older, however, and is expressed throughout the interpretative tradition. P. C. Almond tells us that in the seventeenth century, indeed, it was the majority view (*Adam and Eve in Seventeenth-Century Thought* (Cambridge: Cambridge University Press, 1999), 118–26).

both here in Genesis 1.24–25 and elsewhere in Genesis 1—11, a distinction between non-predatory and predatory wild animals. This in turn has an impact on our interpretation of Genesis 1.29–30, which have sometimes been read as implying that, in Genesis 1, God's original creation is a vegetarian zone, with both humans and animals eating only plants.

However, there is no positive evidence anywhere else in the biblical tradition that its authors believed in an original vegetarian state of creation, in either the human or the animal realms. A prophetic passage like Isaiah 11.6–9 has sometimes been cited as if it had something to contribute to our understanding of the biblical perspective here. This idea arises, however, only from the (faulty) logic that insists that everything that is true about the *future* in biblical thinking must also true about the *past*, which in turn is related to the error noted in our Chapter 5: that 'good' in Genesis 1 means 'perfect', and that the whole biblical narrative is about a return to an original perfection. Once this idea is dismissed from the mind, it is easier to see what is obvious about Genesis 1.29–30, namely, that to affirm that God has given plants for his creatures' sustenance is not to deny that God has also built predation into his good creation, which is indeed what the very existence of categories of wild animals implies. Augustine already addresses the confusion here,[21] as does the noted medieval theologian Thomas Aquinas:

> In the opinion of some, those animals which now are fierce and kill others, would, in that [original] state, have been tame, not only in regard to man, but also in regard to other animals. But this is quite unreasonable. For the nature of animals was not changed by man's sin, as if those whose nature now it is to devour the flesh of others, would then have lived on herbs, as the lion and falcon.[22]

Certainly other parts of the OT tradition that describe creation do not appear to reflect any belief that the existence of carnivorous animals in the world results from anything other than God's good creation purposes (e.g. Pss. 104.21; 147.9).[23] And all of this is consistent with what we read in Genesis 3—8. In Genesis 3.21 we find garments of skin being provided

---

[21] Augustine, *The Literal Meaning of Genesis*, 1.3.16.

[22] Thomas Aquinas, *Summa Theologiae* 1.96.1 (trans. Fathers of the English Dominican Province; 2 vols; New York: Benziger Bros, 1947), 1:486.

[23] For a more extensive discussion, see I. W. Provan, *Seriously Dangerous Religion: What the Old Testament Really Says and Why It Matters* (Waco: Baylor University Press, 2014), chs 9 and 11. Yet many readers of Genesis have not agreed with Augustine and Aquinas, and at least in the seventeenth century theirs was not the mainstream view, which is well expressed in Milton's *Paradise Lost* (10.710–12): 'Beast now with Beast gan war, & Fowle with Fowle, / And Fish with Fish; to graze the Herb all leaving, / Devoured each other.'

for human beings by God, which certainly involves at least animal *death*. Genesis 4.2–4 tells us of Abel's sacrifice of sheep.[24] Genesis 7.2–3 then tells us of Noah, who is instructed to take 'two of every kind of unclean animal, a male and its mate' into the ark in order to ensure survival of all the species. But he is also told to take 'seven of every kind of clean animal, a male and its mate, and seven of every kind of bird, male and female' – and the purpose of this instruction, when added to the previous one, is certainly to ensure that there are enough animals to allow *both* conservation of species *and* also sacrifice (for which people need ritually 'clean' animals). All of this implies a functioning sacrificial system prior to Genesis 9, and much sacrificial ritual in the OT involves the eating of the sacrificial victim. Sacrifice and eating go together. The authors of Genesis, then, clearly do not regard Genesis 9 as the beginning of the carnivorous state, whether among humans or among other animals.

Indeed, the very wording of Genesis 9.2–3 must be carefully attended to. The NIV translation of Genesis 9.2 refers to fear and dread falling upon 'all the beasts of the earth and all the birds of the air, upon every creature that moves along the ground, and upon all the fish of the sea'. However, the Hebrew behind 'the beasts of the earth' here (*chayyat ha'arets*) is exactly the same as the Hebrew we find in Genesis 1.24–25, which the NIV itself correctly translates as '*wild* animals', *not* as (land) animals in general. The NIV also offers the same (correct) translation of the term in Genesis 9.10. It is baffling, then, that its translators offer us 'beasts of the earth' in Genesis 9.2. They thereby mislead the reader into thinking that the verse refers to *all* land animals, not just to a particular *class* of land animal. This is not correct. Instead, we *ought* to understand the creatures in Genesis 9.2 in this way: 'all the wild (predatory) animals and all the birds in the sky, on all the wild, non-predatory animals, and on all the fish in the sea'. This translation immediately allows us to notice something rather striking about the verse: that one class of animals is not mentioned in it at all. There is no mention of *behemah*, 'livestock'. And so we see that Genesis 9.2 only concerns animal life in the *non-domestic sphere*. From the perspective of Genesis, the livestock *already* 'belong' in human hands. It is the wild creatures, and not animals in general, that in the aftermath of the great flood live their lives in fear and dread of human beings.

It is the wild animals that are then, in Genesis 9.3, explicitly singled out as being given over to human beings as food. There are two possibilities

---

[24] Some Jewish tradition states that Adam was, however, the first to offer sacrifice; note *Abodah Zarah* 8a, in *The Babylonian Talmud* (ed. I. Epstein; 18 vols; London: Soncino, 1935–48), 13:37.

for translating this verse, depending on whether we think that the Hebrew word *remes* signifies in this context *all* wild animals or only the non-predatory ones:

> Every wild but non-predatory land-animal (Hb. *remes*) that is living shall be food for you. As I gave green plants to you – everything!

> Every wild land-animal (Hb. *remes*) that is living shall be food for you. As I gave green plants to you – everything!

Whichever option we choose, Genesis 9.2–3 is not a passage about human beings beginning to eat animals. It is a passage about a change in the human relationship with the animal world, whereby wild animals become first and foremost targets of human aggression rather than subjects of human governance and care. A mind to care for creation is replaced with a conquest mentality, and proper distinctions between the domestic and the wild are obliterated. The force of Genesis 9.3 in this context is not 'just as I gave you plants, now I give you animals'. It is, rather: 'just as I gave you the plants of the earth that you had not cultivated, now I give you the wild animals of the earth that you have not domesticated.'[25]

Rights in a fallen world

The *statement* about wild animals becoming human food (Genesis 9.3) is immediately followed, next, by an *instruction* that prohibits any eating of 'meat that has its lifeblood still in it' (9.4). That is, the animal must be definitely and completely dead, which is assured by draining its blood from its carcass. Even in the world of 'fear and dread' there are still rights and wrongs in terms of the treatment of the victims of hunting (cf. Lev. 17.3–4, 11; Deut. 12.23). This statement about animal rights is then connected with a statement about human rights (Gen. 9.5–6). Humans must respect animal life even while taking it away; animals must also respect human life, and are not allowed to take it away at all (9.5); and 'Whoever sheds the blood of man, by man shall his blood be shed; for in the image of God has God made man' (9.6). All of God's creatures have rights, which God takes steps to protect in a world that has been damaged by evil.

Is it inevitable that human beings must persecute wild animals in the post-flood world? Are we to understand the rapacious approach to the animal world envisaged in Genesis 9, not only as a path that *might* be

---

[25] See further Provan, *Seriously Dangerous Religion*, ch. 9.

adopted by human beings, but as a path that will and *should* be adopted, because God has ordained it so? A similar question arose earlier about the curses in Genesis 3 (see our Chapter 6 above). A similar answer is no doubt the correct one here. God's curses are not regarded in biblical thinking as fates or destinies imposed upon creatures who can do nothing to reverse them. God's curses represent, rather, statements of consequences that are bound up very much with a human being's next set of decisions. There are two pathways presented to its readers by the biblical literature – two ways in which its readers might go. One involves obedience and blessing, the other disobedience (autonomy) and cursing. Later biblical passages certainly do not regard it as inevitable that people should choose the path of cursing outlined in Genesis 9, and indeed they hold people accountable for doing so (cf., e.g., Exod. 20.8–11; Hos. 4.1–3; Prov. 12.10); non-human creatures still matter. God's own continuing commitment to all of his creatures is indeed signalled clearly in Genesis 9 itself, in the language of 'covenant' as it is developed in verses 8–17. This is not just a covenant with Noah, we note; it is a covenant with 'all living creatures of every kind' (v. 15).

Noah's drunkenness

Act 4 of Genesis ends with a story that gives the impression of being something of a footnote after a narrative high-point – a transition to the next part of the story (Gen. 9.18–29). Here the sons of Noah are introduced more fully, because 'from them came the people who were scattered over the earth'. Canaan, the grandson, is also introduced because he is at the centre of the particular story recounted here, which concerns Noah's over-indulgence in the fruit of his vines, and Ham's fault in seeing 'his father's nakedness' as Noah lay insensibly in his tent. It is not entirely clear what this entailed. Some have suspected that we have here a euphemism for some kind of serious sexual sin. Certainly Ham is regarded by Noah as having done something very wicked – presumably more than accidentally catching sight of his father's unclothed body. Perhaps the sin lies disguised in his 'telling' of the incident to his brothers – is there perhaps mockery or slander implied in this language? Or is the idea that there is a lack of propriety in speaking of the situation to others rather than taking action to redress the situation (as it were) – notice that Shem and Japheth immediately take such action (Gen. 9.23). Whatever the reason, the situation draws out of Noah a curse on Canaan, Ham's son, and a blessing on Shem and Japheth.

Why is the curse on Canaan and not on Ham? Is it because Noah cannot undo God's blessing on Ham (Gen. 9.1)? Is it because Noah's youngest son sinned against Noah, and Canaan is Ham's youngest son – a kind of poetic justice? It is never made clear in the story. The curse, however, is clearly regarded as one that resounds throughout history. The Canaanites will be slaves of the descendants of Shem, the Semites; the descendants of Japheth will also enslave them (Gen. 9.26). The immediate and obvious point of fulfilment of this curse is probably to be found in Genesis 14, where the Canaanite cities (Gen. 14.4) are said to be enslaved to Elam, the eldest son of Shem according to Genesis 10.22. Among Elam's allies are the Goiim, descendants of Japheth (Gen. 10.5; cf. 14.1, 9). The longer-term fulfilment of the curse was no doubt understood by ancient Israelite readers of the text in relation to the occupation of the land of Canaan by the Israelites, and the following period of domination by David and Solomon.

This particular episode in the Noah story has attracted attention throughout the ages that is out of all proportion to its significance in the Genesis text. It has inspired medieval art that portrays Noah 'unconscious and exposed . . . perhaps soiled by excessive wine' as a type of Christ, 'faint, bloodied, and naked' at his scourging.[26] It has produced drinking songs like the fifteenth-century *Éloge de Noé* by Olivier Basselin; a famous bas-relief from the same period composed on Ghiberti's bronze gates to the Florence Baptistery; and a painting by Michelangelo in the Sistine Chapel.[27] The human obsession with wine, whether by way of warm embrace or fierce rejection, no doubt accounts for just how often literature alludes to its first producer; for example, Scott's *Anne of Geierstein* (1829), Dickens' *Bleak House* (1852–3) and Melville's *The Confidence Man* (1857). Disturbingly, as the first biblical text to reference slavery (as noted by Augustine),[28] Genesis 9.18–29 has also importantly informed a pro-slavery position at different points in history. It was so read by white people, for example, in the eighteenth and nineteenth centuries, 'to justify enslavement of blacks'.[29]

---

[26] Labriola, 'Iconography', 188. G. Herbert, 'The Bunch of Grapes' (1633), sees Noah's *vine* as prefiguring Christ. John Dryden transfers the Noah reference from Christ to King Charles II ('To His Sacred Majesty', 1662): the world once drowned under Puritan waters has recently re-emerged and 'new-born nature in fresh looks appear'd / Thus Royal Sir, to see you landed here/ Was cause enough of triumph for a year.'

[27] Young, Halevy and Hirschberg, 'Noah', 289–90.

[28] Augustine, *City of God*, 19.15.

[29] D. M. Carr, 'Genesis', in *The Oxford Encyclopedia of the Books of the Bible* (ed. M. D. Coogan; 2 vols; New York: Oxford University Press, 2011), 1:316–34 (332). See further W. M. Swartley, *Slavery, Sabbath, War and Women* (Scottsdale, PA: Herald, 1983), ch. 1; and, especially, S. R. Haynes, *Noah's Curse: The Biblical Justification of American Slavery* (Oxford: Oxford University Press, 2002).

Moving On towards Abraham (Gen. 10.1—11.26)

Acts 5 and 6 of Genesis concern, first, 'the descendants of Shem, Ham and Japheth' (Gen. 10.1—11.9), and second, 'the descendants of Shem' (Gen. 11.10–26). We shall focus, first, on the 'Table of Nations' in Genesis 10.1–32, and then on the account of the tower in 'Babel' in Genesis 11.1–9.

The Table of Nations lays out for the reader of Genesis a post-flood world that would have been recognizably 'the world of current history' to an ancient reader – the world in which the patriarchal drama of the remainder of Genesis will be acted out. It opens by briefly describing the descendants of Japheth (10.2–4) – the peoples with whom ancient Israel had the least contact. It moves on, then, to describe at greater length the descendants of Ham, among whom number some of Israel's most influential neighbours (10.6–20). It concludes with an account of the descendants of Shem, the Semites, who include the very ancestors of the ancient Israelites themselves. The total number of names in this list of peoples in Genesis 10 is 70, which appears to be a traditional way of summing up the totality of a people: there are 70 descendants of Jacob in Exodus 1.5, 70 elders of Israel in Exodus 24.1, and 70 disciples of Jesus in Luke 10.1–16. The whole known world is being described here.

The descendants of Japheth include people like the Cimmerians (Gomer), who originated in southern Russia but eventually settled in Asia Minor; the Medes, who lived in Iran; and the Kittim, from Cyprus. These are peoples of the far north-west or the far east, albeit that from Israel's perspective they are simply peoples of the far north, because that is where they come from, and that is where they are encountered. The descendants of Ham include the Egyptians (Mitsraim); the Canaanites; the peoples of Arabia and of Mesopotamia; and the Phoenicians (Sidon). They include all the peoples of Syro-Palestine who are not descendants of Shem. The descendants of Shem include the Elamites and the Arameans, but most importantly from the point of view of the Genesis story, the family of Abraham. All of these together, then, are the descendants of Noah's three sons, who will eventually 'spread out over the earth after the flood' (Gen. 10.32), although it seems that they are regarded as a single community with a single language prior to the time of Eber's son Peleg, when 'the earth was divided' (Gen. 10.25). This comment brings us directly to the story of the tower of Babel in Genesis 11, which explains how the earth was in fact 'divided'.

As one might expect in the case of a single family (Noah's family), initially after the great flood 'the whole world had one language and a common speech' (Gen. 11.1). It was in this state, we are told, that the human community continued on its journey 'eastward' that had first begun with the exit from the garden in Eden, arriving ultimately at 'a plain in Shinar' (Babylonia, 11.2). In this heartland of ancient Mesopotamian civilization they decided to build, in a traditional Mesopotamian manner: 'brick instead of stone, and tar for mortar' (11.3; in Palestine, stone and mortar would have been used). Their intention was to construct a city, possessing a tower that reached 'to the heavens'; their hope in doing so was to 'make a name for ourselves' and not 'be scattered over the face of the whole earth' (11.4). Biblically speaking, of course, it is only God who makes a name for himself (cf. Isa. 63.11–14), and the people in the Genesis story who have previously attempted this task have not been well regarded (the 'men of renown', lit. 'men of the name', in Gen. 6.4). To attempt to build the tower, then, is to attempt once again to grasp at divinity. It is also to ignore the twice-repeated divine commandment in Genesis 9.1 and 9.7, 'Be fruitful and increase in number and *fill the earth*.' These people are not interested in filling the earth; they are intent, instead, on settling down in one place.

It is for these various reasons that God opposes them in this story, taking action to diminish the ongoing human capacity for concerted wickedness. He confuses 'their language so they will not understand each other' (11.7). A play on words in the Hebrew underlines the appropriateness of the punishment: the people say, 'let's make bricks' (Hb. *nilbenah*), to which God responds with 'let us confuse' their language (Hb. *navelah*). The consequence is that the human family is scattered over all the earth. This is why the city is said to be called Babel (Babylon is evidently in mind), for it was there that 'the Lord confused (Hb. *balal*) the language of the whole world' (11.9).

The 'tower' in this story is probably intended as a Mesopotamian ziggurat. These ziggurats – pyramid-like structures associated with temples – are often said in Babylonian texts to have their 'heads in the heavens' (Gen. 11.4). They were dedicated to particular deities, and each had a room at the top set aside for the deity's use. They functioned as gateways between heaven and earth, and indeed the Babylonians understood 'Babel' to mean 'gate of the god'. It was through such a gateway that a god might enter the earthly realm, descending via the staircase to the temple at the ziggurat's foot and receiving there the gifts and worship of his people. Such was the Babylonian view that lay at the foundation of their religious ideology and culture, which in turn brought order and stability to their community life.

The Hebrew view of Babylonian culture, on the other hand, was that it was based on a fundamentally wrong approach to God and the world. Heaven could not be brought to earth by the building of towers; indeed, heaven could not be brought to earth at all. The difference between God (in the singular) and mortals must be respected. In fact, say the authors of Genesis, Babel is not 'gate of god' but 'confusion', and it is not stability and communal order that result from its building, but the fracturing of community. This is one of the perennial biblical indictments of false worship, and Genesis tracks its malevolent effects right back to the beginning of time: the scattering of the first peoples was itself the result of a Babylonian approach to reality. This specific accusation appears to reflect something specific in Mesopotamian culture, for the Sumerian epic *Enmerkar and the Lord of Aratta* tells of a time in human history when all people spoke in one language, until the chief god Enki 'brought contention into it'. No, says Genesis, the confusion of human languages is not the result simply of another disagreement between deities (this time Enki and Enlil), in which human beings have no responsibility. It is the direct result of the Mesopotamian way of thinking about God, the world and themselves. The true and living God who really exists ordained that human languages be diverse so that human wickedness might be contained. He made this decision because, left to themselves, the peoples of the earth with their Mesopotamian religion would have built a corrupt civilization throughout the earth, and there would have been no stopping it.

The story of the tower of Babel has been a source of fascination for biblical interpreters throughout the ages. Associated in Jewish tradition with Nimrod, 'who grew to be a mighty warrior on the earth' (Gen. 10.8) and whose name means 'we will revolt', it appears in Dante's *Inferno* as the starting point of his journey, where

> Languages diverse, horrible dialects
> Accents of anger, words of agony
> And voices high and hoarse, with sound of hands
> Made up a tumult that goes whirling on
> Forever in that air forever black
> Even as the sand doth, when the whirlwind breathes.[30]

Later in the journey Nimrod himself is encountered, 'by whose evil thought / One language in the world is not still used'.[31] In *Paradise Lost*, Milton

---

[30] Dante, *Inferno*, 3.25–30.
[31] Dante, *Inferno*, 31.77–78. He is also one of the imprisoned tyrants in Spenser's *Faerie Queen*, 1.5.48.1 (unfinished, late sixteenth century). See further 'Babel', in Jeffrey, *Biblical Tradition*, 66–9 (68).

has Nimrod's tower built at the very mouth of hell itself,[32] and Lewis also evokes hell when alluding to Babel in *That Hideous Strength* (1945): 'Babble about the *élan vital* and flirtations with panpsychism were ... dragging up from its shallow and unquiet grave the old dream of Man as God.'[33] Human pride is an enduring theme when Babel is alluded to in both literature and art, whether we are thinking of Golding's *The Spire* (1964), about a cathedral's dean and his ambitious church-building programme, or Bruegel's famous 1563 painting, *The Tower of Babel*, in which an impressive-looking Colosseum-type building is revealed upon closer inspection to be in the process of falling down.[34] Oppression is also never far away, when Babel appears. Dostoyevsky's *Summer Notes of Winter Impressions* (1862–3), for example,

> presented the Crystal Palace [in London] as an apocalyptic nightmare of a sort of Tower of Babel where Baal was worshipped. The masses saw escape from the rigid oppression, in the name of utopia on earth, by a mechanized, all-pervasive system not in religious salvation but in the depravity and gin-shops of the Haymarket and Whitechapel.[35]

The Table of Nations and the 'Babel incident' together provide the immediate backdrop for the story of Genesis that follows from Genesis 11.27 onwards. The peoples of the ancient world have now been assigned their proper places; we await the entrance of Abraham, descendant of Shem, which in Hebrew actually means 'name'. If 'making a name for ourselves' (Gen. 11.4) signifies human resistance to God's will for populating the earth and prompts God's judgement, then the biblical story will proceed shortly with a promise of blessing in the midst of this curse – a promise that involves making Abraham's name 'great' (Gen. 12.2).

---

[32] Milton, *Paradise Lost*, 12.24–62, esp. 40–5.

[33] C. S. Lewis, *That Hideous Strength* (rev. ed.; London: Pan Books, 1955), 120.

[34] W. Golding, *The Spire* (London: Faber and Faber, 1974). For more on artistic representation of the tower of Babel, see M. J. Siff, H. L. Ginsberg and I. M. Ta-Shma, 'Babel, Tower of', *EncJud* 3:19–21.

[35] E. Sicher, 'Hard Times in Paradise: An Example of an Inverted Biblical Pattern', in *Biblical Patterns in Modern Literature* (BJS 77; ed. D. H. Hirsch and N. Aschkenasy; Chico, CA: Scholars, 1984), 165–72 (167).

9

Abraham, Sarah and Isaac: Genesis 11.27—25.18

We turn now to Acts 7 and 8 of the book of Genesis, which tell us at length about 'the descendants of Terah' (Gen. 11.27—25.11) and then much more briefly about 'the descendants of Ishmael' (Gen. 25.12–18). Our own focus in this chapter will be first and foremost on Abraham and his wife Sarah, and secondarily on their son Isaac, whose lives get most attention from the authors, even though other characters are also important (e.g. Abraham's concubine Hagar, and his nephew Lot). As the story opens, Abraham is known as Abram, and Sarah as Sarai (11.27, 29), but for convenience's sake we shall refer to them throughout as Abraham and Sarah. The significance of their change of name in Genesis 17.3–8 is unclear. The name 'Abraham' is apparently thought to carry the connotation of 'multitude' in Genesis 17.5 in a way that 'Abram' does not (it means 'exalted father'). We do not know, however, of a Hebrew word *raham* with that meaning in biblical Hebrew. 'Sarah' is simply a different pronunciation of 'Sarai'; both words mean 'princess'. Perhaps it is the *fact* of the change in each case that matters more than the *meaning* of each name: these are the people to whom the promise of Genesis 17 is given, and with whom God's covenant is confirmed, and they are called to make a fresh start after the false fulfilment of the promise in Genesis 16 (see further below).

Overview of the narrative

One of the first things that we are told as Act 7 of Genesis opens is that Sarah is barren (11.30) – an important detail, as it turns out in the story. We are also informed that the family group of which the main characters are a part is living in Haran in northern Syria, having relocated from Ur in Babylonia (11.31). It is in Haran that God appears to Abraham and makes him the promise that will become the driving force of the entire narrative of the Pentateuch that follows (Gen. 12.1–3), sending Abraham, Sarah and Lot to Canaan, the Promised Land (12.7). Famine quickly forces the family to seek food in Egypt, however, where Abraham deceives the

Egyptians and causes them trouble by pretending that Sarah is only his sister, and not his wife (Gen. 12.10–20). Back in Canaan, soon afterwards, Abraham and Lot separate in order to find adequate grazing for their animals. Lot settles in the luxuriant Jordan plain, but falls prey to foreign invaders. Abraham recovers his nephew from these invaders, and subsequently receives the blessing of Melchizedek, the priest-king of Salem (Gen. 13—14).

Following a reassuring vision, Abraham is then promised by God that his childless condition will soon come to an end, and that his offspring will *indeed* occupy the Promised Land. This promise is solemnized with a sacrifice and a covenant (Gen. 15). A child, Ishmael, is then born, but not to Sarah. Ishmael is the son of Abraham and Hagar, who is Sarah's slave, driven out cruelly by Sarah while she is pregnant (Gen. 16). Thirteen years later God renews his covenant with Abraham, changing his name from Abram to Abraham, and Sarai's to Sarah, and imposing circumcision as a sign of membership for all the males in Abraham's household. With this covenant renewal comes the divine promise that Sarah, though old, will bear a son (Isaac) who will receive the covenant. Ishmael at the same time receives a separate promise from God of many descendants (Gen. 17).

Three mysterious visitors then repeat this promise of a son to Sarah and Abraham (Gen. 18.1–15). Lot, meanwhile, has settled in Sodom, which has become totally depraved. Abraham asks that God spare the city if only ten righteous people can be found there, but they cannot, so both Sodom and Gomorrah are destroyed. Only Lot and his two daughters survive (Gen. 18.16—19.29). Abraham, living in southern Canaan, then encounters the king of Gerar, who takes possession of Sarah on her husband's assertion (again!) that she is his sister. However, warned by God, King Abimelek avoids adultery and makes his peace with Abraham (Gen. 20). Then Isaac is born, and Hagar and Ishmael are sent off to wander in the desert, where God provides for them (Gen. 21.1–20). In the same chapter we are told of a treaty between Abimelek and Abraham, intended to solve a water-rights quarrel at Beersheba (Gen. 21.22–34). There follows the surprising story of Genesis 22, where God calls Abraham to offer him Isaac in sacrifice, only staying the father's hand at the last moment. A renewal of God's promise to Abraham follows. At Sarah's death, Abraham buys a cave for her burial from a Hittite of Hebron (Gen. 23). Then he sends his servant back to his relatives in the Haran region to select Isaac's bride (Gen. 24). The succession thus settled, Abraham gives gifts to other sons, and dies (Gen. 25.1–11).

This story is primarily about trusting in God. The key verse is Genesis 15.6, 'Abram believed the LORD, and he credited it to him as righteousness.'

The key passage that relates to this verse is Genesis 22, where Abraham's trust is pushed right to the edge of reason. There are other indications of his trust in God, however. For example, he leaves Haran to enter an unknown land, and he never returns once God has called him away. Yet Abraham's trust is not perfect. For example, his liaison with Hagar in Genesis 16 should probably be read as an attempt to pre-empt God's actions in fulfilling his promise to Abraham. The story explores both trust and the lack thereof, demonstrating how in the midst of both God is at work to move his promise onwards towards fulfilment.

Promise and covenant (Gen. 12.2–3; 15.1–19; 17.1–8; 22.15–19)

The promise to Abraham that lies at the heart of the story of the Pentateuch first appears in Genesis 12.2–3:

> I will make you into a great nation and I will bless you;
> I will make your name great, and you will be a blessing.
> I will bless those who bless you, and whoever curses you I will curse;
> and all peoples on earth will be blessed through you.

This is not the first time in Genesis that we have encountered the idea of divine blessing on humanity, which is already an important idea in Genesis 1—11. Genesis 12 describes only the latest in a series of such blessings, which itself indicates that the purpose of God in calling Abraham out of Haran to travel into Canaan and settle there is tied up intrinsically with the overall purpose of God in creation. Other details of the promise in Genesis 12 confirm this. In verse 2, Abraham will be made into 'a great nation', in a world that is now inhabited by 'nations' (Hb. *goyim*, Gen. 10.5, 20, 31, 32), and his 'name' will be made great (which is what the nations were looking for at Babel). In these words, the divine focus lies on one person and on one nation. However, Abraham will also *be* a blessing to others (also Gen. 12.2) – a *source* of blessing to others, perhaps, or a name invoked by others who are *looking* for God's blessing. One of the ways in which this will work out is that those who bless Abraham will be blessed by God (12.3). Ultimately, all the peoples on earth will find blessing through him (12.3). Gordon Wenham plausibly suggests that we have a particular progression of thought in this passage: Abram is blessed; Abram's name is used as a blessing; Abram's blessers are blessed; all families find blessing in Abraham.[1] So: this one family stands now at the centre of God's

---

[1] G. J. Wenham, *Genesis 1–15* (WBC; Dallas: Word, 1987), 278.

intention to bless his creation; and if this family is cursed, this is at the same time an attack on God and God's plans for the world, so that person doing the cursing will also be cursed. Those who are well disposed to Abraham and his descendants will do well, while those who oppose them will not.

Bound up with the promise just described is a particular land in which Abraham's family will live – a land that God will 'show' him (Gen. 12.1). This land is quickly identified in Genesis 12.7 and 13.14–17 as Canaan. The latter passage also provides further details about the descendants who will make up the 'great nation' mentioned in Genesis 12; they will form a large multitude, 'like the dust of the earth' (13.16). Genesis 15 further describes them as being as many as the stars in the heavens (15.5). It is in this context that we first read of a 'covenant' (Hb. *berit*) being made between God and Abraham that is designed to undergird the promise (15.8–19, confirmed in 17.1–8) – a solemn agreement between the two parties concerned (cf. Gen. 21.25–34; 1 Sam. 18.3; 20.8; 23.18; 2 Sam. 3.12–21; 5.1–5; Ezek. 17.11–16). We encountered this idea already in Genesis 9, where God's response to the disaster that has just befallen the earth is to make a covenant with the whole created order (Gen. 9.1–17): with all of Noah's descendants (i.e. all people), and all living creatures with him (i.e. all other creatures). This Noah covenant is the necessary foundation upon which all the later biblical covenants are built, for it establishes that God will never give up on his 'creation project'. The covenant with Abraham comes next in line. If the Noah covenant is about salvation after judgement for the whole of creation, then the Abraham covenant is about salvation after judgement for one people, and therefore for *all* peoples. The judgement of God falls on all people at Babel; God's response is to bring one family out of Babylonia, so that ultimately all the families of the earth may be blessed, as God originally intended.

The covenantal promise of God to Abraham shows up one more time in his story, in the aftermath of 'the Isaac incident' in Genesis 22.15–19. Some modern source-critical interpreters have found this passage to be superfluous to the story, but in fact it makes an important contribution to its development. Walter Moberly brings out its significance very well when he suggests that 'a promise previously grounded solely in the will and purpose of YHWH has been transformed so that it is grounded *both* in the will and purpose of YHWH *and* in the obedience of Abraham'.[2] Henceforth Israel owes its existence, not just to God, but also to

---

[2] R. W. L. Moberly, 'The Earliest Commentary on the Akedah', *VT* 38 (1988): 302–23 (321).

Abraham.[3] In Jewish tradition, in fact, Israel forever afterwards benefits from Abraham's actions, being spared further testing of the Genesis 22 kind because of him. For example, this is precisely how the 'remembrance' prayers of Rosh Ha-Shanah (the Jewish New Year), where Genesis 22 turns up as the Torah reading for the second day, understand the matter. Pious Jews in the Middle Ages actually recited this passage daily.[4]

The Abraham promise and covenant takes on a particular kind of significance in the NT. Here Jesus, 'son of Abraham' (Matt. 1.1), accepts that his fellow Jews who oppose him are also Abraham's descendants, but points out that they do not do the things that Abraham did, and are in another sense the children of the devil (John 8.31–47). In due course it becomes clear that it is actually all those who accept Jesus as Lord, both Jew and Gentile, who are the true heirs of the promise to Abraham (e.g. Rom. 4.1–25; 9.1–9; Gal. 3.1–14). It is to the new global people of God, the Church, that the promise ultimately points.

Pharaoh and Abimelek (Gen. 12.10–20; 20.1–18; 21.22–34)

There are many threats to the promise to Abraham in the book of Genesis, and one of them is famine; people who do not eat cannot survive. Another is the moral and spiritual character of God's people themselves. Both threats are described for the first time in the immediate sequel to the story of the giving of the promise itself, in Genesis 12.10–20. Famine hits the land of Canaan, and Abraham takes his extended family down to Egypt to weather the storm. Egypt is the obvious place to go, since it was the 'breadbasket' of the ancient world, usually well supplied with food even when other regions were not doing so well. Abraham is only one of many Semites across the millennia to enter Egypt under these and other circumstances. It is nevertheless striking that whereas he enters Canaan at the beginning of Genesis 12 as the result of an explicit divine command to travel (12.1), his departure from it follows no such command. This already raises a slight question in the attentive reader's mind about Abraham's behaviour at this point in the story. Is he still trusting God?

This becomes a full-blown question when we go on to read of Abraham's attempted deception of the Egyptians in Genesis 12.11–16. Here we discover his fear that, as a foreigner, he will be victimized and have his wife stolen away from him. To avoid such trouble, he persuades Sarah to

---

[3] For a similar case, consider the intercessory prayer of Moses in Exod. 32—34.
[4] L. Jacobs and A. Sagi, 'Akedah', *EncJud* 1:555–60 (556).

go along with the lie that she is his sister rather than his wife (12.13).[5] This allows Sarah to enter Pharaoh's harem without any harm coming to Abraham (12.15–16). In the ancient Near East, kings frequently gave their sisters or daughters in marriage to other rulers in such a manner to cement alliances and to demonstrate goodwill. Examples of the practice abound all the way through the second millennium BC in particular – the time frame in which the Abraham story is set. The actions of Abraham may be understood in this context – as an attempt to 'create' an unmarried female relative who could be offered to the Egyptians. The strategy does not ultimately work, however, not because Pharaoh suspects anything, but because Yahweh is the kind of God who takes a dim view of such an approach to marriage and security. 'Serious diseases' befall Pharaoh's household (12.17) – an early version of the plagues of Egypt in the book of Exodus. These diseases save the situation, because they uncover the truth. Abraham is expelled from Egypt. His leaving foreshadows his descendants' leaving in the exodus – a later, more spectacular attempt by God to get his people out of the wrong land and back into the correct one. In spite of his wrongdoing, however, Abraham leaves Egypt a wealthy man (12.16, 20; 13.2). Even an immoral act cannot stand in the way of the divine blessing.

As if to underline the ambiguities in Abraham's character all the way through his story, Genesis 20 provides us with another example of the same kind of strategy, which is frankly described as Abraham's *customary* strategy for dealing with the danger bound up with wandering in foreign lands (Gen. 20.13). Here the ruler who is duped by Abraham is Abimelek, a virtuous man who in Genesis 20.4–5 has his own 'Abrahamic dialogue' with God about innocence, guilt and judgement, matching Abraham's similar dialogue in Genesis 18. Clearly Abimelek is someone who cares about doing what is right, as we discover again later when we read about his making a treaty with Abraham to solve a water-rights quarrel at Beersheba (Gen. 21.22–34).[6] Abraham, on the other hand, reveals himself in Genesis 20 once again in his shadow side, trusting to strategy rather than trusting in God, with all the expected negative consequences that follow. What kind of man would abandon his wife to another man's harem out of self-interest? Fortunately God cares more about Sarah than Abraham

---

[5] Note that the lie is not that she is his sister – she is indeed the daughter of his father (but not his mother, Gen. 20.12). The lie is that she is his sister and not his wife.

[6] He is also apparently portrayed in Gen. 26, however, as a slow learner. For a second time, here, he falls for the 'my wife is really my sister' trick – this time performed by Isaac in respect of Rebekah (26.7–8).

does, and so in this second case of wrong behaviour, as in the first, it is made clear to the innocent offenders (Abimelek and his household) that something is wrong, so that they can put it right and avoid long-term negative consequences (Gen. 20.3, 17–18). Abraham's failure of trust in this instance is all the more striking as the immediate background to chapter 22 – his greatest test in respect of trusting God (see further below).

Lot and Melchizedek (Gen. 13.1–18; 14.1–24; 19.1–38)

When Abraham and Sarah leave Haran to travel to Canaan in Genesis 12.4, Abraham's nephew Lot accompanies them, and his story intersects with theirs in various ways all the way through the subsequent narrative. Our first insight into his character comes in Genesis 13, after the family's visit to Egypt. Given a choice by Abraham about where he wants to settle, Lot chooses 'the plain of the Jordan' (13.10). From one point of view this is a sensible choice, because it is 'well watered'. From another point of view it is a troubling choice, because the region 'looks like the land of Egypt', which does not bring positive associations to the Hebrew mind. Egypt stands for everything that Israel later rejects, and for everything to which they are forbidden to return. So 'looks like the land of Egypt' is an ambiguous phrase, and of course the immediate mention of Sodom and Gomorrah in Genesis 13.10 indicates very well that this region is not as good as it looks. Lot has 'pitched his tents' in a place where people live very wickedly (13.13). This sets us up for the terrible story of Sodom and Gomorrah's end in Genesis 19, which centrally involves Lot and his family.

Before we get to that story, however, we read in Genesis 14 of a more immediate threat to Lot, which arises from an incursion by four foreign kings into the land of Canaan in response to the rebellion of five of its kings against the overlordship of Kedorlaomer, king of Elam (14.1–4). The story reflects the landscape of the Middle Bronze Age before the Old Babylonian period of the famous Hammurabi, king of Babylon. This was a time when Mesopotamia was carved up among a number of less power-ful leaders, and inter-state rivalry was common.[7] The foreign kings them-selves, however, remain unknown outside the narrative of Genesis 14, although Kedorlaomer certainly has an authentic-sounding Elamite name (Kedor stands for a common first element in Elamite royal names, Kudur), and four known Hittite kings were called Tudhaliya ('Tidal'). The four kings, anyway, are victorious over the five, and in carrying off booty from

[7] K. A. Kitchen, *On the Reliability of the Old Testament* (Grand Rapids: Eerdmans, 2003), 320–1.

Sodom and Gomorrah they also carry off Lot. Informed of the disaster, Abraham (now a wealthy and influential man, Gen. 13.2; 14.13) sets off to rescue his nephew, recovering him along with other plunder taken from the Canaanite coalition (14.16).

On his return, Abraham meets a mysterious priest-king of Salem (very probably Jerusalem), who is only otherwise mentioned in the OT in Psalm 110. This is Melchizedek, who is described in Genesis 14 as a priest of El Elyon, 'God Most High' – a deity identified with Yahweh himself (the 'Creator of heaven and earth', 14.19) in the broader context of the book. In this priestly role Melchizedek blesses Abraham, and Abraham gives him in return 'a tenth of everything' he has retrieved from the foreign invaders (14.20). In describing this scene, it seems that the Genesis authors are affirming that the priesthood of the supreme God, the creator of the world, existed in Jerusalem not merely from the time of David or Solomon onwards, but from before Abraham's arrival in the Promised Land. Not only that, they are suggesting that the ancient *priest* of God Most High in Jerusalem was at the same time a king to whom others in the land of Canaan were required to defer. In the biblical story the full significance of these facts becomes clear later, when David conquers the Jebusite city of Jerusalem and Solomon builds the Temple there (2 Sam. 5.6–10; 1 Kings 6). For as Psalm 110 reveals, it is the Davidic king who thereby becomes also 'a priest forever, in the order of Melchizedek' in whom Yahweh's plans for the world are focused. The Davidic dynasty ruling in Zion is in this way understood simply as continuing something that had operated in the same way as far back as Abraham's time.

In the context of the post-exilic book of Psalms, Psalm 110 is already best read as looking far beyond the historical moment of David and Solomon to the coming of some future messianic figure, and it is as such that Melchizedek later appears in a fragmentary midrashic work from Qumran, *11QMelchizedek*. This document interprets a number of verses from Isaiah, Leviticus, and other OT books, dealing with remission of debts and the liberation of slaves at the end of a jubilee cycle, as referring to the last judgement and the final triumph of good over evil during the tenth jubilee of the Essene eschatological era. Psalm 82.1–2 provides a crucial lens through which to view the matter: 'God (*'elohim*) stands in the divine council (*'adat-'el*), in the midst of gods (*'elohim*) he holds judgement. How long will you judge unjustly and show partiality to the wicked?' The first *'elohim* is taken by the Essene interpreter to refer to an angel (Melchizedek), and the 'gods' whom he judges are the wicked spirits associated with Belial, whom he destroys. Here Melchizedek takes on the role of one of two supreme spirits created by God – the spirit of light, opposed to the spirit of darkness – and comes out on top.

Melchizedek also appears in the NT, but in a very different role. Here, in the Epistle to the Hebrews – which may have been addressed to a group of Jewish Christians of Essene background, aimed at overcoming their lingering attachment to the idea of an exclusively Levitical priesthood – the readers are exhorted to recognize that Jesus is a priest, despite his non-Levitical ancestry. The author deploys as a precedent the figure of Melchizedek, whom he supposes to be familiar to the audience, and he applies to Christ the words of Psalm 110.4, 'You are a priest forever, in the order of Melchizedek' (e.g. Heb. 5.6). Abraham's 'tithe' of ten per cent is then drawn into the discourse, as he explains that Melchizedek 'means "king of righteousness"; then also, "king of Salem" means "king of peace". Without father or mother, without genealogy, without beginning of days or end of life, like the Son of God he remains a priest forever.' The fact that Abraham gave a tithe of his spoils to Melchizedek, the author continues, proves that Melchizedek was superior to Abraham and, by implication, to Abraham's descendant Levi, who, as it were, paid tithes *through* Abraham (Heb. 7.10). This notion, in the Epistle to the Hebrews, of Melchizedek as a primeval, immortal being, coeternal with the Son of God, later gave rise to various heterodox opinions in the Christian Church, and there even arose for a while (prior to the fifth century) a sect of Melchizedekians who regarded Melchizedek as equal or superior to Christ.

This NT connection between Christ and Melchizedek greatly influenced the Christian art of the succeeding centuries, and has resulted in many representations of Abraham's encounter with the priest-king. Two parallels have been emphasized in this art: the first, between Abraham offering tithes to Melchizedek and the wise men offering gifts to the infant Jesus (Matt. 2.1–12); and the second, between Melchizedek offering bread and wine to Abraham, and the Eucharist. Among many examples we may mention some fifth-century AD mosaics in the church of Santa Maria Maggiore in Rome, as well as some sixth-century ones in Ravenna; some twelfth-century frescoes in Saint-Savin, Poitou; the thirteenth-century portal of Amiens cathedral; and Rubens' *The Meeting of Abraham and Melchizedek* (*c*.1625).[8]

Another popular subject of Christian art has been Abraham's encounter in Genesis 18, as the story of Lot continues, with three mysterious strangers.

---

[8] N. M. Sarna et al., 'Abraham', *EncJud* 1:280–8 (287–8); T. Nichols, *Tintoretto: Tradition and Identity* (London: Reaktion Books, 1999), 178–9.

Here Yahweh (it seems), appearing in the company of two angels, first repeats to Abraham his promise of a son (Gen. 18.1–15) and then goes on to reveal another purpose in their visit to the region. They have come to see whether Sodom and Gomorrah are as bad as reports have suggested (18.20–21). In the East, these three strangers were often represented artistically as a prefiguration of the Trinity. The most famous example is probably the fifteenth-century icon of the Russian artist Andrei Rublev (*c.*1360–1430), which pictures them seated around an altar, with a chalice representing the Eucharist standing at the centre. The same idea is found in the West in a painting like de Gelder's late seventeenth-century composition *God and the Angels Visit Abraham,* and in Rembrandt's etching *Abraham Entertaining the Angels* (1656). This reading of the story stands in continuity with an earlier tradition represented by Ambrose of Milan:

> Abraham, who was glad to receive strangers, faithful to God and tireless in his service and prompt in fulfilling his duty, saw the Trinity typified. He added religious devotion to hospitality, for although he beheld three, he adored one, and, while keeping a distinction of the persons, yet he called one Lord.[9]

Abraham is drawn into God's confidence in Genesis 18, it seems, precisely because it is through him that 'all nations on earth will be blessed' (18.18). Now two cities are threatened with divine cursing of an ultimate kind, and Abraham looks for blessing instead. Thus it appears in this story that one of the tasks of the chosen people is to *pray* for blessing on the world; we find this theme repeated in Genesis 20.7, where Abimelek is told that Abraham is a prophet, whose prayers will bring him life in spite of being 'as good as dead because of the woman you have taken' (20.3). But the story in Genesis 18 also suggests, centrally, that God is *willing* to bring blessing to the world, since it is clear that only thorough wickedness will lead to the destruction of Sodom and Gomorrah. This theme is already hinted at back in Genesis 15.16, where Israelite possession of the Promised Land needs to wait for four generations, because 'the sin of the Amorites has not yet reached its full measure'. In the case of Sodom and Gomorrah, of course, it turns out that the cities are beyond any help. The story of Genesis 19, in which Lot and his family are central characters, is intended

---

[9] Ambrose, *On the Death of His Brother, Satyrus,* 2.96, cited from *Genesis 12–50* (ACCS 2:61). For a different view, however, see Augustine, *City of God,* 16.29, who insists that we are merely dealing with angels in this story; and this view is also represented in later art, for example in Jewish artist Marc Chagall's *Abraham and the Three Angels* (1966). Chagall was particularly fascinated with the Abraham story, and frequently returned to it in his work.

to indicate this. In the end only Lot and his two daughters survive the catastrophe that follows, as God's justice falls upon a people whose sins are variously remembered in both the Bible and in the later reading tradition as including a lack of justice (e.g. Isa. 1.9–10; 3.9), idolatry (e.g. Deut. 32.15–43), arrogant disregard for the poor (e.g. Ezek. 16.49–50) and sexual perversity (e.g. Jude 7, Philo).[10]

The question as to why Lot's wife did not survive is often asked throughout this tradition (as we saw in our Chapter 2), and a strong note of warning predominates, picking up the Bible's own emphasis. For example, the sixteenth-century ballad 'Of the Horrible and Woefull Destruction of Sodom and Gomorrah' (1570) urges its hearers to amend their lives so as to avoid a similar disaster. Sodom and Gomorrah ultimately become bywords in English literature, in fact, for all that is (from the perspective of authors or characters) dark and damned. In Langland's *Piers Plowman* (late fourteenth century), it is luxury; in Milton's essay 'The Reason of Church Government' (1642), the governance of the Church of England; in Lawrence's story 'Things' (1928), industrial materialism.[11] As such, they become a subject of interest for many artists as well, including Dürer (*The Destruction of Sodom and Gomorrah*, 1493), Raphael (*Lot Flees from Sodom*, 1518–19), Turner (*The Destruction of Sodom*, 1805) and Corot (*The Burning of Sodom*, 1843). The 1963 film *The Last Days of Sodom and Gomorrah*, starring Stewart Granger as Lot, departs substantially from this tradition, however, and 'plays so fast and loose with the story . . . that it is almost unrecognizable . . . The plot is, frankly very confusing.'[12]

Hagar and Ishmael (Gen. 16.1–16; 21.8–21)

Before we get to the narrative of Sodom and Gomorrah's end in Genesis 19, we are told (in Genesis 16) an interesting story about Sarah's slave-girl Hagar. Abraham and Sarah have apparently grown weary of waiting for God to act in the matter of 'descendants', and they devise a strategy of their own to solve the problem. Abraham takes Hagar as his concubine, in order to produce an heir through that means (16.1–4). This leads on

---

[10] Philo, *On Abraham*, 48.137–8, in *The Works of Philo* (trans. C. D. Yonge; Peabody, MA: Hendrickson, 1993), 411–44 (423).

[11] These examples are taken from M. W. Twomey, 'Sodom and Gomorrah', in D. L. Jeffrey, *A Dictionary of Biblical Tradition in English Literature* (Grand Rapids: Eerdmans, 1992), 720–1.

[12] J. S. Lang, *The Bible on the Big Screen: A Guide from Silent Films to Today's Movies* (Grand Rapids: Baker Books, 2007), 166. Contrastingly, Lang thinks that the story is told well in the 1966 film *The Bible . . . In the Beginning*.

to great unhappiness, as is characteristically the case in Genesis when Abraham and Sarah act on their own initiative (cf. 12.10–20). Hagar causes marital friction between husband and wife, and as a result of Sarah's harsh treatment of her (16.6), the pregnant girl ends up fleeing the family home. The result is that she herself receives an 'Abraham-like' promise from God (16.10): 'I will so increase your descendants that they will be too numerous to count.' The son who starts this line, Ishmael, is of course not the son that is in view in God's own promise to Abraham, even though it seems that Abraham would prefer him to be (17.18).

Yet the story underlines that God is not just interested in Abraham (and Israel), but also in other people. Notice that Hagar is, in fact, described in Genesis 16 explicitly in terms that *evoke* the 'chosenness' of Israel itself. In Genesis 16.6, we read, she is 'afflicted' by Sarah (Hb. *'anah*, NIV 'mistreated'). This is the same verb that is used in Exodus 1.12 and 15.13 of the Egyptian affliction of Israel before the exodus. Moreover, Hagar the Egyptian 'flees' from this affliction just as Israel later flees before the Egyptians (Hb. *barach*, Gen. 16.6 and Exod. 14.5) – although she runs back towards Egypt, rather than away from it.[13] Hagar is also told, just like Abraham, that suffering and the multiplication of descendants will be bound up with each other in God's plan for her (Gen. 16.9–10; cf. 15.13– 16). Hagar is herself 'chosen'; and out of her submission and suffering will come a Bedouin people who enjoy the freedom in the desert that Hagar seeks in fleeing from Sarah. That is where the wild donkeys live that are alluded to in Genesis 16.12 (cf. Jer. 2.24; Hos. 8.9). Untamed, they do not have to live in conformity with the wishes of anyone else; and this is how Hagar's descendants will be, defining themselves over against settled peoples (Gen. 16.12).[14] All of this will happen because Yahweh 'sees' Hagar (in the sense of 'looks after', 16.13). Yahweh cares for her.

This truth is borne out later in Genesis 21.8–21. Here God cares for Hagar and Ishmael in the desert, and is present with Ishmael as he grows up, after Isaac has been born and Sarah has finally had both Hagar and her son ejected from her home. Ishmael is significantly older now – already in his teens – although the reader would not guess this from some of the English translations of the chapter.[15] The NIV, for example, speaks of Hagar

---

[13] The road to Shur is one of the roads to Egypt that runs through the Sinai Peninsula (Gen. 16.7).

[14] The NIV's 'live in hostility toward' is better translated 'live over against' or 'live apart from'.

[15] Ishmael is already 13 years of age in Gen. 17.25, when Abraham is said to be 99 years old. Isaac is born when Abraham is 100 years old (Gen. 21.5). The story in Gen. 21 is set in the period after Isaac has been weaned (Gen. 21.8), which in ancient times would be around two to three years old. So Ishmael must be around 16 or 17 years old.

'putting' the boy under a bush, and describes him 'crying' (21.15, 17), thereby giving the impression that we are still dealing with a much younger child. It is better to translate Genesis 21.15 as referring to Hagar 'leaving the boy' under a bush (in a weakened, dying state, perhaps), and to translate Genesis 21.17 as referring to God hearing the boy's voice, perhaps as he prays.

The theme of Hagar's descendants defining themselves over against settled peoples is revisited in Act 8 of the book of Genesis, where we find described, briefly, Ishmael's descendants (Gen. 25.12–18). This accords with the general custom in Genesis: the account of the 'unchosen' son (in this case, Ishmael) is provided prior to the (more extensive) account of the chosen son (in this case, Isaac). Ishmael is said in this passage to have had 12 sons, fulfilling the divine promise concerning Ishmael in Genesis 17.20 and paralleling the 12 sons of Jacob who will later produce the tribes of Israel. His descendants apparently include the Nabateans ('Nebaiot', Gen. 25.13), the Qedarites, and other people groups of Arabia and the Sinai Peninsula. These various tribes lived in settlements and encampments, we are told in Genesis 25.16, reflecting their wandering lifestyle – Israel's Bedouin-like, Ishmaelite neighbours, who plied the trade routes in times of peace (Gen. 37.25), and pounced on the settlements of Israel in times of war (Judg. 8.24).

Hagar's role in the story of Genesis is reflected to a significant degree in later literature, drama, art and music. In Philo, she represents allegorically 'the academic subjects with which the soul must "sojourn" temporarily on its way to wisdom and truth', whose attainment is symbolized by the birth of Isaac, after which 'Hagar' may be cast out into the wilderness.[16] In the NT she becomes, as a slave-woman, a picture of the slavery to the Jewish law that the apostle Paul wants to see abolished in the church of Galatia (Gal. 4.21–31). By the middle of the third century Hagar has come to stand for Judaism as such, over against the Church, and this theme is clearly articulated in the fifth century by Augustine, who argues that all Jews have descended from Hagar rather than from Sarah: 'Christians, not Jews, are the seed of Abraham, the inheritors of the promise through Isaac.'[17] In Islam, by contrast, Hagar is 'a woman of true faith, indeed a

---

[16] A. Reinhartz and M.-S. Walfish, 'Conflict and Coexistence in Jewish Interpretation', in *Hagar, Sarah, and Their Children: Jewish, Christian, and Muslim Perspectives* (ed. P. Trible and L. M. Russell; Louisville: Westminster John Knox, 2006), 101–25 (104).

[17] E. A. Clark, 'Interpretive Fate amid the Church Fathers', in Trible and Russell, *Hagar*, 127–47 (136). See Augustine, *Letter 196*, in *Saint Augustine: Letters, Volume IV* (FC 30; trans. W. Parsons; Washington, DC: The Catholic University Press, 1955), 342–44.

monotheist in a pagan world. As "mother of the Arabs", she not only gave birth to Ishmael but was herself a faithful messenger appointed by the one God.'[18] This appropriation of Hagar and Ishmael by Muslims in turn leads on to a Christian criticism of Hagar that is allied to criticism of Muslims, as in Martin Luther's lectures on Genesis delivered between 1535 and 1545.[19]

In the seventeenth century Hagar's exile in the desert then becomes a popular theme among Dutch artists such as Rubens (*Hagar Leaves the House of Abraham*, c.1615) and Rembrandt (*Abraham Dismissing Hagar and Ishmael*, 1640). Her story is also the subject of oratorios like Scarlatti's *Agar et Ismaele esiliati* (1683) and Giovanni Battista Vitali's *Agar* (1671). In the eighteenth and nineteenth centuries she becomes the subject of plays like *Hagar dans le désert* (1781), written by the French Comtesse de Genlis, and *Hagar* (1848), written by the Dutchman Isaac da Costa. Schubert writes a song about her (*Hagars Klage*, 1811), and Étienne Nicolas Méhul an opera (*Agar au désert*, 1806, never performed).[20] Hagar has also attracted significant attention from the nineteenth century to the present day from African American artists and writers like Toni Morrison, who have focused on themes like sexual exploitation, slavery and survival.[21] A growing body of feminist literature has also arisen during this period, asking questions (for example) about how the struggle between Sarah and Hagar represents 'part of a broader picture of power dynamics in which patriarchy constrains their motherhood'.[22]

Ishmael, in turn, shows up in the later reading tradition as a person who is outside God's grace (Augustine),[23] and therefore a representative of people outside the Church like the Saracens (in *Mandeville's Travels*, 1357). In Shakespeare's *Merchant of Venice*, Shylock finds himself, ironically (as one of the chosen people), in the position of Ishmael – an outcast from society.[24] In Coleridge's *Zapolya* (1817), Ishmael denotes exile and alienation. He is, according to James Baird, 'the overseer of every major

---

[18] P. Trible and L. M. Russell, 'Unto the Thousandth Generation', in Trible and Russell, *Hagar*, 1–29 (9). See further in the same volume R. Hassan, 'Islamic Hagar and Her Family' (149–67). This Islamic view stands in contrast to some Jewish views, according to which 'Hagar's Egyptian origins mark her as an unreformed idolater' (Reinhartz and Walfish, 'Conflict', 106, citing the c. ninth-century text *Pirqe Rabbi Eliezer*).

[19] Trible and Russell, 'Generation', 15–21.

[20] Sarna et al., 'Abraham', 287–8.

[21] D. S. Williams, 'Hagar in African American Biblical Appropriation', in Trible and Russell, *Hagar*, 171–84.

[22] L. M. Russell, 'Children of Struggle', in Trible and Russell, *Hagar*, 185–97 (187).

[23] Augustine, *City of God*, 15.2.

[24] The irony is especially apparent in Shakespeare, *The Merchant of Venice*, 2.5.44.

work in [Melville's] literary record'.[25] Yet in modern art and literature Ishmael can also be portrayed as an 'insider', at least at the end of time (as in Blake's *Vision of the Last Judgement*, 1808). He can even become heroic, as in Byron's *The Island* (1823) and Daniel Quinn's *Ishmael* (1992), in which the central character is a wise gorilla who functions as a teacher for 'civilized humanity'.

The binding of Isaac (Gen. 22.1–19)

Of all the well-known stories about the patriarchs in the book of Genesis, it is perhaps the one told in Genesis 22.1–14 that has most attracted the attention of both Jews and Christians down through the centuries – 'the binding of Isaac' (the Akedah), as it is known in Jewish tradition, or 'the sacrifice of Isaac', as it has more often been described among Christians. It is a powerful and disturbing story, which begins with a few stark words: 'After these things God tested Abraham' (NRSV). These words remind us of the context: it is the Abraham who has already left family, country and religion in pursuit of a God who makes implausible promises who is now to endure this experience. It is the Abraham, in other words, who has already been well tested; this is not his first test, even though it is the first occasion upon which the Hebrew verb *nasah*, 'to tempt, to test', is used of him. Rabbinic tradition speaks of this test in actuality as his *tenth*.[26] Why is it necessary? We are not explicitly told, of course, but it is plausible to understand it as addressing a lingering question in the Abraham story, given his patchy record in trusting God. How *deep* is Abraham's trust, and (connectedly) how deep is Abraham's desire for obedience? Biblical faith gives evidence of interest in this kind of testing elsewhere – the process of refining, in which it becomes clear what is pure and true, and what is counterfeit and worthless. 'Testing is no marginal notion in the faith of Israel.'[27]

Abraham himself does not know that it is a test – or at least, he is not told this. *The readers* are told this, as privileged insiders; but Abraham is

---

[25] Quoted in A. Westenbroek, 'Ishmael', in Jeffrey, *Biblical Tradition*, 382–3 (382), from whom most of the other information in this paragraph is also drawn. For an extended set of reflections on Melville's use of Ishmael, see I. Pardes, 'Modern Literature', in *Reading Genesis: Ten Methods* (ed. R. Hendel; Cambridge: Cambridge University Press, 2010), ch. 9: 'Ishmael – far more than Adam – allows Melville to translate Genesis into American landscapes and inscapes, to capture the diverse manifestations of the American frontier in big strokes, to envision a biblical scene no European could have imagined' (177).

[26] *Pirqe R. El.*, 31.

[27] W. Brueggemann, *Genesis* (Interpretation; Atlanta: John Knox, 1982), 190.

not. The situation is similar to the one in the book of Job, where the reader is given some insight into the reasons for Job's suffering, but Job is not. This connection between the two patriarchs, Abraham and Job, is already picked up and developed early in the reading tradition, in the book of *Jubilees*. Here the Akedah is preceded by a debate in the heavenly council, in the course of which one of the participants proposes just such a test, so that God may find out if Abraham is faithful (cf. Job 1—2).[28] Abraham knows nothing about such matters; all that *he* knows is that God has once again spoken to him. His response is characteristic – 'Here I am.' We meet it again in Genesis 22.7 (where the NIV unhelpfully disguises it behind the 'yes' in Abraham's response to Isaac) and in Genesis 22.11. As these recurrences suggest, Abraham is open to and ready to respond to both God and his son in this story. The dilemma, it seems, is that he will have to choose between them.

This reality is quickly and shockingly introduced in Genesis 22.2. The word order in the Hebrew of the first part of the verse seems designed for maximum effect, building to a crescendo until the son who is to be taken is at last named: 'take your son, your favored one, the one whom you love, Isaac' (my translation). The emphasis, clearly, lies on what this son means to the father. The command, then, to 'go . . . to a land' (my translation) is not very disturbing, and is indeed familiar to the reader (and to Abraham); it reminds us of Genesis 12.1 ('go to the land I will show you'). Set in that context, it is not a very demanding instruction; Moriah is a mere three-day journey away. The last part of the verse, however, is darkly unfamiliar: 'sacrifice him there on one of the mountains' (my translation). The shock is heightened by the prior familiarity. Isaac, so long promised and so long awaited, and the one whom God himself has provided so that all the nations of the world shall be blessed, is to be taken away. The first command to 'go' in Genesis 12 sent Abraham off into the land of promise; the second sends him off now to bring an end (apparently) to the promise altogether. And the question is: will Abraham obey God?

Perhaps there is a prior question, however: *should* Abraham obey God? Some interpreters have wondered.[29] They have particularly wondered about

---

[28] *Jub.* 17.16.

[29] This 'wondering' takes various forms; for a few examples see R. W. L. Moberly, The *Theology of the Book of Genesis* (OTT; Cambridge: Cambridge University Press, 2009), ch. 10: 'Genesis 22: Abraham – Model or Monster?' In quite recent times the 'wondering' even underlies a popular video game called 'The Binding of Isaac', in which a contemporary mother receives a message from God demanding the life of her son, Isaac, as proof of her faith, and the son takes refuge from her in the monster-filled basement of their home.

the apparent dissimilarity between the Abraham of Genesis 18 and the Abraham of Genesis 22. In chapter 18, faced with the likelihood that God would destroy Sodom and Gomorrah because of their inhabitants' wickedness, Abraham dialogues with God and explores with him the question of innocent suffering. Yet in Genesis 22, with not a wicked person in sight, and faced with an apparent divine severity that is counter to the divine promise, Abraham says nothing. Without a word, 'Early the next morning Abraham . . . took his son' (Gen. 22.3). Some have found this puzzling. Yet in truth the issue in Genesis 18 is not the same as in Genesis 22. In the first passage the question is whether God should treat the righteous and the unrighteous alike in terms of dispensing justice. Genesis 22 is not a story about justice, however. The issue at the heart of this passage is whether God, who is the creator of everything, has the right to give life and to take it away. The biblical answer to this question, as the book of Job reminds us, is that he does indeed possess such a right. So we cannot assume that we are meant to think, or to read Abraham as thinking, that there is something fundamentally wrong about what God is asking him to do here, and therefore that his lack of objection to the divine command requires an explanation.

Given that God has the right to give and to take away life, how are we to read his particular command in respect of Isaac? Here we must also look to the broader context for help. A major theme of the whole preceding narrative in Genesis has been the tension between God's plan for the world, on the one hand, and the desire of human beings to control their own destiny, on the other. Genesis 1—11 is largely about that. Abraham, too, has previously succumbed to a desire to control *his own* destiny, conceding to Sarah's demand for a child in Genesis 16 – a false climax to the cycle of stories in Genesis 12—22. He even somewhat argues with God about God's promise in Genesis 17.18; he wishes that Ishmael might be blessed by God instead of the promised son. In such a context, Abraham's silence in the face of God's command in Genesis 22 makes perfect sense. We can read it as a sign that he has *understood* that God is God, and that in this whole matter of life and destiny, he and his beloved son are entirely in God's hands. The depth of his attachment to his son may well be indicated in the very words of address in Genesis 22.2, which refer to Isaac as Abraham's *only* son (which he is not), and which specify Isaac alone as the object of Abraham's devotion.[30] So does Abraham perhaps

---

[30] The Hb. word *yachid* might not necessarily mean 'only', but if it does not, it certainly means 'darling', and it has the sense of sole devotion.

love his son more than he loves God? This key issue is identified explicitly in Genesis 22.12, 'Now I know that you fear God, because you have not withheld *from me* [i.e. from God, emphasis added] your son, your only son.'

And so we find in Genesis 22.3 that preparations are made for the journey to the mountain, which is reached on the third day (Gen. 22.4). Soon there is a question from Isaac: 'The fire and the wood are here . . . but where is the lamb for the burnt offering?' (Gen. 22.7). It is an intriguing question; the reader inevitably asks how Isaac cannot hitherto have noticed the lamb's absence. Are we reading here of a dawning realization that this is not a normal sacrifice – perhaps even of Isaac's acceptance of his own role as 'the lamb'? Along these lines, Jewish tradition later made much of the *willingness* of Isaac to endure his fate, *Genesis Rabbah* asking whether it is really possible to bind a man of Isaac's age without his consent.[31] In such a way of thinking, Isaac becomes the archetypal martyr, willingly dying for the faith.

Abraham's response to Isaac's question is apparently confident, but is in fact ambiguous: 'God himself will provide', literally, God will 'see to it' (Hb. *ra'ah*). But what will God provide: Isaac, whom he has already 'provided', or a substitute? The matter is settled very quickly in our canonical biblical text (Gen. 22.10–12): an angel speaks, and Abraham obeys in not killing his son. Josephus tells us that Abraham and Isaac embraced when they heard the angel's words – as we might well imagine.

However, not every ancient interpreter took such a straightforward view. *Genesis Rabbah* has Abraham anxious to kill Isaac even after the angel has told him not to do so, and even after the angels' tears have dissolved the knife.[32] This suggests, perhaps, an insistence that only the actual sacrifice of Isaac himself will do, if Abraham's faithfulness to God is truly to be demonstrated. The same text actually has Abraham praying to God that he would *regard* it as though Isaac had been sacrificed first, and only afterwards the ram. *Pirqe Rabbi Eliezer* has the angels supporting the idea of abandoning the sacrifice, but having to struggle with God over this, since *God* wants to go ahead.[33] *Tanhuma Genesis* has Satan throwing away the knife, which Abraham tries to recover to fulfil the divine commission; this text suggests that Abraham was unsure whether the angel was truly speaking for God. Clearly this was a vexed issue for early readers of the story.

---

[31] *Gen. Rab.* 56.8. Isaac is reckoned here to be either 26 or 37 years old.
[32] *Gen. Rab.* 5.7.
[33] *Pirqe R. El.* 31.

In the biblical version of the story, anyway, it is all over quickly and straightforwardly, and Abraham returns to rejoin his servants (Gen. 22.19). Isaac is not mentioned further as the story ends, perhaps surprisingly; but after all, this is not really a story about Isaac. It is a story about Abraham and, beyond that, about Israel and the whole world. We should therefore probably not read too much into the (apparent) absence of the son.

As we have just seen, the Akedah has been very important for Jewish readers throughout the ages, and Jewish art from the earliest times reflects this.[34] Its impact on Jewish literature is still profoundly felt in the modern period, as in Adele Wiseman's novel *The Sacrifice* (1956), which tells the story of an orthodox Jew with Old World values (Abraham) whose life turns to chaos and tragedy in the New World of Canada. Musically, it has been the subject of works like Hugo Adler's *Akedah* (1938) and Judith Eisenstein's *The Sacrifice of Isaac: A Liturgical Drama* (1972).[35] It is even alluded to in one of Bob Dylan's early songs, 'Highway 61 Revisited' (1965),

> in the line about God telling Abraham to kill his son on Highway 61. Dylan does not use the first-person singular, but the lyrics suggest this is another self-referential writing because Abraham is the name of Bob's father, and Highway 61 runs through Duluth, Minnesota, where Bob was born.[36]

The story also has political importance in Judaism, functioning for many as 'the deepest symbol of modern Israeli existence, epitomizing the Zionist revolution and the sacrifices it exacted'. In such a view, 'Isaac becomes the paradigmatic Zionist pioneer, representing an entire generation: rather than being passive victims, the modern Isaacs assume responsibility for their destiny and sacrifice themselves on the altar of national renaissance.'[37]

For Christian readers, the story of Abraham and Isaac has provided *one* important example of self-sacrifice in obedience to God's will, but not the supreme example. It provides in this Christian frame of reference only

---

[34] The art of the early synagogues of Dura-Europos (on a wall) and Beth-Alpha (on the mosaic floor) depicts God himself (not an angel) stretching out his hand to restrain Abraham. See D. M. Carr, 'Genesis', in *The Oxford Encyclopedia of the Books of the Bible* (ed. M. D. Coogan; 2 vols; New York: Oxford University Press, 2011), 331. For a much more modern Jewish composition on the theme, consider Marc Chagall's etching, *Sacrifice of Abraham* (1931–9).

[35] See further L. A. Berman, *The Akedah: The Binding of Isaac* (New York: Jason Aronson, 1997), ch. 23: 'The Akedah in Music and Literature'.

[36] M. J. Gilmour, 'Bob Dylan's Bible', in *The Oxford Handbook of Reception History of the Bible* (ed. M. Lieb, E. Mason, J. Roberts and C. Rowland; Oxford: Oxford University Press, 2011), 355–68 (364).

[37] Jacobs and Sagi, 'Akedah', 558. There is an interesting account on this and the following page of modern Jewish literature that both reflects this view (e.g. U. Z. Greenberg, 'Morning Offering', 1972) and questions it (e.g. Y. Laor's 'This Fool, Isaac', 1985).

a foreshadowing of the sacrifice of Christ. The NT itself already connects Isaac with Jesus early on in the Gospels with this thought in mind, when it is announced in Mark 1.11 and parallels that Jesus is 'the beloved son' of God. The word here is *agapētos*, the Greek that renders the Hebrew *yachid* in the LXX of Genesis 22.2, 12 and 16. The Genesis 22 passage is thus strongly evoked by Mark 1.11. We also hear echoes here of Isaiah 42.1 ('in whom I delight') and its surrounding context, which speaks of a suffering servant, persecuted unto death yet bringing redemption to others. Jesus is in this way associated with notions both of binding and of sacrifice. Elsewhere he is connected directly with the lamb of the Passover feast who takes away the sins of the world (John 1.29), developing a stream of Jewish tradition that by the first century AD had already associated the Akedah with Passover.[38] It is this association that explains the later Jewish traditions that tell us that Isaac's blood was, after all, in some sense shed – that he was *truly* a martyr, and not merely an *almost*-martyr. It also explains the way in which from the first century AD onwards, Isaac himself (and not Abraham) stands at centre stage in the story, in a way that is not true of Genesis 22 itself. In these traditions, the crucial thing about the story is that *Isaac's* willing sacrifice effects atonement for many; some of them even have him experiencing, after his death, a resurrection.[39]

It is in the context of the early association of the Passover lamb and the binding of Isaac that the NT representation of Jesus as 'beloved son' becomes especially meaningful. Here is the Son of God given up by the Father for the sake of the redemption of many, carrying the instrument of his death with him to the place of execution (as Isaac also did, Gen. 22.6). Thus, for the writers of the NT, the Akedah prophesied a higher truth, the divine mystery proclaimed in Christ. We see this reflected in the Gospel of John, 'God so loved the world that he gave his one and only Son' (John 3.16). We see it also in Paul, with his 'he who did not spare his own Son, but gave him up for us all' (Rom. 8.32). Jesus is the supreme example of parental sacrifice, the supreme example of willing martyrdom, as the averted death of the son becomes the literal death – and resurrection – of the Son. Christ is the beloved son par excellence – 'the offspring', in an ultimate sense, mentioned in Genesis 13.15 and 17.8 (Gal. 3.13–16). This is how the story is read, for example, by Tertullian.[40]

---

[38] *Jubilees* makes it clear, e.g., that the sacrifice of the lamb in the Akedah story takes place on Passover (*Jub.* 17.15–16). Abraham is the originator of Passover, Isaac the paschal lamb – a willing victim, according to (e.g.) Josephus, in *Ant.*, 1.232.

[39] E.g. *Pirqe R. El.* 31.

[40] Tertullian, *Against Marcion*, 3.18 (*ANF* 3:336).

This Christian interpretation of Genesis 22 inevitably plays out among Christian writers, musicians and artists of the succeeding centuries. The story figures in all the important English miracle-play cycles, and numerous later dramas; it is reflected in the artistic works of Donatello (*The Sacrifice of Isaac*, c.1418), Caravaggio (*The Sacrifice of Isaac*, 1601–2) and Rembrandt (*The Sacrifice of Isaac*, 1635), among others; and it was turned into a sacred ballad by Stravinsky (*Abraham and Isaac*, 1963).[41] One of the most famous treatments in literature comes from Kierkegaard, in his *Fear and Trembling* (1843), who understands the story as an invitation to radical self-abandonment to God, even as it takes the believer beyond the bounds of the moral law.

---

[41] M. Stern, *Bible and Music: Influences of the Old Testament on Western Music* (Jersey City, NJ: Ktav, 2011), 41–55.

10

The Jacob story: Genesis 25.19—37.1

In this chapter we shall focus on the substantial Act 9 of the book of Genesis (Gen. 25.19—35.29), which tells us about 'the descendants of Isaac', passing over the much briefer Acts 10 and 11 (Gen. 36.1—37.1), which account for the family history of Esau, Isaac's 'unchosen' son. Isaac himself appears in Act 9: he is the recipient of the promise to Abraham, signalled by the repeated expression that God was with him and blessed him (e.g. Gen. 25.11); he faces similar threats to the fulfilment of the promise; and like Abraham, he responds with a certain lack of trust (Gen. 26). Yet Isaac remains throughout this section of Genesis a rather 'flat' character – a pale reflection, only, of his father. It is upon his younger son Jacob that the spotlight falls; it is he who lends Act 9 all of its dynamism.

Birthing, naming and plot

The Jacob story begins in Genesis 25.19–34, with the births of Jacob and his twin brother Esau. It is in this opening story that Jacob receives his name, which in Hebrew is *ya'aqov*. This name is connected to two other Hebrew words. First, there is the noun *'aqev*, 'heel', which makes sense of the naming in the immediate context of his birth: he was born clutching the heel of his brother Esau (Gen. 25.26). As the story develops, however, another connection becomes clear, for there is also a Hebrew verb *'aqav*, 'to cheat'. The connection in this case is not with the circumstances of Jacob's birth, but with two important events that take place during his early years and drive the plot of this entire section of Genesis. Esau will shortly claim that Jacob has cheated him twice, taking first his birthright and then his blessing (Gen. 27.36). It is this reality of 'cheating' that dominates the entirety of the first part of the Jacob story, resulting in his hasty flight from Canaan and his long residence abroad, in order to avoid his brother's revenge.

Later, when Jacob returns to Canaan, he receives a quite different name, this time from God himself. It is the name 'Israel' (Gen. 32.29; 35.10). This name informs the reader not so much about Jacob's *character* (as a cheat), but about his *role*. He is the chosen one of God, and the father of many descendants who will also be identified by this name ('children of Israel'). The connection between the movements out of and into the Promised Land, on the one hand, and the different namings of Jacob/ Israel, on the other, suggest that the whole of Act 9 is designed to answer two important and related questions. The first is, how did the duplicitous Jacob become one of the ancestors of God's people in the first place, given that this people is called to holiness? The second is, how did he manage to inherit the promise made to Abraham and Isaac about the Promised Land after he willingly left it for an extended period of time? The latter question is especially pointed in view of Genesis 26.2–6, where Isaac is explicitly instructed by God to remain in the land even under conditions of famine, and he obeys this command.

Genesis 25.19—35.29 is structured in a very evident way to allow reflection on these two questions. The various components of the story are presented in a concentric pattern that we can identify in part by noting similarities of both vocabulary and theme. Each 'half' of the chiastic structure contains seven segments, presented thematically in reverse order as they move into and out from the centre of the chiasm, which concerns the birth of Joseph and Jacob's decision to return to Canaan:

A Beginnings, including the early conflict between Jacob and Esau
  (Gen. 25.19–34)
  B Relations with the indigenous population (Gen. 26.1–35)
    C Jacob obtains the blessing (Gen. 27.1–40)
      D Jacob's flight from Esau (Gen. 27.41—28.5)
        E Jacob encounters God's agents (Gen. 28.10–22)
          F Jacob arrives in Haran (Gen. 29.1–30)
            G Jacob acquires a family (Gen. 29.31—30.24)
Jacob's intention to return to Canaan is revealed as soon as Joseph is born
            G′ Jacob acquires wealth (Gen. 30.25–43)
          F′ Jacob departs from Haran (Gen. 31.1–55)
        E′ Jacob encounters God's agents (Gen. 32.1–2)
      D′ Jacob approaches Esau (Gen. 32.3–32)
    C′ The blessing is returned (Gen. 33.1–20)
  B′ Relations with the indigenous population (Gen. 34.1–31)
A′ Endings: Jacob and Esau together (Gen. 35.1–29)

The *thematic* correspondences between the 'mirrored' segments are clear enough, but so too are specific *linguistic* ones. For example, segments E and E′ both employ the Hebrew verb *paga'* (Gen. 28.11; 32.2). In the latter it is used in its more usual sense of 'to meet or encounter', but in the former it means 'to reach a place'. This suggests that the author chose the verb deliberately in the former, even though it involved an unusual usage, in order to signal the connection between E and E′. Again, the occurrence of *laqach . . . berakah*, 'take . . . blessing', in both Genesis 27.35–36 and 33.11 (NIV's 'accept my present') explicitly connects segments C and C′.

Birthright and blessing (Gen. 25.19—27.40)

The Jacob story begins in Genesis 25.19–34 with the well-known account of the birth of the twin brothers and the early loss of Esau's birthright to Jacob. The two events are connected by the oracle that Isaac's wife Rebekah elicits from God concerning the jostling of the babies in her womb (Gen. 25.23). This makes clear that her children will be ancestors of separate peoples of unequal power, and that 'the older will serve the younger'. Although the oracle does not explicitly name these peoples, their identity is not in question: they are the Israelites (descended from Jacob) and the Edomites (descended from Esau). The way in which Esau is described in this story itself alludes to this reality, because we are told that he had a hairy appearance at birth (Hb. *saʿir*, Gen. 25.25; 27.11). This term alludes to the country of Seir where Esau is later said to live (Gen. 33.16) – a mountainous region that traditionally marked the south-eastern border of Edom with Israel. We are also told that he came out of the womb coloured 'red' (Hb. *'admoni*, Gen. 25.25), another word that alludes to Edom. Later, we read of his preference for red stew (Hb. *ha'adom*, Gen. 25.30); on this occasion the author explicitly references Edom.

How did the elder son come to serve the younger? First of all, Jacob took advantage of Esau's fatigue and hunger by requiring him to trade his birthright for some food (Gen. 25.27–34). The 'birthright' (Hb. *bekorah*) represents Esau's inheritance rights as firstborn – his right to receive a double share in the family property (i.e. twice as much as other brothers, Deut. 21.15–17). Esau is not without blame in this incident; he is characterized as 'despising' his birthright (Gen. 25.34). However, Jacob's behaviour is not intended to be regarded as exemplary either. In this story, as in Genesis 27 later, his 'hand' lies already on Esau's 'heel' (25.26) – that is, he is grasping and manipulative. Whatever the faults and weaknesses of other ancestors of Israel in this Genesis story (Abraham and Isaac), we do not find them behaving in such an avaricious way; it is not, indeed, how the reader probably *expects* an ancestor to behave (which is why Jacob is often 'rewritten' in the reading tradition, so as to make him more virtuous; see further below).

The gap between expectation and reality is perhaps heightened by the curious description of the twins' way of life in Genesis 25.27, just prior to the report of the birthright incident. Opposite the assessment 'Esau became a skilful hunter', we read (translating the Hb. first in a normal manner) that 'Jacob was a blameless man' (Hb. *'ish tam*). This is exactly what we read of the morally blameless Job (Job 1.8; 2.3). It is a curious juxtaposition of terms in the Genesis context, however, since no blame attaches in the OT to hunting as such. Just for this reason, translators have typically used an English word for the Hebrew *tam* that avoids any moral connotation. The old KJV would like us to think that Jacob was a 'plain' man, while the more recent Revised Standard Version (RSV) and NIV portray him as 'quiet', and the Jewish Publication Society (JPS) translation as 'mild'. No doubt this is indeed how we *must* understand the word in this particular context, but it is an exceedingly unusual usage, which begs for an explanation. Why use a term that so clearly evokes moral excellence, when that is not really what is primarily being expressed?

A plausible explanation comes to mind when we note the immediately preceding *tom* of Genesis 20.5–6 (referring to Abimelek's 'clear conscience' or integrity of heart), and the adjective *tamim* in both Genesis 6.9 and 17.1, referring to Noah's and Abraham's moral uprightness. The author has chosen *tam* in Genesis 25.27 *precisely* to raise in the reader's mind the tension that exists at this point in the Jacob story between what Jacob *should* be and what he *is*. He is *tam* in one sense (he is a home-bird), but not in the usual sense (he is not 'blameless'). Moral excellence is Jacob/Israel's vocation, but it is not currently a vocation that he is pursuing.

The same question about Jacob's character and lifestyle arises when we turn from the loss of Esau's birthright (Hb. *bekorah*) to the loss of his 'blessing' (Hb. *berakah*). These two words not only sound alike, but are also visually similar in their consonants on the written page (*bkrh* and *brkh*), being distinguishable only by the transposition of the middle two. That is, the language directly mirrors the reality, that the *bekorah* and the *berakah* are closely associated, but different from each other. When Esau loses the 'blessing' of his father, this goes beyond the question of how much property he will receive. Now the question is (as Gen. 27.27–29 make clear), who is going to be head of the family? The action in this part of the story is initiated by the parents. Isaac is old and his eyesight is poor; it is in this condition that he summons Esau to discuss the matter of the patriarchal blessing (Gen. 27.1–5). This is already an interesting beginning to the story, since elsewhere in the OT it is normal for a dying man, when organizing the succession, to summon *all* his close male relatives and to bless them publicly (cf. Gen. 49; 50.24–25). If Isaac is in danger of imminent death, then his behaviour is strange (why summon Esau alone?); and if he is not, then it is also strange (why summon Esau at all?). In either case, it immediately raises this further question: why does Isaac (apparently) wish to bless Esau and not Jacob, since (as the story goes on to suggest in vv. 34, 38) both are entitled to some blessing? The most likely answer has to do with favouritism within the family – something that is already signalled in Genesis 25.28, where we are told that Isaac loved Esau, but Rebekah loved Jacob.

This favouritism is further indicated in Genesis 27.5–6, where Esau is explicitly '*his* son' and Jacob '*her* son'. This family is divided, and the mother and father each pursue their own interests. Isaac's interest lies in giving Esau his blessing; Rebekah's lies in making sure that this does not happen. It is for this reason that Rebekah takes such decisive action when she discovers what her husband intends to do – decisiveness indicated not least by the strong verb 'command' (Hb. *tsiwwah*) with which she addresses Jacob in Genesis 27.8. This is not a verb usually found with a feminine subject.[1] Rebekah exerts all the maternal authority she can muster in order to make Jacob carry out her scheme, and Jacob complies. Consistent with what we have discovered about him so far, he expresses no moral qualms about her plan; he is only concerned that he may be found out (27.12). His character is in fact further alluded to even in his physical self-description in Genesis 27.11 – literally, 'I am a smooth man' (Hb. *'ish chalaq*). The same adjective, *chalaq*, occurs elsewhere in the OT precisely of deceptive speech:

> Proverbs 5.3   For the lips of an adulterous woman drip honey,
> and her speech is smoother than oil.
> Proverbs 26.28 A lying tongue hates those it hurts, and a flattering
> [smooth] mouth works ruin.

Jacob is not a 'blameless man' (Gen. 25.27), but a 'slippery man'.

A tense scene follows in Genesis 27.14–29. Jacob asserts his identity with Esau in the face of Isaac's immediately suspicious attitude (27.18). He almost overdoes it, speaking so much that he all but betrays himself ('The voice is the voice of Jacob, but the hands are the hands of Esau', 27.22). In the end, however, Isaac is apparently satisfied, and he blesses Jacob (27.27–29). Since it is a blessing intended for Esau but pronounced over Jacob, it explicitly reflects this reality as it begins, mentioning 'the

---

[1] G. J. Wenham, *Genesis 16–50* (WBC; Dallas: Word, 1994), 207.

smell of a field' – the open, uncultivated land where men like Esau hunt (27.27). It goes on to mention rainfall, however, and the rich harvests that it produces in terms of 'grain and new wine' (27.28); these are the concerns of the farmer more than the hunter. As it comes to an end the blessing then echoes (unwittingly on Isaac's part, we assume) the earlier birth oracle (27.29; cf. 25.23), and before that the even earlier promise to Abraham: 'May those who curse you be cursed and those who bless you be blessed.' Unbeknownst to Isaac, Jacob has now taken his place within the 'succession' of the inheritors of the Abrahamic promise.

The scene that follows in Genesis 27.30–40 is designed to underline the fact that Isaac's blessing is irrevocable. Esau arrives just too late, and is greatly shocked to discover what has happened (27.33–34): 'he trembled a very great trembling' and 'screamed a great scream' (my translation). The deed is done, however: 'Your brother came deceitfully and took your blessing' (27.35). Now Esau is left with nothing (27.37), condemned to a wandering existence like Cain and Ishmael. A warlike nation often hostile to his brother Israel (27.40; cf. passages like Num. 20.18; 1 Kings 11.14–16; 2 Kings 14.7–10), he will haunt the wilderness to the south and east of Canaan, 'away from the earth's richness' (Gen. 27.39). His only hope lies far in the future, when Edom will regain its independence from Israel (27.40; cf. 2 Kings 8.20–22).

It is intriguing to note how the relationship between Jacob and Esau is handled in early post-biblical Jewish literature, where the biblical account 'is subjected to a thorough reinterpretation, with a view to discrediting the enemies of Israel, while glorifying Jacob – regarded as virtually identical with the Jewish people'.[2] Even while *in utero*, according to *Genesis Rabbah*, Jacob would try to escape the womb if Rebekah passed by a synagogue, while Esau would do so while she was near a pagan place of worship.[3] Their physical appearances were taken to suggest the spiritual beauty of Israel, on the one hand, and the ugliness of the pagan world on the other. Jacob was not to be criticized in his quest for the birthright, because his motives were good: he wanted to be able to offer the sacrifices, at that time the firstborn's prerogative.[4] Indeed, when Jacob went to see his father, 'the Garden of Eden entered with him', but only 'Gehenna' accompanied Esau; and Jacob did not deceive Isaac, who was in fact deceived about Esau.[5] For the rabbis, indeed, Jacob was the greatest of the patriarchs, and it could be said that the entire universe had been created only for his

---

[2] N. M. Sarna et al., 'Jacob', *EncJud* 11:17–25 (20).
[3] *Gen. Rab.* 63.6.
[4] *Gen. Rab.* 63.13.
[5] *Gen. Rab.* 63.10; 65.13, 22; 67.1–2.

sake.[6] Only occasionally is he criticized in rabbinic literature, as in *Genesis Rabbah* 67.4, where Esau's grief (Gen. 27.34) is recompensed in the days of the Israelite Mordecai, who is found 'wailing loudly and bitterly' in Esther 4.1. For the most part, Jacob is depicted as a great and holy man.

This same approach to the story as concerning 'insiders' and 'outsiders' is also found in Christian literature, where the identifications are naturally different. The twelfth-century allegorical drama *Ordo de Ysaac et Rebecca et Filiis Eorum*, for example, has Esau as the Jews and Jacob as the Christians.[7] Nicholas Udall's *The Historie of Jacob and Esau* (1557–8), on the other hand, sees Jacob as the righteous Hebrew (i.e. a Protestant) and Esau as a pagan (i.e. a Catholic). Milton's *Eikonoklastes* (1649) differentiates between the independent Puritans (right) and the Presbyterians (wrong). Whatever their differences, however, all of these texts build on earlier Christian reading that, like the Jewish reading, 'cleans up' the portrait of Jacob in the biblical text (as well as that of his mother, Rebekah), making Jacob simply a saint (and as such, prefiguring Christ), and Esau simply a sinner.

The ninth-century Benedictine monk Rabanus Maurus, for example, reads Rebekah as the holy Church, directing Isaac's blessing to Jacob. Ambrose sees her as self-sacrificial in this respect, since she knew that her action would separate her from Jacob.[8] Chrysostom exalts Rebekah's love for her son, as well as her wisdom.[9] Jacob, for his part, did not lie to Isaac (according to Augustine), but spoke figuratively to him, and indeed Isaac 'knew what was happening since he had the spirit of prophecy, and he himself was acting symbolically'.[10] Pelagius agrees with Augustine as to Jacob's virtue (and Esau's contrasting vice), and makes use of these realities to argue (against Augustine) that 'God's foreknowledge of merits was the cause of his subordinating Ishmael to Isaac and Jacob to Esau'.[11] Ambrose urges his readers to imitate Jacob in precisely this virtue.[12]

---

[6] *Gen. Rab.* 76.1; *Lev. Rab.* 36.4, in *Midrash Rabbah* (ed. M. Simon; trans. H. Freedman; 3rd ed.; 10 vols; London: Soncino, 1983), 4:461.

[7] A long line of interpretation lies behind these identifications, beginning with Church Fathers like Augustine, who held that the Genesis statement about the elder serving the younger signified that the Jews would serve their younger brother, the Christians. Augustine, *City of God*, 16.35.

[8] M. O'Kane, *Painting the Text: The Artist as Biblical Interpreter* (BMW 8; Sheffield: Sheffield Phoenix, 2007), 115–16.

[9] Chrysostom, *Homilies on Genesis*, 53.5–7 (ACCS 2:169, 171).

[10] Augustine, *Sermon* 4.21 (ACCS 2:174).

[11] M. Edwards, 'Augustine and Pelagius on Romans', in *The Oxford Handbook of Reception History of the Bible* (ed. M. Lieb, E. Mason, J. Roberts and C. Rowland; Oxford: Oxford University Press, 2011), 609–20 (618).

[12] Ambrose, *On the Death of His Brother Satyrus* 2.100, in *Funeral Orations by Saint Gregory Nazianzen and Saint Ambrose* (FC 22; ed. R. J. Deferrari; trans. J. J. Sullivan and M. R. P. McGuire; Washington, DC: Catholic University Press of America, 1968), 161–259 (242).

It is only with the Enlightenment that we see a general shift away from regarding Jacob in such a favourable light. Dryden finds Jacob's vices in many of his descendants (in *Absalom and Achitophel*, 1681–2), and Robert Browning laments that 'smooth Jacob still robs homely Esau' ('The Flight of the Duchess', 1845).[13] Rebekah herself 'virtually disappears as a reference or subject in English literature' after the Middle Ages; she is noticeable by her absence, for example, in both Shakespeare and Milton, to name but two significant authors.[14] Her name lives on in the nineteenth century and afterwards, however, in works like Scott's *Ivanhoe* (1820) and du Maurier's *Rebecca* (1938).

The Jacob and Esau story has inspired not only subsequent literature, but also art and music. Musically, the story of Jacob, Esau and the birthright is told (for example) in *Il vecchio Isaac* by Anerio (1619). In art, the birth of the two boys is represented in fourteenth-century manuscripts such as the *Queen Mary Psalter* and the *Sarajevo Haggadah*, and in a fifteenth-century painting by the Florentine artist Gozzoli (1420–97) at the Campo Santo in Pisa. Their adult life is represented in a pastoral landscape by the Renaissance painter Bassano (1515–92) in the sixteenth century. From the seventeenth century onwards we find renewed interest both in the narrative about Esau selling his birthright to Jacob – not least in two famous ink drawings by Rembrandt – and in the story of Isaac (ultimately) blessing Esau, which is captured by both Raphael (1483–1520), in his frescoes for the Loggia in the Vatican, and (again) Rembrandt.[15] The account of Isaac blessing Jacob, already represented in fourth-century mosaics at Santa Maria Maggiore in Rome, in thirteenth-century frescoes at Assisi, and in various medieval manuscripts, held particularly great appeal for Renaissance artists (note, e.g., Ghiberti's relief on the doors of the Baptistery in Florence, *c.*1439) and those who came later. To identify only a few examples, it is portrayed in Setti's *Isaac Blessing Jacob* (1570), as well as works of the same name by the Dutch artist Stom (*c.*1635), by the Spanish Baroque artist Ribera (1637) and by Rembrandt (1652). Of the seventeenth-century Dutch artists in particular, Martin O'Kane says this:

---

[13] J. Dryden, 'Absalom and Achitophel', 2.6, in *Poems and Prose of John Dryden: A Selection by Douglas Grant* (Saint-Lambert, Montreal: The Penguin Poets, 1955), 18–63; R. Browning, 'The Flight of the Duchess', line 42, in *The Complete Poetical Works of Robert Browning* (ed. A. Birrell; New York: Macmillan, 1915), 356–66 (366). See further 'Jacob', in D. L. Jeffrey, *A Dictionary of Biblical Tradition in English Literature* (Grand Rapids: Eerdmans, 1992), 385–8.

[14] R. A. Peck, 'Rebekah', in Jeffrey, *Biblical Tradition*, 656–7 (657).

[15] Many of the leads on the compositions mentioned in the two preceding paragraphs were originally taken from Sarna et al., 'Jacob', 22–4.

The manner in which artists interpreted and depicted the story changed radically ... in the seventeenth century. Not only did they tend to concentrate on the very specific episode of the blessing ... but, more often than artists of any other age, they were much more inclined to interpret the story generally on purely human terms, as one of sibling rivalry, guile and deception.[16]

O'Kane sees this as a welcome development, capturing depth dimensions of the story lost in the stereotyping found in much prior post-biblical reading. Some earlier rabbis would no doubt have agreed with him, for against the grain of much that we have described so far, they 'emphasized that the Bible neither suppresses unpleasant stories about its heroes nor tries to beautify their image'.[17] This is surely true.

Jacob's dream at Bethel (Gen. 27.41—28.22)

We pick up the biblical story once again at the point when Esau's understandable anger at Jacob forces the latter to flee his homeland. He sets off for the far north to stay with his uncle Laban for a while. Once again Rebekah stands at the centre of the plan, manipulating both Jacob and Isaac to do as she wishes (Gen. 27.41—28.5). This leads on to a brief but pivotal episode in the Jacob story, as he finds himself at nightfall near the city of Luz (cf. 27.19), unable or perhaps unwilling to find a place to stay for the night. Travellers in other biblical stories are accommodated for the night by residents, but not always with happy outcomes (e.g. Gen. 19.1–3); travelling in the ancient world could be a dangerous activity. Jacob beds down, therefore, in what appears to be an area outside the city, using a stone as a pillow. In this lonely place, he has a dream. He sees a 'ladder', or better a ramp or stairway, which links earth and heaven. Most likely this is meant to be something like an ancient Babylonian ziggurat – a tower with a shrine at the top and a ramp or flight of stairs leading to the upper levels, connecting the world of mortals to the world of the gods. This 'stairway' could be conceived of as the means by which the gods or the messengers of the gods moved between heaven, earth and the netherworld (see our Chapter 8 above). Here in Genesis the stairway is likewise a symbol of the accessibility of divine help and presence. It is not the gods, however, that Jacob sees using this stairway, but the 'messengers' of God – the Hebrew *mal'akim*, often translated 'angels' (Gen. 28.12).

[16] O'Kane, *Painting the Text*, 117.
[17] Y. Zakovitch, 'Inner-Biblical Interpretation', in *Reading Genesis: Ten Methods* (ed. R. Hendel; Cambridge: Cambridge University Press, 2010), ch. 5 (101).

Where God himself is to be found, and whether he has used the stairway to get there, is a matter of debate. Traditionally, the beginning of Genesis 28.13 has been understood as saying that Jacob saw Yahweh standing *above* 'it' (the stairway), and thus still in heaven (so KJV, NASB, and NIV main text). He stands there to receive the angels who report back to him after patrolling the earth (cf. 1 Kings 22.19–22; Job 1.6–8; 2.1–3; Zech. 1.10). NRSV differs, however, in understanding the text to say that Yahweh was standing, not above the ladder, but 'beside *him*', i.e. Jacob (see also NIV footnote). This is the better interpretation, since the combination of the verb and preposition found here (Hb. *nitstsav 'al*) usually means 'stand beside' in other contexts, and never clearly means 'stand above'. Indeed, thus far in Genesis we have already read that 'Abraham looked up and saw three men standing nearby' (i.e. possibly above, but *certainly* near, Gen. 18.2); and we have encountered Abraham's servant saying, 'See, I am standing beside this spring' (i.e. also possibly above, but *certainly* near, Gen. 24.13). The traditional reading speaks of 'the sovereign ruler of heaven and earth, who is ministered to by angels', and it 'gives the promises that follow a majestic authority and weight'.[18] The alternative reading speaks of intimacy – God comes down the stairway to be with Jacob where he is.

Why has God come? He has come to announce himself to Jacob as 'The LORD, the God of your father Abraham and the God of Isaac'. This title occurs nowhere else in the OT; it is part of the divine address specifically to Jacob. The divine promise that follows most closely parallels the one found in Genesis 13.14–16. This is interesting, because Genesis 13.14–16 is also associated with Bethel (cf. 13.3–4). Yahweh thus reveals himself to be the very same God who spoke to Abraham, and confirms that Jacob stands in the chosen line. The very promise first made to Abraham as he was *settling* in the land is reaffirmed to Jacob as he is *fleeing* from it. Indeed, although he is fleeing, he will one day return – God will be with him and preserve him and bring him back to the land (28.15).

Jacob apparently wakes up from this dream in two stages or, perhaps, wakes up in the night but waits until first light to get up (28.16–18). Certainly he responds in two ways to his dream. First, he experiences a feeling of awe at having been in the presence of God – he recognizes that this place in which he has slept is none other than the 'house of God' (28.16–17). The point of access to God turns out, not to be at the top of a man-made temple, but on the very earth where a person sleeps – in the world that this same God has created. It is here that the living God can

---

[18] Wenham, *Genesis 16–50*, 222.

be encountered. Second, Jacob transforms his pillow into a sacred pillar, dedicating it by pouring oil on it (28.18) – a gesture frequently associated with consecrating cultic items (e.g. Exod. 40.9–13; Lev. 8.10–12) – and he calls the place Bethel ('house of God'). He does this because he intends in the future, when he returns to the land, that the pillar will be God's house so far as he is concerned (Gen. 28.22). He has seen in his dream a stairway standing (Hb. *mutstsav*, 28.12) on the earth; now he sets up a 'pillar' (Hb. *matstsevah*, 28.18) to mark this spot. He has come to the conclusion that this place is the very 'house of God' (Hb. *bet 'elohim*, v. 17), so he calls it Bethel (Hb. *bet-'el*, v. 19).

The words with which Genesis 28 ends are Jacob's last words within the land of Canaan for 20 years. They comprise a vow, which appears at first sight to cement this first personal encounter with God in the story, and to take Jacob off in a new direction. However, upon closer inspection, it is striking just how far short this vow falls of a hearty embrace of the promise to Abraham that has just been repeated in Genesis 28.13–15. In reiterating God's words, Jacob omits all references to land, progeny, expansion and the families of the earth – essential elements in the patriarchal promise. Comparing Genesis 28.15 and 28.20–21 in particular, we discover that 'I [the Lord] will bring you back' becomes 'if I [Jacob] return', and 'this land' becomes 'my father's house'. This suggests, perhaps, that Jacob wants to retain the initiative in this new relationship with God, and is more interested in the family estate than in the Promised Land. This interpretation is consistent with the preoccupation generally evident in Genesis 28.20–21 with personal well-being: note the addition of food and clothes to the list of divine benefits in verse 20, when compared with verse 15. In short, although the Bethel event marks Jacob's awakening to God and to the divine promise, he is apparently still a 'slippery man' in this story, and his vow appears to be as much a bargain as a commitment.

Along with the story of Jacob's struggle with the angel in Genesis 32, the incident at Bethel has proved to be one of the most popular scenes in the Jacob story for artists down through the ages, beginning with the third-century frescoes of the synagogue at Dura Europos. The earliest artwork shows a simple ladder as the mode of angelic transport; no doubt accidentally, Raphael manages to capture something of the *original* intent (a stairway) in his painting in the Loggia in the Vatican (1513–14), in which he portrays Jacob as lying asleep at the foot of a monumental staircase. The Bethel scene has also been captured by Chagall (*Jacob's Ladder*, 1973), and by many other artists, including Harriet Powers (1837–1910), a former slave who could neither read nor write but who made quilts that are now 'celebrated as masterpieces of African American folk art'.[19] Her Smithsonian quilt (*c.*1886), for example, depicts 11 biblical scenes, including Jacob's dream.

Musically, we find the story reflected from the sixteenth century (which produced motets composed on the basis of Jacob's dream) right through to the twentieth, in works like Schoenberg's unfinished oratorio *Jacob's Ladder* (1917–22), Rathaus' *Jacob's Dream* (1941) and Milhaud's *The Dreams of Jacob* (1949).[20] In literature, the question of the meaning of the ladder is much to the fore. In early Christian writings, the main emphasis is inevitably Christological, as in Augustine: 'Christ is the ladder reaching from earth to heaven, and from the carnal to the spiritual.'[21] The Protestant Reformers tend to follow him in this view, as do later hymn writers like Charles Wesley. In the Middle Ages, however, the ladder typically represents spiritual progress in the individual believer, as in the Rule of St Benedict and in the teaching of Bonaventure, who uses the ladder to represent six stages of the ascent of the soul to God. 'The English title of Walter Hilton's vernacular classic *The Ladder of Perfection* draws upon these same associations.'[22] This notion of the ascent of the soul to the heavens noticeably marks the later literary tradition also, appearing there in various guises: for example, in Dryden's *The Hind and the Panther* (1687) and in Wordsworth's 'Humanity' (1829). Shaw's *Back to Methuselah* (1921), on the other hand, envisages movement in the opposite direction, humanity 'crashing down all the steps of this Jacob's ladder' into death.[23]

In the far north (Gen. 29.1—31.55)

Moving on from Bethel, Jacob eventually approaches Haran. The story of his residence there will take up the entirety of segments F–G and G′–F′ of the Jacob story. It begins with an encounter at a well where shepherds are gathered with their flocks, and Jacob is able both to demonstrate to Laban's daughter Rachel his physical strength and to ingratiate himself to the family by ensuring that the flocks are watered in a timely fashion (Gen. 29.10). Ultimately this leads to a contract between Laban and Jacob.

---

[19] C. Crown, 'One Bible, Two Preachers: Patchwork Sermons and Sacred Art in the American South', in Lieb, *Reception History*, 340–54 (340).

[20] Many of the leads on the compositions mentioned in this paragraph were originally taken from Sarna et al., 'Jacob', 22–4. See further, on Schoenberg's *Jacob's Ladder*, M. Stern, *Bible and Music: Influences of the Old Testament on Western Music* (Jersey City, NJ: Ktav, 2011), 57–75.

[21] Augustine, *Reply to Faustus the Manichean*, 12.26 (*NPNF*, Series 1, 4:192).

[22] 'Jacob's Ladder', in Jeffrey, *Biblical Tradition*, 388–90.

[23] 'Jacob's Ladder', in Jeffrey, *Biblical Tradition*, 388–90.

Jacob will work seven years for Laban, and he will then marry Rachel (29.14–30). When the time comes, however, Laban substitutes his older and less attractive daughter Leah for Rachel, a deception that Jacob does not discover until the next morning.[24] When Jacob protests, Laban pleads local custom, and offers to give him Rachel as well, in exchange for another seven years of work. Thus it is that Jacob comes to have two wives.

In the context of the whole Jacob story, of course, this is poetic justice. Jacob had grasped the rights of the firstborn son (i.e. Esau, Hb. *bekor*, Gen. 27.32), and now this grasping ultimately gets him the firstborn daughter as well (i.e. Leah, Hb. *bekirah*, Gen. 29.26). He had eschewed the place of the younger son (*tsa'ir*, Gen. 25.23), and now, at first, he is denied the younger daughter (*tse'irah*, Gen. 29.26). The man who has just deceived him in this way (Laban) is the brother of the woman (Rebekah) who led Jacob to deceive Isaac in the first place. All of this leads us to revisit what Laban says in Genesis 29.14, 'You are my own flesh and blood.' He says this after Jacob tells him all that has happened (29.13), presumably including the reason for his flight from home. It is possible to read Laban's words, then, as a recognition that 'you are certainly a member of *this* family!' There is certainly just such a family likeness reflected in the story. Jacob, the cheat, has just met someone who can out-cheat him – a character noted in his own younger days for his greed (Gen. 24.22, 29–31).

Segment G of the Jacob story (Gen. 29.31—30.24) concerns the expansion of Jacob's family through the birth of 12 children, including his daughter Dinah. The sense of dysfunction in the family in this part of the story is very strong: favouritism, rivalry and hostility ultimately make the narrative a very sad one. Jacob 'loved Rachel more than Leah', we are told in Genesis 29.30, and so it begins. Leah is miserable even in motherhood (Gen. 29.31–32), desperate for her husband's love, which never comes her way (Gen. 29.33–34). Eventually she gives up on Jacob entirely (Gen. 29.35). Meanwhile, Rachel is not a happy woman either, and becomes jealous of her sister's childbearing success (Gen. 30.1). She comes to see her relationship with Leah as a battle, eventually claiming victory in Genesis 30.7–8. This prompts Leah to re-engage (Gen. 30.9), and Rachel to persist (Gen. 30.22–24). The contest eventually kills Rachel, as she gives birth to Benjamin (Gen. 35.18).

---

[24] The subsequent theme in Western literature of the 'exchanged woman', as it appears in such works as Shakespeare's *Measure for Measure* and *All's Well That Ends Well*, is explored by Z. Jagendorf, '"In the Morning, Behold, It Was Leah": Genesis and the Reversal of Sexual Knowledge', in *Biblical Patterns in Modern Literature* (BJS 77; ed. D. H. Hirsch and N. Aschkenasy; Chico, CA: Scholars, 1984), 51–60.

The prior birth of Joseph is especially important for the narrative, since it marks the midpoint of the Jacob story, and comes about because 'God remembered Rachel' (30.22). This is the kind of expression that gets alert Bible-readers thinking, because it reminds them of other stories: God remembering Noah at the height of the flood (Gen. 8.1), or the people of Israel under Egyptian oppression (Exod. 2.24), or Hannah in the midst of her own childlessness (1 Sam. 1.19) – all of them turning points in their respective narratives. Here too, in Genesis 30, we have a turning point. No sooner has Joseph been born than Jacob announces his intention to return to Canaan (Gen. 30.25). Just as the waters of the flood rose to their height and then receded after God 'remembered', so here the tide that has taken Jacob out as far as Haran has now turned, and will eventually take him all the way back home.

Before he returns home, however, the growth in his family must be matched by a growth in his wealth (segment G', Gen. 30.25–43). Here competitiveness and trickery re-emerge with a vengeance. Jacob proposes to take with him all the irregularly coloured sheep and goats from Laban's flocks. Laban agrees, but immediately removes those animals from his flocks, so that Jacob still has nothing. Jacob responds with certain obscure procedures by which Laban's animals produce irregularly coloured offspring. In the end, his large family is equalled by his enormous holdings of servants and livestock (30.43). Jacob steals away from Haran (segment F', Gen. 31.1–55), pursued by Laban, who eventually overtakes him near the land of Canaan itself. Warned by God not to mistreat those he has pursued, Laban nevertheless berates Jacob and accuses him of stealing his household idols, which indeed Rachel has done – but she manages to deceive her father about this by way of a clever ruse (Gen. 31.33–35). Now it is Jacob's turn to berate Laban, accusing his uncle of wrongdoing and referring to his own conscientious service and God's protection (31.36–42). An amicable settlement is reached.

Laban is treated in rabbinic literature even more negatively than Esau: as the personification of greed, and as the master of deceivers who changed Jacob's wages no fewer than 100 times.[25] This part of Jacob's story is also picked up in later artistic representation. Fourth-century mosaics at Santa Maria Maggiore in Rome, for example, show the scene in which Jacob, upon leaving Laban, divides the flocks with him. Later, Ribera shows us Jacob tending Laban's flocks (*Jacob with the Flock of Laban*, 1638), and Lorrain portrays both men standing in an idyllic landscape (*Landscape*

---

[25] *Gen. Rab.* 70.13; 74.11; 75.5.

with Jacob and Laban and Laban's Daughters, 1654). The appropriation of Laban's household idols in Genesis 31 ultimately becomes a very popular subject, appearing in Raphael's frescoes in the Vatican, and in paintings by the Spanish Baroque artist Murillo (1618–82), the Dutch genre painter Steen (1626–79), and Rembrandt's teacher, Lastman (1583–1633).[26]

Jacob wrestles with God (Gen. 32.1–32)

Parting from Laban, Jacob continues his journey towards an encounter with Esau. Expecting his brother to attack him, he breaks his retinue into two camps so that at least half might escape a battle (Gen. 32.7–8). He then prays for help, which is a 'first' in this Jacob story (32.9–12), and he devises a strategy that will hopefully placate his brother (32.13–21). So it is that we come to the famous story of Jacob's encounter with God at the River Jabbok (Gen. 32.22–32). Here, we are told, 'a man wrestled with him till daybreak' (Gen. 32.24). The Hebrew verb is *'avaq*, and in the entire OT it only appears in this passage. There can be no doubt that it has been chosen here precisely because of its value for wordplay, since *wayye'aveq*, 'he wrestled', is a play on the name of the stream 'Yabbok' (*yabboq*) and on the name of Jacob himself, *ya'aqov*. Wenham thus suggests a paraphrase as follows: a man 'Yabboked him' or 'Jacobed him' till daybreak.[27]

A little ancient Near Eastern background to this story will help us to read it well. First of all, river fords were commonly understood in the ancient world as gateways into the lands to which they gave entry. As such, they were believed to be guarded by the gods or their servants, just as a city, temple or palace had guards to protect it. Genesis reflects this background, but appropriates it in its customarily distinctive way. Although it is not clear as the Jabbok narrative opens, either to the reader or to Jacob (who is wrestling in the dark), the 'man' with whom he wrestles is in fact the one, living God (Gen. 32.24). He is the one who 'guards' the Jabbok ford, as he guards all other fords – since there are no other gods. It is with Yahweh, then, that Jacob must deal before he can cross the river.

Second, some ancient peoples believed that there was an advantage to be gained from holding on to gods and refusing to let them go. The closest parallel to our Genesis account in this respect is found in the literature of the ancient Hittites. A Hittite ritual text describes a situation where the

---

[26] Sarna et al., 'Jacob', 22–4.
[27] Wenham, *Genesis 16–50*, 295.

image of the goddess Khebat, consort to the storm god and king of the gods, Teshub, is locked in a particular building, apparently intending to withhold her blessing from her worshippers. The king begs her to return to them, and she answers, 'If I come back, will you in whatever manner – such as with horses and chariots – (strive to) prevail over me?' The king then confirms, 'I shall (strive to) prevail over you.'[28] In the Genesis story, it is of course only the one, true and living God who can give a blessing, and it is to him that Jacob clings in the hope of obtaining one.

As the wrestling match continues, the 'man', it turns out, is not able to overpower Jacob (Gen. 32.25). This would be strange, even if we were to think of him as an ordinary man; Jacob is at this point in the story 97 years old! Indeed, the 'man' is seemingly able to damage Jacob physically precisely when he chooses to do so. This suggests that there must be more to this struggle than simply a physical contest. Another battle is being fought – a spiritual battle, concerning identity and vocation – and Jacob will not yield. The instant injury does seemingly alert him, however, to the identity of his opponent, and he asks for a blessing. He is, of course, a man obsessed with gaining blessings! However, when he deceived Isaac and cheated Esau he was in control of the situation; here he is not. He gets the blessing – unsurprisingly, since in our Genesis story, God is always more than willing to bless – but he is required to give something up in return: his name, which evokes all the cheating in Jacob's life up to this point ('Isn't he rightly named Jacob?' Gen. 27.36). Indeed, he gives it up in a more profound sense than merely revealing it (Gen. 32.27). He is no longer to be called Jacob, but Israel (32.28). If the name Jacob reflects a particular character, now a new character is to be forged. The crossing of the river symbolizes a new beginning, marked by a new name – just as, earlier, Abram and Sarai became Abraham and Sarah.

Jacob, it seems, has lost this fight by the end of it. In what sense, then, has he 'overcome' (32.28)? John Walton is probably close to the mark when he says this:

> His persistence has brought him success in his dealings with people, and now it is responsible for success in his struggle with God – not because God has surrendered but because Jacob has conceded. As always, with God one has to lose in order to win.[29]

So is Walter Brueggemann: 'The *new name* cannot be separated from the *new crippling*, for the crippling is the substance of the name . . . his prevailing

---

[28] J. H. Walton, *Genesis* (NIVAC; Grand Rapids: Zondervan, 2001), 606–7.
[29] Walton, *Genesis*, 606.

is a defeat as well as a victory.'[30] There is a cost involved in having seen God face to face, in this story – as Jacob realizes he has done, when he names the place Peniel, 'face of God' (Gen. 32.30).

Jacob's wrestling match became a popular subject for artists in the Middle Ages, and we find it variously interpreted. God remains central to the struggle in Christian art: for example, in an eighth-century fresco in Santa Maria Antica in Rome; in an eleventh-century fresco in the cathedral of Hagia Sophia in Kiev; and in later paintings by Rembrandt (*Jacob Wrestling with the Angel*, c.1659) and Doré (*Jacob Wrestling with the Angel*, 1865). The French Romantic artist Delacroix (1798–1863), however, in depicting the struggle in a fresco in the church of Saint Sulpice in Paris (1857–61), appears to have intended his painting to represent the artist struggling with Nature in order to wrest away her secrets. Musically, the wrestling match forms the basis for Johann Sebastian Bach's cantata, *Ich lasse dich nicht, du segnest mich denn* (1727), as well as for a motet for double choir written by Johann Christoph Bach (1642–1703), published in English in the nineteenth century as *I Wrestle and Pray*.[31] In early Jewish literature, Jacob's opponent is often the angel Michael; in early Christian literature, either God the Father, or Christ (the latter certainly also being Luther's later choice).[32] Calvin generalizes, seeing all of God's servants as wrestlers, and Christina Rossetti picks up this idea in her poem 'Alas My Lord' (1874).[33] The wrestling match is further alluded to in more recent literature, in sometimes profound and sometimes less profound ways: for example, in Dickinson's 'A Little Over Jordan' (1924), in Hawthorne's *The House of Seven Gables* (1851) and in Laurence's *Stone Angel* (1964).[34]

After Peniel (Gen. 33.1—35.29)

The 'rescue' of Jacob from the God who wants to bless him, and through him the entire cosmos, points forward to the 'rescue' of Jacob from Esau that is next described. Jacob has already asked God for this rescue, in Genesis

---

[30] W. Brueggemann, *Genesis* (Interpretation; Atlanta: John Knox, 1982), 270.

[31] Sarna et al., 'Jacob', 22–4.

[32] M. Luther, *Lectures on Genesis*, 32.29–31.

[33] See further E. Ludlow, 'Christina Rossetti', in *The Blackwell Companion to the Bible in English Literature* (ed. R. Lemon et al.; Oxford: Wiley-Blackwell, 2009), 551–62. Before Rossetti, the same idea appears in C. Wesley's poem 'Wrestling Jacob' (eighteenth century), which became the well-known hymn, 'Come, O Thou Traveller Unknown'. C. Wesley, 'Wrestling Jacob', in *Eighteenth Century Poetry and Prose* (2nd ed.; ed. L. I. Bredvold, A. D. McKillop and L. Whitney; New York: Ronald Press Co., 1956), 509–10.

[34] 'Wrestling Jacob', in Jeffrey, *Biblical Tradition*, 852–4.

32.11, 'Save me (Hb. *natsal*), I pray, from the hand of my brother Esau.' Now he has been spared at Peniel (Hb. *natsal* again, Gen. 32.30), even though he has seen God 'face to face'. What happens next is that he sees Esau face to face (Gen. 33.10), and recognizes that 'to see your face is like seeing the face of God, now that you have received me favourably'. For Esau, it turns out, does not want to fight Jacob at all. There is reconciliation, and the brothers go their separate ways, Esau to Seir and Jacob to Canaan, where he buys a piece of land near the ancient city of Shechem. This is the background to the terrible story in Genesis 34.1–31 about the rape of Dinah, Jacob's daughter, by Shechem, son of the city's chief, Hamor, and the events that unfold in its aftermath. Jacob's own involvement in this story is minimal; his sons are the main actors, deceiving the people of Shechem into thinking that they intend peaceful co-existence, but then attacking the city and killing the entire male population, before taking for themselves the women and the children and all the city's wealth. The story closes with Jacob's weak protest that Simeon and Levi in particular have made him 'odious' in the land.

The violence and duplicity of this story surpass anything ever done by Jacob, Rebekah or Laban, and it is a particularly striking story when compared to its counterpart in segment B (Gen. 26.1–35), where Isaac's treaty with Abimelek is described. The Jacob story as a whole may therefore be seen as presenting two paradigms for relationships between the descendants of Abraham and the other residents of the Promised Land: on the one hand, mutual acceptance and respect, represented by Isaac and Abimelek, and on the other, murder and vindictiveness rooted in 'deceit' (Hb. *mirmah*, Gen. 34.13), represented by Simeon and Levi. The 'deceitfulness' of the father, Jacob (Hb. *mirmah*, Gen. 27.35) is now found in his sons, and it does not augur well either for the family (as we shall see in Genesis 37) or for anyone else.

The Jacob story comes to a close in Genesis 35.1–29 (segment A') with a passage that has generally puzzled interpreters because of its fragmented nature. Yet everything in it plays a role in bringing the story's themes to a conclusion, not least by deliberately echoing aspects of segment A. For example, Genesis 35.1–7 describes Jacob leading a pilgrimage to Bethel, preceded by religious reforms involving his own household and his Shechemite captives. The language of his speech, especially 'Get rid of the foreign gods you have with you' (35.2), makes him a prototype of later reformers who likewise called on God's people to turn away from idolatry (e.g. Joshua and Samuel). The sly opportunist of segment A has ended up as a zealous religious leader; the one who scarcely understood anything about God when he first arrives at Bethel in Genesis 28 returns there in Genesis 35 a very different man.

11

The Joseph story: Genesis 37.2—50.26

The final section of the book of Genesis tells us about 'the descendants of Jacob' (Gen. 37.2—50.26). It is typically referred to as the 'Joseph story', because the spotlight in the narrative mainly falls on this *one* of Jacob's descendants (as it does in the brief retelling of the story in Ps. 105.16–23). As we shall see, however, to a significant extent it is also a 'Judah story'. It is a narrative about how the promise to Abraham continues to work its way out through his early descendants, even though later OT tradition does not name Joseph as one of the first 'patriarchs' of Israel (only Abraham, Isaac and Jacob are typically listed as such. e.g. Exod. 2.24; 3.6, 15; 5.5). Nevertheless, like the patriarchal narratives proper, Genesis 37.2—50.26 demonstrates powerfully how the promise survives in spite of significant obstacles, in this case (again) the threat represented by famine. By the end of Act 12 of our Genesis drama, the promise is still alive, and Joseph himself foresees a time when 'God will surely come to your aid and take you up out of this land to the land he promised on oath to Abraham, Isaac and Jacob' (Gen. 50.24).

Joseph thus occupies a pivotal place in the biblical story, and comes to be reckoned in the interpretative tradition, as we shall see, as one of the greats of biblical history (e.g. in Sir. 49.15; Acts 7.9–16; Heb. 11.22) – an outstanding personality, a model breadwinner, an astute administrator, an example of chastity and even an outstanding scientist.[1] Arguably, indeed, no biblical character has inspired more subsequent literature than Joseph – a character whose story, as late as the middle of the twentieth century, is still capable of filling three of Thomas Mann's four large volumes on *Joseph and His Brothers*.[2] He has also inspired at least one great oratorio: Handel's *Joseph and His Brethren* (1743).

The style of the Joseph narrative is significantly different from what we find in the patriarchal narratives proper, which for the most part are made up of short episodes linked together, albeit clearly intended to be read in

---

[1] L. Jovanović has recently addressed this last theme, noting the popularity of the Joseph story in the Hellenistic period and 'the Hellenistic identification of Joseph with the popular notion of the contemporary scientist'. L. Jovanović, *The Joseph of Genesis as Hellenistic Scientist* (HBM 48; Sheffield: Sheffield Phoenix, 2013), 9.

[2] T. Mann, *Joseph and His Brothers* (trans. J. E. Woods; Toronto: A. A. Knopf, 2005). The original German volumes were written between 1926 and 1943.

concert with each other. The Joseph narrative, by contrast, has a novella-like quality to it, developing a single plot from its originating point to its conclusion. This reality led to early questioning of the nineteenth-century Documentary Hypothesis with respect to Genesis 37—50 – that the sources J and E run all the way through the Joseph story – and to the competing idea that it was originally written as one, well-crafted, continuous narrative.[3] We are dealing here with a story that displays an 'unparalleled continuity of narrative' (Nahum Sarna), such that even the most enthusiastic source critics have often felt compelled to accept the vulnerability of the Hypothesis in this section of Genesis.[4]

Brother against brother (Gen. 37.2–36)

The opening chapter of the story presents Joseph as a brash young man possessing little tact. It is important to begin by saying this, given that some interpreters through the ages have wished to portray him in rather glowing terms. His righteousness, in particular, is frequently stressed in both rabbinic and early Christian tradition.[5] Athanasius and Cyprian, for example, consider him to be 'a model of constancy to God in the face of enemies, temptations and trials'.[6] This reading has a lot to do with the associated reading of Joseph as a 'type' of Christ, most extensively developed in Ambrose's *On Joseph the Patriarch*, where the author notes many correspondences between Joseph and Jesus, including their suffering at the hands of others and their betrayal by Judah/Judas.[7] As late as the nineteenth century, Franz Delitzsch's commentary on Genesis (1852) still represents this stream of the interpretative tradition.[8]

---

[3] See R. N. Whybray, 'The Joseph Story and Pentateuchal Criticism', *VT* 18 (1968): 522–8.

[4] N. M. Sarna, *Understanding Genesis* (New York: Schocken Books, 1966), 160–1. See further G. A. Rendsburg, 'Redactional Structuring in the Joseph Story: Genesis 37–50', in *Mappings of the Biblical Terrain: The Bible as Text* (Bucknell Review; ed. V. L. Tollers and J. Maier; Cranbury, NJ: Associated University Presses, 1990), 215–32. Rendsburg believes that once the reader has engaged in careful literary analysis of Genesis 37—50 'the failings of this traditional approach to source criticism become readily apparent . . . the standard division of the Joseph story into J, E, and P strands should be discarded' (228). This has not, of course, prevented scholars from continuing to work with this model; e.g. B. J. Schwartz, 'How the Compiler of the Pentateuch Worked: The Composition of Genesis 37', in *The Book of Genesis: Composition, Reception, and Interpretation* (VTSup 152; ed. C. A. Evans, J. N. Lohr and D. L. Petersen; Leiden: Brill, 2012), 263–78.

[5] *Gen. Rab.* 84.5. On *Gen. Rab.*'s interpretation of Joseph more generally, see M. Niehoff, *The Figure of Joseph in Post-Biblical Jewish Literature* (New York: Brill, 1992), ch. 5.

[6] A. Jacobs, 'Joseph the Patriarch', in D. L. Jeffrey, *A Dictionary of Biblical Tradition in English Literature* (Grand Rapids: Eerdmans, 1992), 414–16.

[7] Ambrose, *On Joseph*, 3.13–14; 4.19.

[8] F. Delitzsch, *A New Commentary on Genesis* (trans. S. Taylor; 2 vols; Minneapolis: Klock and Klock, 1978), 2:252–3.

Notwithstanding these later readings, we note that Genesis 37 begins by putting on display the same favouritism that has marked the family of Jacob throughout its history, now evident in the special gift given to Joseph by his father, who 'loved Joseph more than any of his other sons' (Gen. 37.3). Jacob prefers Rachel's child to his other children, just as he had once preferred Rachel to Leah (Gen. 30.30). Jacob can be criticized in both rabbinic and Christian tradition for favouring his son in this way, and it was surely the intent of the author that we should indeed think critically of him.[9] The gift in question is a robe of some kind, variously understood by interpreters as possessing 'many colours' (LXX, Vulgate, KJV), or being 'richly ornamented' (NIV), or possessing 'sleeves' (RSV). These are all guesses from the context, although it is the first possibility that has most grasped the imagination through the ages, from Ambrose down to Andrew Lloyd Webber and Tim Rice's popular modern musical, *Joseph and the Amazing Technicolor Dreamcoat* (1968–76).[10] Clearly it is a remarkable robe, but for reasons that are strictly speaking unknown. It certainly elevates Joseph in status, however, and it is somewhat prophetic of his future role in Egypt.

From early Christian times this robe is associated with Christ's assumption of humanity in the Incarnation; as Cyril of Alexandria puts it, 'The multicolored garment is the symbol of the multiform glory with which God the Father clothed the Son made similar to us through his human nature.'[11] This early reading is then developed in later Western literature such as the Old English *Physiologus* (tenth century), three brief poems 'dealing with the mythical traits of a land-animal, a sea-beast, and a bird respectively, and deducing from them certain moral or religious lessons', in which the panther's coat in the first poem is compared to 'Joseph's many-colored coat'.[12] George Herbert's poem 'Joseph's Coat' (1633) later picks up this theme, identifying the Christian believer's sufferings with those of Christ:

> he hath spoil'd the race; and giv'n to anguish
> One of Joyes coats, ticing it with relief
> To linger in me, and together languish.

---

[9] *Shabbath* 10b., in *The Babylonian Talmud* (ed. I. Epstein; 18 vols; London: Soncino, 1935–48), 2:38; Ambrose, *On Joseph*, 2.5–6 (ACCS 2:230), who notes that 'even parental love does harm to the children unless it is practiced with restraint; for it may give the beloved child free rein out of excessive indulgence or, by preference shown to one child, may alienate the others from the spirit of brotherly love.'

[10] Ambrose, *On Joseph*, 2.5–6; M. Stern, *Bible and Music: Influences of the Old Testament on Western Music* (Jersey City, NJ: Ktav, 2011), 77–88.

[11] Cyril of Alexandria, *Glaphyra on Genesis*, 6.4 (ACCS 2:231–2).

[12] A. S. Cook (ed.), *The Old English Physiologus* (Yale Studies in English 63; text and prose translation A. S. Cook; verse translation J. H. Pitman; New Haven: Yale University Press, 1821).

It is because Joseph is their father's favourite that his brothers hate him; no doubt it is also (as *Genesis Rabbah* suggests) because he tells tales about them.[13] What really provokes them, however, is the dreaming that Joseph unwisely reports to them, and then also to his father (Gen. 37.5–10). These dreams of lordship over his family drive the brothers further into hatred, and into jealousy. Jacob does not like the dreams much better than they do, although he is at least open to what the future might bring ('his father kept the matter in mind', 37.11). We remember at this point that Jacob himself dreamed significant dreams earlier in the Genesis story, and possesses some prior experience of the younger gaining the upper hand on the older.

The consequences of the hatred and the jealousy are described at length in Genesis 37.12–36. Joseph, charged by *Genesis Rabbah* not only with wearing a special robe but with 'painting his eyes, curling his hair, and walking with a mincing step', is sent by Jacob to find his brothers and to submit a report about them.[14] He finds them near Dothan, an area regularly traversed by traders travelling from Gilead to the coast and thence to Egypt (which land shortly becomes important in this story). The brothers make a plan to kill Joseph, throw his body into a water cistern, and tell Jacob that he was eaten by a wild animal (37.19). Reuben and Judah, however, develop different strategies to save Joseph's life (37.21–27). Reuben's strategy is to have him flung into the pit *instead of* killing him, and certainly this is what initially happens. Judah's words in Genesis 37.26 suggest, however, that the brothers as a group still intend to kill Joseph later – that this is only a temporary respite. Indeed, they have already 'stripped him of his robe' (37.23), suggesting that they intend to go through with their plan (cf. 37.31–33).

Judah's proposal, instead, is that they *sell* Joseph to some traders who have just shown up. These traders, when they are first seen, are referred to as Ishmaelites (37.25, 27), used in the general sense of 'Bedouin' (Judg. 8.24; cf. Gen. 16.12, where Ishmael is represented as a wild ass of a man, possibly indicating his itinerant lifestyle). It becomes clear when they 'come by', however (Gen. 37.28), that they are 'Midianites' in particular (37.28). It is to these traders, then, that Joseph is sold for the price of 20 shekels, which was the standard price for slaves in the first half of the second millennium BC.[15]

---

[13] Gen. 37.2; *Gen. Rab.* 87.3, which holds that Joseph was appropriately punished for wrongly charging his brothers with serious offences.

[14] *Gen. Rab.* 84.7.

[15] K. A. Kitchen, 'Genesis 12–50 in the Near Eastern World', in *He Swore an Oath: Biblical Themes from Genesis 12–50* (ed. R. S. Hess, G. J. Wenham and P. E. Satterthwaite; 2nd ed.; Grand Rapids, 1994), 67–92 (79). Inflation took the price up to 30 shekels in the second half of the second millennium, and up to 50 shekels in the first millennium.

Reuben, who is apparently away when the traders ride through, is aghast when he discovers that Joseph has gone (37.29), but apparently falls in with the original plan to deceive Jacob about his loss after all. The robe given to the dreamer is now evidence, it seems, of the death of the dreamer and his dream, as it is dipped in goat's blood and presented to Jacob, who deduces that 'Some ferocious animal has devoured him' (Gen. 37.33). It is this very moment that is later alluded to in literature such as Melville's *Billy Budd* (1924), when the false accuser Claggart 'surveys Captain Vere's face with "a look that might have been that of the spokesman of the envious children of Jacob deceptively imposing on the troubled patriarch the blood-dyed coat of young Joseph"'.[16]

Joseph in trouble (Gen. 39.1—40.23)

Passing over for a moment the story about Judah in Genesis 38, we next encounter Joseph as a slave in Egypt, in the household of a powerful man named Potiphar. This Potiphar is said in Genesis 39.1 to be 'captain of the guard', in Hebrew literally 'captain of the butchers' or 'cooks' – a title that has no doubt outstripped its original meaning, or may even be intended in a grimly humorous way to refer to what royal officers often had to do (i.e. 'butcher' people). Potiphar is also explicitly called an 'Egyptian', because high officials of Pharaoh were not necessarily Egyptians, and could indeed be Semites. The fact that the family is Egyptian and Joseph is not (he is a 'Hebrew', 39.14) becomes an important aspect of the plot in Genesis 39, since it enables Potiphar's wife to play 'the race card' to get herself out of the trouble that soon arises from her lust for this handsome slave (Gen. 39.13–17; cf. 39.6–7) – a physical attractiveness that is often commented upon in the early interpretative literature. The non-canonical romance *Joseph and Asenath*, for example, written around the second century BC, has Asenath asking about Joseph, 'who among men will ever father such beauty, and what mother will ever bear such a light?'[17] Josephus later correlates this same extraordinary beauty with Joseph's moral excellence.[18] *Joseph and Asenath* goes on to tell us that Joseph's looks became quite a problem for him in Egypt,

[16] Jacobs, 'Joseph', 415.

[17] *Joseph and Asenath*, 6.4 (ed. J. Charlesworth; trans. C. Burchard; vol. 2 of *The Old Testament Pseudepigrapha*; Garden City, NY: Doubleday, 1985), 177–247 (209).

[18] Josephus, *Ant.*, 2.9–10. On Josephus' interpretation of Joseph more generally, see Niehoff, *Figure of Joseph*, ch. 4, who claims that Josephus' attempts to present Joseph as a moral paragon, extricating him from all ambiguity, reflects 'his apologetics about his relationship with other leaders of the early Jewish Revolt. He thus highlights the innocence of his behaviour among his family' (144).

for all the wives and daughters of the lords and satraps of all the land of Egypt used to solicit him to lie with him. And many of the wives and daughters of the Egyptians suffered much, after seeing Joseph, because he was so handsome; and they would send emissaries to him with gold and silver and valuable gifts.[19]

It is this same beauty that entices Potiphar's wife in the *biblical* story, and her subsequent actions in it have given her a long literary afterlife.[20] Jewish tradition from *Jubilees* and the *Testament of the Twelve Patriarchs* onwards alludes to them in the course of exhortations to sexual morality, Potiphar's wife becoming the prototype of the immoral pagan woman who must be avoided by the virtuous man.[21] Joseph is that virtuous man, ultimately becoming master of Egypt (according to 1 Macc. 2.53) precisely because he keeps God's commandments under great duress. Pre-modern Christian readers referred to Joseph in much the same way. Ambrose, for example, tells us that

> although he was good-looking . . . he did not direct the charm of his countenance toward another's wrongdoing but kept it to win grace for himself . . . That is the true beauty that does not seduce the eyes of others or wound their fragile hearts but gains the approval of all.[22]

John Chrysostom declares that 'it was remarkable and unprecedented that this remarkable young man had his clothes torn from him by this frenzied and intemperate woman without yielding to her'.[23] The story could also be read typologically in the pre-modern period; for example, in Bede's *Commentary on the Pentateuch* (eighth century) Joseph is Christ, who did not commit adultery by accepting the teaching of the scribes and the Pharisees, but left his life in their hands (as Joseph left his garment in the hand of the temptress).[24] As we move towards the modern period, we find Bunyan in the seventeenth century picking up the theme of chastity in *The Pilgrim's Progress* (1678–84), in which Potiphar's wife appears as

---

[19] *Joseph and Asenath*, 7.3–4, in Charlesworth, *Old Testament Pseudepigrapha*, 210.

[20] She would perhaps have become even more prominent than she did had not Tertullian in his *To the Nations* (AD 197) cut her and her husband out of the story and made the queen of Egypt Joseph's would-be seducer. It is this tradition that sometimes vies with the biblical story for later attention, appearing e.g. in the Middle English *Iacob and Ioseph* (thirteenth century).

[21] *Gen. Rab.* 87.4–5 describes this immorality as involving not only lust, but also murderous intent with respect to her husband. On early Jewish interpretation generally, including *Jubilees*, see Niehoff, *Figure of Joseph*, ch. 2.

[22] Ambrose, *On Joseph*, 5.22 (ACCS 2:251).

[23] Chrysostom, *Homilies on Genesis*, 62.19 (ACCS 2:252–3).

[24] Bede, *Commentary on the Pentateuch*, referred to in M. Siebald, 'Potiphar's Wife', in Jeffrey, *Biblical Tradition*, 625–6 (625).

the character Wanton, who attempts to seduce Christian's companion Faithful. At the same time Christiana's son, also named Joseph, is exhorted to be like his biblical counterpart, 'Chaste, and one that flees from Temptation'.[25] Fielding returns to the theme in *Joseph Andrews* (1742), where the hero must resist the charms of Lady Booby.[26] Scott also alludes to Potiphar's wife in *Woodstock* (1826), and Trollope in *The Last Chronicle of Barset* (1867).

Where is God in all of this? The biblical Joseph story to this point has been curiously silent, at an explicit level, as to where God is to be found in the narrative. In Genesis 39, however, it becomes explicitly clear that God is 'with Joseph' in Egypt, and that he is providentially in control of the whole affair. We note, indeed, the *concentration* of occurrences of the divine name 'Yahweh' in Genesis 39 (vv. 2, 3, 5, 21, 23 – a total of eight occurrences), setting Joseph's current predicament within the framework of such divine providence.[27] Yahweh, our narrator tells us, was 'with Joseph' and 'gave him success in everything he did' (Gen. 39.2–3). This in turn resulted in blessing on Potiphar's household – the blessing that all Gentile peoples are ultimately promised through Abraham (Gen. 39.5; cf. Gen. 12.1–3) – since 'Potiphar put him in charge of his household, and he entrusted to his care everything he owned' (Gen. 39.4). The biblical text does not elaborate on the details of Joseph's employment, which has not, of course, prevented later interpreters from speculating about it. The 1962 Italian film *Giuseppe venduto dai fratelli*, for example, shows Potiphar and Joseph hunting for lions and elephants in the jungles of Egypt. The plausibility of this scenario is much reduced, unfortunately (as Stephen Lang points out), by the fact that Egypt possesses no jungles![28]

An important key to the development of the entire storyline in Genesis 39—41, although translators often obscure its importance by the translation choices they make, is the presence throughout of the Hebrew word *yad*, 'hand'. God causes everything to prosper in Joseph's 'hand' (Gen. 39.3, 'gave him success'), so that everything belonging to Potiphar is given *into* Joseph's 'hand' (Gen. 39.4, 6, 8, variously translated). Yet this 'everything'

[25] J. Bunyan, *The Pilgrim's Progress* (ed. R. Pooley; London: Penguin Classics, 2008), 250.

[26] See further H. Fisch, 'Biblical "Imitation" in *Joseph Andrews*', in *Biblical Patterns in Modern Literature* (BJS 77; ed. D. H. Hirsch and N. Aschkenasy; Chico, CA: Scholars, 1984), 31–42.

[27] This divine name only otherwise appears in the Joseph story on one occasion (in Gen. 49.18).

[28] J. S. Lang, *The Bible on the Big Screen: A Guide from Silent Films to Today's Movies* (Grand Rapids: Baker Books, 2007), 157. For a better Joseph film, see the made-for-television *Joseph*, which won an Emmy Award for best miniseries in 1995.

does not mean, from Joseph's point of view, that he is permitted to sleep with Potiphar's wife. Displaying the 'fear of the LORD' that the book of Proverbs commends (e.g. Prov. 1.7), he refuses to succumb to the charms of the adulteress (Prov. 6.23–26; 7.10–20), and he flees her embrace. Unfortunately, he leaves his garment in the temptress's 'hand' (Gen. 39.12). The first garment that was stripped from Joseph in Genesis 37 was used as evidence of his death; the second is used as evidence of his lust (Gen. 39.17–18). Lying in the woman's hand, the garment represents the extent to which *Joseph* is also 'in her hand' (i.e. in her power).

Yet because God has more power than anyone else in this story, Joseph eventually prospers once again. In prison for his alleged offence, the other prisoners are given into his 'hand' (39.22, my translation); that is, he is put in charge of them. He exercises this newfound power so well that the warden gives no thought to anything 'in his hand' (39.23, my translation), since he can depend completely upon Joseph's competence. Ultimately, Joseph's prospering is seen in his elevation to the highest administrative position in Egypt (Gen. 41.41–45). At this point in the story, Pharaoh himself takes a ring from his own hand and transfers it to the 'hand' of Joseph (41.42). He also dresses Joseph in garments of fine linen; at last, and after many trials, Joseph once again possesses the clothing of nobility.

The path to this happy outcome is in this story, however, a thorny one. The victim for a second time of a conspiracy involving the deceptive use of garments, Joseph endures a second spell in a 'pit' (i.e. a prison, Gen. 40.15 – the same word used in Gen. 37.22–24 of the cistern).[29] It is in this prison that he comes into contact with two high-ranking Egyptian officials, the royal cupbearer and the royal baker, both of whom have displeased Pharaoh and find themselves now under lock and key. For a moment it appears that there is hope for Joseph. Both men dream dreams that they do not understand, and complain that there is 'no one to interpret them' (Gen. 40.8) – there is no professional interpreter available to them in prison. Joseph believes, however, that interpretation belongs to God, and not to mortal beings.[30] He explains the dreams, predicting the release of both dreamers (Gen. 40.12–19). Both men will in fact have their heads 'lifted up' by Pharaoh, which might be taken to imply a restoration of honour (cf. 2 Kings 25.27). In reality, however, only the cupbearer later

---

[29] Joseph might well have expected death for his alleged assault on his master's wife. For whatever reason, he is not in fact put to death; perhaps we are supposed to think that Potiphar does not really believe his wife's story.

[30] This same theme is prominent in the later story of Daniel, where a Hebrew 'non-professional' is also the crucial character in interpreting a foreigner's dreams (Dan. 1—4).

finds himself in Pharaoh's good graces (his head is lifted up); the baker is executed (*his* head is lifted *off*, Gen. 40.20–21). One survivor is enough reason, perhaps, for Joseph to continue to hope; but unfortunately, the cupbearer's 'kindness' (40.14, Hb. *chesed*) fails to match the kindness of God (39.21, same word), and he forgets to speak to Pharaoh about Joseph's plight.[31] Joseph's future at this point looks uncertain. Will God remember what the cupbearer has forgotten?

Joseph, Pharaoh and the famine (Gen. 41.1—47.27)

Two years pass (Gen. 41.1), and now it is the turn of Pharaoh to dream a dream. It involves the River Nile, the source of Egypt's fertility, but now producing devouring need (seven gaunt cows) as well as abundance (seven sleek cows, Gen. 41.1–7). The dream is troubling, not least because of the importance of cows to the Egyptian economy. It leads Pharaoh to consult his dream-interpreters ('all the magicians and wise men of Egypt', 41.8) – a professional class found throughout the ancient world, where dreams were routinely regarded as a means of divine communication. As in the book of Daniel, none of these professionals can help; only Joseph, in touch with the living God, can do so, and happily the cupbearer now remembers him (41.9–13). The wisdom that Joseph thus brings to his task is often celebrated in the interpretative tradition.[32]

The dream is repeated to Joseph by Pharaoh, and Joseph is able to tell him that the numbers represent years (41.26–27). There will be seven years of plenty and seven years of famine in the region – a plausible prediction within the context of an Egyptian history, where seven-year cycles are not unknown.[33] He also takes the chance to create a job opportunity for himself, as the official in charge of preparations for the famine (41.33–36). A 'discerning and wise man' is required; and it so happens that Joseph has just displayed discernment and wisdom in interpreting Pharaoh's dream, thereby revealing that he has in him 'the spirit of God' (41.38). This idea,

---

[31] It is this reality that is reflected in *Gen. Rab.* 89.7, 'Accursed are the wicked, for they never do a kindness thoroughly.' See also *Tanh.* (Buber), Gen. 10.1, in *Midrash Tanhuma* (trans. J. T. Townsend; 3 vols; Hoboken, NJ: Ktav, 1989), 1:251–2.

[32] E.g. in *Wis.* 10.13–14, where Joseph's wisdom is regarded as preserving him in his Egyptian trials. On how to interpret this wisdom 'that is central to the Joseph Story', in relation to the broader category 'Wisdom Literature', see M. V. Fox, 'Joseph and Wisdom', in Evans, Lohr and Petersen, *Genesis*, 231–62 (quote from 261).

[33] A text from the twenty-eighth century BC, concerning the reign of the Third Dynasty king Djoser, already 'reports on a severe famine attributed to the failure of the Nile to rise for seven years'. N. M. Sarna et al., 'Joseph', *EncJud* 11:406–13 (407).

that special insight and aptitude arise from the indwelling of the Spirit, is also found in a passage like Exodus 31.3, which refers to Bezalel, the craftsman working on the Tabernacle furniture, although when the idea is expressed by a non-Israelite king, it is perhaps better to render the Hebrew *'elohim* in the plural (as in Dan. 4.9, and the NIV footnote): 'Can we find anyone like this man, one in whom is the spirit of the gods?' Joseph possesses divine power of a general kind; that is what qualifies him for the task.

His elevation to his new position is marked by Pharaoh giving him his 'signet ring' (Gen. 41.42), typically used in sealing documents; the vizier of Egypt was known as the 'sealbearer of the king of lower Egypt' as far back as the third millennium BC. He is also given new clothing – effectively replacing his original robe (Gen. 37), and bringing this part of the story full circle; and a new name, indicating his new status and vocation (as elsewhere in Genesis). It was common in Egypt (as it was later in Babylon – note that Daniel is renamed Belteshazzar in Dan. 1.7) for slaves to be given indigenous names by their masters. The meaning of *Joseph's* new name has attracted some attention in the interpretative tradition: 'revealer of secrets' (Josephus, Syriac, Targum, working with the Hb.); 'saviour of the world' (Vulgate, deriving from the Coptic); 'the god speaks and he lives' (working with the Egyptian language itself). It is impossible to be certain what is intended.

The final indication of Joseph's change in status, beyond the ring, the clothing and the name, is his marriage into an important priestly family (Gen. 41.45). The high priest of On – Heliopolis, just to the north-east of modern Cairo – was an important figure in ancient Egypt, since Heliopolis was an ancient seat of worship of the sun god Ra. From the Egyptian point of view, then, this marriage is no doubt a good thing. From the biblical point of view, however, it raises questions. Abraham approaches the matter of getting a wife for Isaac from among his own people very seriously (Gen. 24.1–4), and Solomon's later marriage to an Egyptian princess (and many other foreign wives) leads him into apostasy (1 Kings 3, 11). Read in this biblical context, it is not surprising that Joseph's marriage to an Egyptian woman so closely associated with an Egyptian god was problematic to many early Jewish readers. The author of *Joseph and Asenath* in fact rewrites the Joseph story in order to avoid the problem. In this text, our hero first *rejects* Asenath as a suitable wife, and later marries her only after she repents of her idolatry and converts to true religion. Later midrashim solve the problem in a different way: they portray Asenath as Dinah's daughter (and thus Joseph's niece), later adopted by Potiphar/Potiphera. According to this view, Asenath did not convert from paganism, but was one of God's own people from the beginning.[34]

So it is that in Genesis 41 the foreign slave, Joseph, rises to a position of great power in one of the dominant kingdoms of the ancient world – just like other Semitic people before him:

> The possibility of the rise of a foreigner to high station in the Egyptian court and administration is well substantiated. A Semite named Yan☐amu was Egyptian commissioner for Canaan and Syria in the time of Akhenaten (14th century B.C.E.), and a certain Ben-Ozen from northern Canaan rose to the position of marshal at the court of Merneptah (13th century B.C.E.). This same king's brother married the daughter of a Syrian sea captain named Ben-Anath, and in the following century one of the judges in the trial of the murderers of Ramses III bore the Semitic name Mahar-Baal.[35]

For many early Jewish readers, Joseph's elevation in status was a reward for his virtuous life.[36] We have already seen reason in our reading of Genesis 37, however, to qualify such claims of virtue, and the unfolding story of the famine in Genesis 41—47 gives us further reason to do so. The stated plan is to store food during the years of abundance that can later function as a food reserve, 'so that the country may not be ruined by the famine' (Gen. 41.36). However, it is important to note that this food is later sold (not given) to the Egyptian populace by Joseph (41.56). He *gives* food to his family when he resettles *them* in Egypt (see further below), but he *sells* it to the Egyptians, and to the Canaanites (47.11–14). When the Egyptians' money is gone, he then gives them food in exchange for their livestock, and when their livestock are gone, he gives them food in exchange for their land, making them Pharaoh's serfs (47.15–21). The people are grateful enough to be alive (47.25), but these are oppressive arrangements – precisely the kind of oppression from which God will shortly rescue the Israelites in the exodus.

Called out as a descendant of Abraham to be a blessing to the Gentile nations, Joseph fails to bless *any* Gentile in *this* part of the story, with the exception of the Egyptian god-king himself. We are bound to notice this precisely because the Abrahamic promise is explicitly brought to mind in relation to the grain accumulation by the wording of Genesis 41.49. 'Joseph stored up huge quantities of grain, like the sand of the sea', we are told, and Genesis 22.17 echoes in our ears: 'I will surely bless you and make your descendants as numerous as the stars in the sky and as the sand on

---

[34] *Pirqe R. El.* 38; *Tg. Ps.-J.* to Gen. 41.45 and 46.20.
[35] Sarna et al., 'Joseph', 408.
[36] E.g. *Gen. Rab.* 90.3.

the seashore.' Joseph might have used the grain to bless the Egyptians. Instead, he creates a reality that 'corresponds to the situation of state slavery that prevailed in Egypt following the expulsion of the Hyksos [non-Egyptians who immigrated into the Nile Delta during the eighteenth century BC] toward the end of the 16th century B.C.E.'[37]

Joseph and his brothers (Gen. 42.1—45.15)

It is in the context of this famine that Jacob sends all of his sons except Benjamin down to Egypt to get food, since 'All the countries came to Egypt to buy grain from Joseph, because the famine was severe in all the world' (Gen. 41.57). Again we see Jacob's favouritism at play: he does not send Benjamin along because he is 'afraid that harm might come to him' (Gen. 42.4). The key to what happens next lies in the fact that Joseph recognizes his brothers, but they do not recognize him (42.6–8), and they bow down to this great Egyptian lord just as Joseph's dream had predicted (Gen. 37.7). This allows Joseph to toy with his brothers, accusing them of being spies.[38] Their defence is that they are all 'sons of one man'; that is, they do not comprise a diverse group sent by a foreign power (42.10–17). Crucial to this defence is the claim that there is another son still at home (42.13). Joseph demands that they prove this claim to be true – that they bring this other brother to Egypt as well.

Joseph's motives at this point in the story are opaque. Is he simply out for revenge? Does he want to teach his brothers a lesson – to make them understand what it feels like to be treated as victims? Or does he want the whole family down in Egypt with him, and he cannot trust the ten guilty brothers to tell his father that he is alive? Whatever is the case, he has his brothers thrown into prison to give them time to think it over (42.17). Why do they need this time? Perhaps we are to imagine that no one wants to be the one to go and tell Jacob that he has lost the other brothers in Egypt, and that he is now taking Benjamin to Egypt as well. Or perhaps

---

[37] Sarna et al., 'Joseph', 409. This interpretation of this part of the Joseph story is very different from the one found in many early Christian sources (e.g. Ambrose, *On Joseph*, 7.41), which makes him unambiguously a hero who takes 'special care of the orphans, widows and every needy person in Egypt' (Ephrem, *Commentary on Genesis* 36.1, in ACCS 2:272). This same heroic interpretation turns up in the later reading tradition too: see G. Reedy, 'John Dryden', in *The Blackwell Companion to the Bible in English Literature* (ed. R. Lemon et al.; Oxford: Wiley-Blackwell, 2009), 297–309 (302).

[38] Rabbinic tradition was evidently disturbed by some aspects of Joseph's treatment of his brothers at their reunion, and felt compelled to defend him (e.g. *Gen. Rab.* 91.7). Some modern readers have been less inclined to let him off the hook (e.g. R. W. L. Moberly, *The Theology of the Book of Genesis* (OTT; Cambridge: Cambridge University Press, 2009), 237–41).

the brothers are reluctant to allow *one* of their number to leave Egypt out of fear that he will simply abandon them there. We need to remember the character of Joseph's brothers as we ponder this text (Gen. 37).

The spell in prison, however, does not lead the brothers to sort themselves out, so Joseph comes up with a different plan (Gen. 42.18–24): one of the brothers will stay, and the rest will go back to Canaan. Joseph himself does the choosing of the hostage (42.24), selecting Simeon, the second oldest brother. Perhaps he is chosen because Joseph has just learned of Reuben's actions back when Joseph was handed over to the Ishmaelites (42.22), and he realizes that Reuben, at least, may try to do the right thing after he leaves Egypt (as, indeed, he does, 42.37). Simeon remains, and the other brothers are sent off back to Canaan with grain and provisions, as well as the silver they had originally brought to spend on the grain. The silver, when it is discovered, unsettles them – what does it mean (42.35)? Joseph has perhaps intended generosity, but the brothers clearly fear that they will be accused of dishonesty (43.12). In the short term, however, there is nothing to worry about, because it turns out that Jacob does not agree to Joseph's plan (42.36–38); he would rather sacrifice Simeon than risk Benjamin. So Simeon is abandoned to his fate, and the family settles down to eat – until the food runs out (43.2).

At this point Jacob is forced to return the ten brothers to Egypt, along with Benjamin (43.3–15), sending with them so many choice trade items that the Egyptians (he hopes) will not think of harming him (43.11). Ironically, some of these (spices, balm and myrrh) are the very items that accompanied Joseph down to Egypt in the first place (37.25). Joseph as Egyptian lord is now to receive the gifts from the brothers that originally accompanied him on his way down to Egypt as a slave. The plan works, however; the siblings are received warmly by Joseph (Gen. 43.16), and the problem of the silver is resolved (Gen. 43.19–23).

On the return journey, however, a serious problem arises – engineered by Joseph himself, for reasons that are initially unclear. A silver cup is put into Benjamin's sack, used by Joseph for 'divination' (Gen. 44.5) – the science of discovering the unknown by supernatural means, here presumably by pouring oil on water. Before they know that it is in their baggage, the brothers respond to the accusation of theft with a rash vow (44.9): they offer the death of the culprit, and the enslavement of all the other brothers, if the cup is found among them. The steward modifies their words in line with what he knows Joseph's wishes to be: the culprit will be the slave, and the remainder will be blameless (44.10, 17). It now appears that Joseph's plan is to keep Benjamin with him. Understandably, this causes consternation among the other brothers, and draws out of Judah an impassioned speech, in which he pleads on behalf of his father, and offers himself, self-sacrificially, in Benjamin's place (44.18–34). With this speech, it is clear that Joseph has managed in the course of Genesis 42—44 to bring all of his brothers to a degree of understanding of their guilt and of Joseph's own experience at their hands, and that he has to some extent changed them. Where there was once only jealousy, hatred and a willingness to sacrifice a favoured younger brother (a son of Rachel) in order to be rid of an annoyance, now we see a desire to sacrifice *on behalf of* a favoured younger brother (and another son of Rachel) in order to save him from slavery, and to save their father from further grief.

This brings us to the climactic scene in Genesis 42—45, as Joseph breaks down and reveals himself to his brothers, delivering in the midst of his tears a theological reflection on the entire preceding story:

> And now, do not be distressed and do not be angry with yourselves for selling me here, because it was to save lives that God sent me ahead of you. For two years now there has been famine in the land, and for the next five years there will not be ploughing and reaping. But God sent me ahead of you to preserve for you a remnant on earth and to save your lives by a great deliverance. So then, it was not you who sent me here, but God.
>
> (Gen. 45.5–8)

Certainly the brothers did sell Joseph into slavery, but in the midst of all their wicked actions, God was also at work, turning evil to good, and moving his redemptive plan along. This is of course what God has been doing throughout the whole book of Genesis, so it is no surprise to find that we return to this theme as the book comes to an end in Genesis 50. Here the brothers become concerned that Joseph has only shown them kindness out of love for their father. Now Jacob is dead, and they wonder if Joseph will pay them back for all the wrongs they have done to him; but Joseph reassures them (Gen. 50.15, 19–21).

Jacob's family in Egypt (Gen. 45.16—50.26)

In the aftermath of Joseph's self-revelation to his brothers, the whole family is welcomed to live in Egypt – the kind of migration from Canaan that was not unusual in these ancient times. Nahum Sarna refers to an Egyptian papyrus that describes a parallel case, 'bearing a report of an official on the eastern frontier to his superior relating how he had granted Edomite shepherd tribes permission to make use of the Nile Delta pasturage "to keep them and their flocks alive."[39] Those who settled in Egypt with Jacob are carefully listed in the remainder of Genesis 46 – traditionally totalling 70 in number (46.27), corresponding to the later number of the Israelite clans (cf. Exod. 24.1, 9; Num. 11.6). Joseph had already promised his family that they would live in the region of Goshen (Gen. 45.10; cf. Exod. 8.22; 9.26), traditionally in the north of the country, on the eastern edge of the Delta near the desert. Pharaoh had been less specific (Gen. 45.18). The stratagem devised in Genesis 46.31–34, and acted out in Genesis 47.12, is designed to get Pharaoh to agree to what Joseph wants. If the family states that they are herders, they will be allowed to settle in Goshen, which is also referred to as 'the district of Rameses' (47.11). This is no doubt related to Joseph's plan to look after his own family well in the midst of the ongoing famine, in an area apparently far away from the royal court where he can act without others knowing too much about it, while at the same time progressively bringing the Egyptians and Canaanites into servitude to Pharaoh (Gen. 47.13–26).

One important event that is described as occurring during the family's stay in Egypt is the death of Jacob (Gen. 49.29–33), which is preceded by the blessing of Joseph's sons Manasseh and Ephraim (Gen. 48.1–22), and then of all of Jacob's sons (Gen. 49.1–28). Jacob apparently cannot see very well as he comes to bless Manasseh and Ephraim, and he wants to confirm their identity before blessing them (48.8–10). It is tempting to think that he remembers the trick he played on his own father Isaac in Genesis 27 – that the author of Genesis is drawing our attention to the parallel. Although Jacob is not in fact deceived in the same way as Isaac in this story, the outcome is interestingly the same in both cases: the 'wrong' child gets the better blessing (Gen. 48.13–20). The natural order of things has been turned upside down (again). The new, *de facto* order is reflected in Israel's later history: Ephraim was so much the more dominant tribe in later times that this name could be used for the whole of the northern kingdom (e.g. Isa. 7.1–9, 17; Hos. 5.12–14).

The order in which Jacob's sons are then blessed in Genesis 49 is partly genealogical and partly geographical. Geographically, we may distinguish a southern group (Reuben, Simeon, Levi and Judah), a northern group (the following six tribes) and a central group (Joseph and Benjamin). Genealogically, the six Leah tribes come first, corresponding to the order of birth in Genesis 29—30, save that Zebulun and Issachar change places (Gen. 49.3–15). The tribe of Reuben's relative insignificance in later history is explained in terms of his illicit sexual encounter with his father's

---

[39] Sarna et al., 'Joseph', 409.

concubine Bilhah (Gen. 35.22; 49.3–4). Simeon and Levi's ultimate fates as dispersed tribes (assimilated into Judah, on the one hand, and becoming a priestly tribe without land, on the other) is connected with their role as protagonists in the story of the rape of Dinah (Gen. 34; 49.5–7). To Judah we shall return in the next section of this chapter. There is probably an implicit reproach for Zebulun in Genesis 49.13 – a rebuke regarding aspirations for sea commerce. As for Issachar, overly enamoured with the fertility of the Promised Land, his fate is to be assimilated by the Canaanites and forced into servitude (Gen. 49.14–15).

After the Leah tribes come the 'concubine tribes' (descended from Zilpah and Bilhah), but not in the correct order: the two Zilpah tribes, Gad and Asher, come between the two Bilhah tribes, Dan and Naphtali (Gen. 49.16–21). Dan will punch above his weight, we are told, just as a snake can bring down a mighty horse (Gen. 49.16–17). Gad will likewise repulse invaders (Gen. 49.19).[40] Asher will be rich in agriculture, and Naphtali will be noted for its beauty (Gen. 49.20–21). Finally, the two Rachel tribes are blessed (Gen. 49.22–27). Joseph's blessings are extensive, as we might expect; they include the fact that he will be a 'prince among his brothers' (49.26; cf. Gen. 37). Benjamin will be a warlike tribe (cf. Judg. 19–20).

It has often been argued that this section of Genesis is entirely unrelated to its narrative context. Walter Brueggemann states, for example, that

> the poem of chapter 49 seems to have no important connection with its
> context . . . [it] ignores the dramatic movement of the narrative and presents
> an unrelated statement on the power relations of the tribes (sons?) at a later
> time when Judah-David is preeminent.[41]

This begs an important question, however, about the role of Judah in the preceding narrative, to which we now turn.

The importance of Judah (Gen. 38.1–30; 43.3–10; 44.18–34; 49.8–12)

If we ask who is the most prominent of the brothers in the narrative of Genesis 37—50, apart from Joseph, the answer is surely 'Judah'. He is, after all, the only brother who has an entire, separate narrative devoted to him in the Joseph story – the narrative in Genesis 38. Modern readers of Genesis have often had difficulty in reading this chapter as part of the Joseph story

---

[40] There is extended wordplay here. Four of the six words in Gen. 49.19 are derived from Hb. *gadad*, 'cut, penetrate, gather in bands'.
[41] W. Brueggemann, *Genesis* (Interpretation; Atlanta: John Knox, 1982), 365–6.

at all, and they are not alone in this. Already in the closing centuries BC, the author of *Jubilees*, in his retelling of the Genesis story, delays the account of Judah and Tamar until he has reported the Joseph story up to the point of Joseph's gathering of food in preparation for the famine (Genesis 41). He clearly thinks that this is a more 'natural' position for the account. Yet we have already noted in our Chapters 2 and 3 above (when discussing Robert Alter's *Art of Biblical Narrative*) the good reasons we have for thinking that the author of Genesis 37—50 inserted Genesis 38 into the Joseph account quite deliberately. The question is, why did he do this? What did he mean by it? And the most plausible answer to this question is that he meant to introduce Judah as the other major player in the drama, and to tell us some facts about him that are of importance for understanding the story that follows.

By way of getting to the heart of the matter, let us first consider where the 'Judah story' ends up in Genesis 37—50. It ends up in Jacob's oracle about Judah in Genesis 49.8–12. Here it is striking that, after the highly ambivalent through to negative comments made about the first three sons mentioned (Gen. 49.3–7), Judah is praised unreservedly, and indeed celebrated as the premier tribe: 'your father's sons will bow down to you' (49.8). It may have been Joseph who dreamed the dream about his brothers bowing down to him, but it is Judah who ultimately inherits the dream. In Genesis 49.10, indeed, he is pictured as seated with his royal sceptre held upright in front of him, ruling 'until he comes to whom it belongs', at which point the nations will give their obedience to that person. The precise meaning of the Hebrew behind this phrase has long been a matter of discussion, although early Jewish interpretation already regarded it as a messianic passage, with the final word *shiloh* sometimes being regarded as the place to which the Messiah comes (Shiloh), and sometimes as a personal name of the Messiah.[42] A descendent of King David of the tribe of Judah appears to be in view.

As one might expect, then, the NT picks up the language of Genesis 49.9–10 in relation to Jesus Christ. Revelation 5.5 deploys the 'lion of Judah' language in this way, and Hebrews 7.14 stresses more generally the Judaean lineage of Jesus. This handsome king who is to come, we are told, will be associated with abundance (Gen. 49.11–12): vines will be so common that they are used for tethering donkeys (which we would expect to feed on them and destroy them), and wine will be so abundant that it will be used

---

[42] E.g. *Sanh.* 98b, in Epstein, *Babylonian Talmud*, 12:667: 'What is his [the Messiah's] name? – The School of R. Shila said: His name is Shiloh, for it is written, *until Shiloh come.*'

for washing clothes. This paradise imagery is very similar, of course, to that found in other passages about the Judaean king who is still to come in the future (e.g. Ezek. 34.23–31; Amos 9.13–15; Ps. 72). Judah's line is crucially important to the biblical story; ultimately it inherits the dream of lordship not only over the others brothers, but over the whole earth.

Now let us return to Genesis 38 – a story precisely about Judah's line! As the chapter opens, we find that it is a line in danger of extinction. It is saved only by the actions of a resourceful Canaanite woman, Tamar, which ensure that two dead sons (Er and Onan, 38.7, 10) are replaced by two twin boys, Perez and Zerah (38.29–30). Tamar is not the only non-Israelite woman who gets involved in the business of maintaining the Judah/David line in the biblical story, of course. Later, the genealogy of Jesus in Matthew 1.1–17 scandalously draws attention to this fact, most notably in reminding us that Solomon's mother was the 'wife of Uriah', a Hittite soldier in the army of King David. Genesis 38, then, for a moment moves attention away from Joseph and on to Judah, while Joseph is 'out of sight' on his journey down to Egypt. In doing so, it anticipates the way in which the whole book of Genesis in the end (and much more permanently) will move the spotlight away from Joseph and on to Judah. This in turn anticipates the way in which the descendants of Judah will turn out in the entire biblical story to be much more important than the descendants of Joseph.

Who is this Judah who is such an important ancestor of the Israelites? Like his father Jacob, he is not very promising material for use in God's redemptive plans for the world, as his story opens. We meet him in Genesis 37 as someone who is happy to rid himself of a troublesome brother when the opportunity presents itself, and more than able to treat him as a piece of merchandise. Genesis 38 then develops Judah's character further, and in a wholly negative way. He marries a Canaanite woman, we are told (38.2), which is not a good thing to do (see above regarding Joseph's marriage). Moreover, he 'sees, takes and lies with' this woman (the Hb. verbs of this verse). This language does not possess positive associations for the Genesis reader: almost the same set of verbs is used in Genesis 34 concerning the rape of Dinah.

Throughout the story of Genesis 38, Judah is presented as someone who does not care much about other people, even in his own family (which is certainly consistent with Genesis 37). He does not mourn for any of the three deaths in the chapter (contrast Jacob's refusal to be consoled in mourning in Gen. 37.35), and upon the death of his wife, in fact, he goes straight off to a prostitute (38.12–16). This, too, does not reflect well upon him. Later, he condemns the widow Tamar for having illicit sex, even

---

The Joseph story

though he as a widower has just done the same (Gen. 38.24). He is a man with double standards. And all the way through the story, there is no hint that Judah has any kind of relationship with God. When his two sons die, he does not even *blame* God, but instead holds Tamar responsible, as a kind of bad-luck charm (Gen. 38.11). Like Jacob at the beginning of his story, Judah is in need of redemption.

It is interesting, then, to notice the way in which Judah in particular (and not just the brothers in general) becomes a different person in the course of the narrative that follows. Judah does not care much about other people in Genesis 37—38: later he comes to care at least about Benjamin and his father (43.8–10; 44.18–34), and he behaves self-sacrificially in respect of both of them. In Genesis 37—38, Judah does not yet have any sense of the universe as a moral place where divine providence is working out its ways in pursuit of the good and in judgement on the bad. By the time we reach Genesis 44, Judah is apparently in a very different space: 'God has uncovered your servants' guilt' (44.16). Like Jacob in his story, Judah is on a journey in Genesis 37—50 – which turns out to be as much a 'Judah story' as a 'Joseph story'. Indeed, it turns out to be more importantly the former than the latter.[43]

All of this explains why those scholars are mistaken who argue that Genesis 49 is unrelated to its narrative context. It is in fact intrinsically bound up with its narrative context, reorienting Joseph's dream so as to make it clear that it is the admittedly reprobate Judah, and not the victimized Joseph, who will ultimately 'rule' over the family, and indeed the nations.

On receiving Joseph

We return in the end to Joseph, however, because our comments on the reception of the Joseph story scattered throughout our treatment above have not yet done justice to its impact throughout history. Joseph not only appears in most of the medieval European mystery cycles, but also in a medieval Turkish poem on the theme of Joseph and Potiphar's wife, based on the Qur'an (which knows them as Yusuf and Zulaikha). Towards the end of the fifteenth century, the Persian poet Jāmī writes his own romance, *Yūsufo Zuleikhā*, based on the same ideas; and the Jews of medieval Spain also create a tradition of their own, found in definitive form in Abraham de Toledo's, *Coplas de Yosef ha-□addik* (1732). By 1560, Bathja Bayer tells

---

[43] For a recent reading that presses to some extent in the same direction, see R. J. Clifford, 'Genesis 37–50: Joseph Story or Jacob Story?', in Evans, Lohr and Petersen, *Genesis*, 213–29.

us, there were in Christian Europe '12 English plays on the subject [of the Joseph story] and dozens more in French, Spanish, Italian, Dutch, and German'.[44] Interest in this story then continues through the subsequent centuries, producing such English-language works as Charles Wells' *Joseph and His Brethren* (1824) and John Eyre's *The Story of Joseph and His Brethren* (1854). These are followed in the twentieth century by works such as Louis Napoleon Parker's play, *Joseph and His Brethren* (1913).

Although Joseph does not appear in early Christian art, he does later become an important figure, especially as we reach the Renaissance. His story is represented, for example, on Ghiberti's bronze doors for the Baptistery in Florence, in the frescoes in the Campo Santo in Pisa by Gozzoli, and in Raphael's frescoes in the Vatican. Rembrandt paints him relating his dreams to his family (1638), Murillo portrays him being dumped into the pit (*c.*1670), and both Ferrari (1640) and Madox Brown (1866) show Jacob receiving his bloodstained coat. The attempted seduction of Joseph by Potiphar's wife is a very popular story among sixteenth- and seventeenth-century artists, among them Tintoretto (1555) and (yet again) Rembrandt (1634). Cuyp paints Joseph interpreting the dreams as he sits in prison (*c.*1630), Pontormo portrays his brothers begging for help (1515), and (who else?) Rembrandt shows Joseph standing over the dying Jacob while the latter lays his hands on Manasseh and Ephraim (1656). Musically, Joseph and his brothers really begin to dominate the cultural stage in Europe in the eighteenth century. Leaving aside the Handel oratorio already mentioned earlier in the chapter, we may mention here only Neri's *Giuseppe che interpreta i sogni* (1726) and Metastasio's *Giuseppe riconosciuto* (1733). Nineteenth- and twentieth-century compositions include Méhul's opera *Joseph* (1807), Richard Strauss's ballet *Die Josephslegende* (1914), Werner Josten's *Joseph and His Brethren* (also a ballet, 1936), and Sternberg's suite for string orchestra, entitled *The Story of Joseph* (1942).

And so it turns out in this way, as we bring this final chapter and also our small contribution to understanding the book of Genesis as a whole to a close. It may well be, in Genesis itself, that it is Judah who inherits Joseph's dream, and becomes the one to whom all the other brothers bow down (Gen. 37.5–7). In the reception history of Genesis 37—50, however, there is no question about who it is that comes out on top – the one to whom the cultural and intellectual 'sun and moon and eleven stars' defer (Gen. 37.9). It is clearly Joseph, whether with his technicolor dreamcoat or not.

---

[44] Sarna et al., 'Joseph', 411. I depend heavily on Bayer throughout this final section of the chapter.

Bibliography

Abelard. 'Dedication Letter to the Commentary on the Six Days of Creation.' Pages 52–63 in *Letters of Peter Abelard: Beyond the Personal*. Translated by Jan M. Ziolkowski. Washington, DC: Catholic University of America Press, 2008.

Allert, Craig D. *A High View of Scripture? The Authority of the Bible and the Formation of the New Testament Canon*. ER; Grand Rapids: Baker, 2007.

Almond, Philip C. *Adam and Eve in Seventeenth-Century Thought*. Cambridge: Cambridge University Press, 1999.

Alter, Robert. *The Art of Biblical Narrative*. London: Allen & Unwin, 1981.

Ambrose. *Cain and Abel*, in *Saint Ambrose: Hexameron, Paradise, and Cain and Abel*. FC 42. Translated by John J. Savage. Washington, DC: Catholic University of America Press, 1961.

Ambrose. *Hexameron, Paradise, and Cain and Abel*. FC 42. Translated by John J. Savage. Washington, DC: Catholic University of American Press, 1961.

Ambrose. *On the Death of His Brother Satyrus*. Pages 161–259 in *Funeral Orations by Saint Gregory Nazianzen and Saint Ambrose*. Edited by Roy J. Deferrari. Translated by John J. Sullivan and Martin R. P. McGuire. FC 22. Washington, DC: Catholic University Press of America, 1968.

Aquinas, Thomas. *Summa Theologiae*. Translated by Fathers of the English Dominican Province. 5 vols. Westminster, MD: Christian Classics, 1948.

Armstrong, Karen. *A Short History of Myth*. Toronto: Knopf, 2005.

Augustine, *City of God*. FC 14. Translated by Gerald G. Walsh and Grace Monahan. Washington, DC: Catholic University of America Press, 1952.

Augustine. *Letter 196*. Pages 342–4 in *Saint Augustine: Letters, Volume IV*. FC 30. Translated by Wilfrid Parsons. Washington, DC: The Catholic University Press, 1955.

Augustine. *On the Trinity: Books 8–15*. CTHP. Edited by Gareth B. Matthews. Translated by Steven McKenna. Cambridge: Cambridge University Press, 2002.

Bacon, Roger. *The Opus Majus of Roger Bacon*. Translated by Robert B. Burke. Philadelphia: University of Pennsylvania Press, 1928.

Barbour, Ian. G. *Western Man and Environmental Ethics*. Reading: Addison-Wesley, 1973.

Barthes, Roland. *Image, Music, Text: Essays Selected and Translated by Stephen Heath*. London: Fontana, 1977.

Barton, John. *Reading the Old Testament: Method in Biblical Study*. Philadelphia: Westminster, 1984.

Basil of Caesarea. *On the Holy Spirit*. Translated by David Anderson. Crestwood, NY: St Vladimir's Seminary Press, 1980.

Becking, Bob, and Susanne Hennecke, eds. *Out of Paradise: Eve and Adam and Their Interpreters*. HBM 30. Sheffield: Sheffield Phoenix, 2011.

Begg, Christopher T. 'Genesis in Josephus.' Pages 303–29 in Evans, Lohr and Petersen, *The Book of Genesis*.

Beichner, Paul E. 'The Allegorical Interpretation of Medieval Literature.' *PMLA* 82 (1967): 33–8.

Ben-Sasson, Haim Hillel, Raphael Jospe and Dov Schwartz. 'Maimonidean Controversy.' Pages 371–81 in vol. 13 of Berenbaum and Skolnik, *Encyclopaedia Judaica*.

Berenbaum, Michael, and Fred Skolnik. *Encyclopaedia Judaica*. 2nd ed. Detroit: Macmillan Reference USA, 2007.

Boitani, Piero. 'Dante and the Bible: A Sketch.' Pages 281–93 in Lieb et al., *Reception History*.

Bowker, John. *The Targums and Rabbinic Literature: An Introduction to Jewish Interpretations of Literature*. Cambridge: Cambridge University Press, 1969.

Brooke, John H. 'Samuel Wilberforce, Thomas Huxley, and Genesis.' Pages 397–412 in Lieb et al., *Reception History*.

Browning, Robert. *The Complete Poetical Works of Robert Browning*. Edited by Augustine Birrell. New York: The Macmillan Company, 1915.

Bunyan, John. *The Pilgrim's Progress*. Edited by R. Pooley. London: Penguin Classics, 2008.

Byron, Lord. *Dramatic Works of Lord Byron*. New York: A. V. Blake, 1840.

Calvin, John. *Commentaries on the First Book of Moses Called Genesis*. GSC. Edited and translated by John King. London: Calvin Translation Society, 1847.

Calvin, John. *Commentary on the Harmony of the Evangelists, Matthew, Mark, and Luke*. Translated by W. Pringle. 3 vols. Edinburgh; Calvin Translation Society, 1846.

Carr, David M. 'Genesis.' Pages 316–34 in vol. 1 of *The Oxford Encyclopedia of the Books of the Bible*. Edited by Michael D. Coogan. 2 vols. New York: Oxford University Press, 2011.

Charles, R. H., ed. *The Apocrypha and Pseudepigrapha of the Old Testament*. 2 vols. Oxford: Clarendon, 1976.

Charlesworth, James, ed. *The Old Testament Pseudepigrapha*. Vol. 1. Garden City, NY: Doubleday, 1985.

Childs, Brevard S. *Biblical Theology of the Old and New Testaments: Theological Reflection on the Christian Bible*. Minneapolis: Fortress, 1992.

Childs, Brevard S. *Introduction to the Old Testament as Scripture*. Philadelphia: Fortress, 1979.

Clement of Alexandria. *Christ the Educator*. FC 23. Translated by Simon P. Wood. Washington, DC: Catholic University of America Press, 1954.

Clines, David J. A. *The Theme of the Pentateuch*. JSOTSup 10. 2nd ed. Sheffield: Sheffield Academic Press, 1997.

Coleridge, Samuel Taylor. *The Works of Samuel Taylor Coleridge*. WPL. Hertfordshire: Wordsworth Editions, 1994.

Crown, Carol. 'One Bible, Two Preachers: Patchwork Sermons and Sacred Art in the American South.' Pages 340–54 in Lieb et al., *Reception History*.

Crowther, Kathleen M. *Adam and Eve in the Protestant Reformation*. Cambridge: Cambridge University Press, 2010.

Danielson, Dennis. 'Eve.' Pages 251–4 in Jeffrey, *Biblical Tradition*.

Danielson, Dennis, ed. *Paradise Lost by John Milton: Parallel Prose Edition*. Vancouver: Regent College Publishing, 2008.

Dante Alighieri. *Inferno*. Vol. 1 of *The Divine Comedy*. Translated by Henry Wadsworth Longfellow. Boston: Ticknor and Fields, 1867.

Delitzsch, Franz. *A New Commentary on Genesis*. Translated by Sophia Taylor. Minneapolis: Klock and Klock, 1978.

Dershowitz, Alan M. *The Genesis of Justice: Ten Stories of Biblical Injustice That Led to the Ten Commandments and Modern Law*. New York: Warner Books, 2000.

Dorsey, David A. *The Literary Structure of the Old Testament: A Commentary on Genesis–Malachi*. Grand Rapids: Baker, 1999.

Dressler, H., ed. *Homilies on Genesis and Exodus*. FC 71. Translated by R. E. Heine. Washington, DC: Catholic University of America Press, 1947.

Driver, Samuel R. *The Book of Genesis*. 2nd ed. London: Methuen, 1904.

Dryden, John. *The Hind and the Panther*. London: Jacob Tonson, 1687.

Dryden, John. *Poems and Prose of John Dryden: A Selection by Douglas Grant*. Saint-Lambert, Montreal: The Penguin Poets, 1955.

Dunderberg, Ismo. 'Gnostic Interpretations of Genesis.' Pages 383–96 in Lieb et al., *Reception History*.

Edwards, Katie B. *Admen and Eve: The Bible in Contemporary Advertising*. BMW 48. Sheffield: Sheffield Phoenix, 2012.

Epstein, Isidore. *The Babylonian Talmud*. 18 vols. London: Soncino, 1935–48.

Evans, Craig A., Joel N. Lohr and David L. Petersen, eds. *The Book of Genesis: Composition, Reception, and Interpretation*. VTSup 152. Leiden: Brill, 2012.

Exum, J. Cheryl. '"Mother in Israel": A Familiar Figure Reconsidered.' Pages 73–85 in Russell, *Feminist Interpretation*.

Finan, T., and V. Twomey, eds. *Scriptural Interpretation in the Fathers: Letter and Spirit*. Dublin: Four Courts, 1995.

Flood, John. *Representations of Eve in Antiquity and the English Middle Ages*. RSMRC 9. New York: Routledge, 2011.

Foster, Michael B. 'The Christian Doctrine of Creation and the Rise of Modern Natural Science.' *Mind* 43 (1934): 446–68.

Foucault, Michel. *The Archaeology of Knowledge*. Translated by Alan M. Sheridan-Smith. London: Tavistock, 1972.

Fulk, Robert D., ed. and trans. *The Beowulf Manuscript: Complete Texts and the Fight at Finnsburg*. DOML 3. Cambridge, MA: Harvard University Press, 2010.

García Márquez, Gabriel. *One Hundred Years of Solitude*. New York: Harper and Row, 1970.

Gilmour, Michael J. 'Bob Dylan's Bible.' Pages 355–68 in Lieb et al., *Reception History*.

Goethe, Johann Wolfang von. *Faust: Part One and Part Two*. LOLA. Translated by Charles E. Passage. Indianapolis: Bobbs-Merrill, 1965.

Golding, William. *Lord of the Flies*. London: Penguin, 1999.

Golding, William. *The Spire*. London: Faber and Faber, 1974.

Gordis, Robert. 'The Knowledge of Good and Evil in the Old Testament and the Qumran Scrolls.' *JBL* 76 (1957): 123–38.

Gottwald, Norman K. *The Tribes of Yahweh: A Sociology of the Religion of Liberated Israel, 1250–1050* BCE. Maryknoll, NY; Orbis, 1979.

Gunkel, Hermann. *Genesis*. Translation of the 1910 ed. by Mark E. Biddle; Macon: Mercer University, 1997.

Habel, Norman. 'Playing God or Playing Earth? An Ecological Reading of Genesis 1:26–28.' Pages 33–41 in *'And God Saw That It Was Good': Essays on Creation and God in Honor of Terence E. Fretheim*. Word and World Supplement Series 5. Edited by Frederick J. Gaiser and Mark A. Throntviet. St Paul, MN: Luther Seminary, 2006.

Halkin, Abraham Solomon, et al. 'Saadiah (ben Joseph) Gaon.' Pages 606–14 in vol. 17 of Berenbaum and Skolnik, *Encyclopaedia Judaica*.

Halton, Thomas P. *Saint Augustine on Genesis*. FC 84. Translated by Roland J. Teske. Washington, DC; Catholic University of America Press, 1947.

Halton, Thomas P. *Saint John Chrysostom: Homilies on Genesis 1–17*. FC 74. Translated by R. C. Hill. Washington, DC: Catholic University of America Press, 1985.

Hamilton, Victor P. *Genesis 1–17*. Grand Rapids: Eerdmans, 1990.

Hassine, Juliette. 'The Creation of Eve in the Writings of Marcel Proust.' Pages 95–104 in Hirsch and Aschkenasy, *Biblical Patterns*.

Hauser, Alan J., and Duane F. Watson, eds. *A History of Biblical Interpretation*. 2 vols. Grand Rapids: Eerdmans, 2003 and 2009.

Haynes, Stephen R. *Noah's Curse: The Biblical Justification of American Slavery*. Oxford: Oxford University Press, 2002.

Hayward, C. T. Robert. 'Genesis and Its Reception in Jubilees.' Pages 375–404 in Evans, Lohr and Petersen, *The Book of Genesis*.

Hayward, C. T. Robert. *Saint Jerome's Hebrew Questions on Genesis*. OECS. Oxford: Clarendon, 1995.

Hendel, Ronald, ed. *Reading Genesis: Ten Methods*. Cambridge: Cambridge University Press, 2010.

Herr, Moshe David. 'Midrash.' Pages 182–5 in Berenbaum and Skolnik, *Encyclopaedia Judaica*.

Hess, Richard S., Gordon J. Wenham and Philip E. Satterthwaite, eds. *He Swore an Oath: Biblical Themes from Genesis 12–50*. 2nd ed. Grand Rapids: Michigan, 1994.

Hill, Christopher. *The World Turned Upside Down: Radical Ideas during the English Revolution*. New York: Viking, 1972.

Hirsch, David H. and Nehama Aschkenasy, eds. *Biblical Patterns in Modern Literature.* BJS 77. Chico, CA: Scholars, 1984.

Hirst, Wolf Z. 'The Reassertion of Biblical Views in European Romanticism.' Pages 73–83 in Hirsch and Aschkenasy, *Biblical Patterns.*

Jacobs, Louis, and David Derovan. 'Hermeneutics.' Pages 25–9 in vol. 9 of Berenbaum and Skolnik, *Encyclopaedia Judaica.*

Jacobs, Louis, and Avi Sagi. 'Akedah.' Pages 555–60 in vol. 1 of Berenbaum and Skolnik, *Encyclopaedia Judaica.*

Jaspers, Karl. 'The Axial Age of Human History: A Base for the Unity of Mankind.' *Commentary* 6 (1948): 430–5.

Jeffrey, David L. *A Dictionary of Biblical Tradition in English Literature.* Grand Rapids: Eerdmans, 1992.

Jennings, Theodore W. 'Theological Anthropology and the Human Genome Project.' Pages 93–111 in Thistlethwaite, *Adam, Eve, and the Genome.*

Joyce, James. *Ulysses.* Harmondsworth, Middlesex: Penguin, 1954.

Korte, Anne-Marie. 'Paradise Lost, Growth Gained: Eve's Story Revisited – Genesis 2–4 in a Feminist Theological Perspective.' Pages 140–56 in Becking and Hennecke, *Out of Paradise.*

Kramer, Samuel N. 'Cuneiform Studies and History of Literature.' *APSP* 107 (1963): 485–527.

Lang, J. Stephen. *The Bible on the Big Screen: A Guide from Silent Films to Today's Movies.* Grand Rapids: Baker Books, 2007.

Lemon, Rebecca, Emma Mason, Jonathan Roberts and Christopher Rowland, eds. *The Blackwell Companion to the Bible in English Literature.* Oxford: Wiley-Blackwell, 2009.

Lerner, Anne L. *Eternally Eve: Images of Eve in the Hebrew Bible, Midrash, and Modern Jewish Poetry.* HBISJW. Waltham, MA: Brandeis University Press, 2007.

Levison, John R. *Portraits of Adam in Early Judaism: From Sirach to 2 Baruch.* JSPSup 1. Sheffield: University of Sheffield Press, 1988.

Lévi-Strauss, Claude. *The Savage Mind.* Chicago: Chicago University Press, 1967.

Lewis, Clive S. *The Lion, The Witch, and the Wardrobe.* New York: HarperCollins, 2000.

Lewis, Clive S. *That Hideous Strength.* Rev. ed. London: Pan Books, 1955.

Lieb, Michael. 'John Milton.' Pages 269–85 in Lemon et al., *Bible in English Literature.*

Lieb, Michael, Emma Mason, Jonathan Roberts and Christopher Rowland, eds. *The Oxford Handbook of Reception History of the Bible.* Oxford: Oxford University Press, 2011.

Lin, Yan. 'Re-reading Genesis 1–3 in the Light of Ancient Chinese Creation Myths.' Pages 65–80 in *Genesis.* TatC 1. Edited by Athalya Brenner, Archie C. C. Lee and Gale A. Yee. Minneapolis: Fortress, 2010.

Luther, Martin. *Lectures on Genesis: Chapters 26–30.* Edited by Jaroslav Pelikan and W. A. Henson. Translated by G. V. Schick and P. D. Pahl. 55 vols. St Louis: Concordia Publishing House, 1968.

MacDonald, George. *Lilith: A Duplex*. London: Chatto & Windus, 1895. Reprint Whitehorn, CA: Johannesen, 1994.

MacLeish, Archibald. *Nobodaddy*. Cambridge, MA: Dunster House, 1926.

Maimonides. *The Guide for the Perplexed*. Translated by M. Friedlander. 2nd ed. New York: Dover, 1904.

Marsman, Hennie J. *Women in Ugarit and Israel: Their Social and Religious Position in the Context of the Ancient Near East*. Leiden: Brill, 2003.

Mellinkoff, Ruth. *The Mark of Cain*. Berkeley: University of California Press, 1981.

Melville, Hermann. *Moby Dick*. Edited by Hershel Parker and Harrison Hayford. 2nd ed. New York: W. W. Norton and Company, 2002.

Metz, Walter C. 'Adapting Genesis.' *Literature Film Quarterly* 35 (2007): 229–36.

Mews, Constant J., and Micha J. Perry. 'Peter Abelard, Heloise and Jewish Biblical Exegesis in the Twelfth Century.' *JEH* 62 (2011): 3–19.

Milburn, Robert. *Early Christian Art and Architecture*. Los Angeles: University of California Press, 1988.

Moberly, R. Walter L. *The Old Testament of the Old Testament: Patriarchal Narratives and Mosaic Yahwism*. OBT; Minneapolis: Fortress, 1992.

Moberly, R. Walter L. *The Theology of the Book of Genesis*. OTT. Cambridge: Cambridge University Press, 2009.

Morello-Frosch, Marta. '*One Hundred Years of Solitude* by Gabriel Marquez, or Genesis Re-Written.' Pages 155–63 in Hirsch and Aschkenasy, *Biblical Patterns*.

Muilenburg, James. 'Form Criticism and Beyond.' *JBL* 88 (1969): 1–18.

O'Fearghail, Fearghus. 'Philo and the Fathers: The Letter and the Spirit.' Pages 39–59 in Finan and Twomey, *Scriptural Interpretation in the Fathers*.

O'Kane, Martin. *Painting the Text: The Artist as Biblical Interpreter*. BMW 8; Sheffield: Sheffield Phoenix, 2007.

Pagels, Elaine. *Adam, Eve, and the Serpent: Sex and Politics in Early Christianity*. New York: Vintage Books, 1989.

Pardes, Ilana. 'Modern Literature.' Pages 176–95 in Hendel, *Reading Genesis: Ten Methods*.

Parker, Robert. 'Greek Religion.' Pages 248–68 in *Greece and the Hellenistic World*. Vol. 1 of *The Oxford History of the Classical World*. Edited by John Boardman, Jasper Griffin and Oswyn Murray. Oxford: Oxford University Press, 1988.

Phillips, John A. *Eve: The History of an Idea*. San Francisco: Harper and Row, 1984.

Potter, Jane. 'The Great War Poets.' Pages 681–95 in Lemon et al., *Bible in English Literature*.

Provan, Iain W. *Convenient Myths: The Axial Age, Dark Green Religion, and the World That Never Was*. Waco: Baylor University Press, 2013.

Provan, Iain W. 'The Land Is Mine and You Are Only Tenants: Earth-Keeping and People-Keeping in the Old Testament.' Pages 33–50 in *Many Heavens, One Earth: Readings on Religion and the Environment*. Edited by Clifford C. Cain. Lanham, MD: Lexington, 2012.

Provan, Iain W. 'Pain in Childbirth? Further Thoughts on "An Attractive Fragment" (1 Chronicles 4:9–10).' Pages 285–96 in *Let Us Go Up to Zion: Essays in Honour of H. G. M. Williamson on the Occasion of His Sixty-Fifth Birthday.* Edited by Iain Provan and Mark Boda. Leiden: Brill, 2012.

Provan, Iain W. *Seriously Dangerous Religion: What the Old Testament Really Says and Why It Matters.* Waco: Baylor University Press, 2014.

Provan, Iain W., V. Philips Long and Tremper Longman III. *A Biblical History of Israel.* 2nd ed. Louisville: Westminster John Knox, 2015.

Quasten, Johannes, and Walter J. Burghardt, eds. *St. Augustine, The Literal Meaning of Genesis.* ACW 41 and 42. Translated by John H. Taylor. 2 vols. New York: Newman, 1982.

Quasten, Johannes, and Joseph C. Plumpe, eds. *The Didache. The Epistle of Barnabas. The Epistles and The Martyrdom of St. Polycarp. The Fragments of Papias. The Epistle to Diognetus.* ACW 6. Translated by James A. Kleist. New York: Newman, 1948.

Quasten, Johannes, and Joseph C. Plumpe, eds. *The Epistles of St. Clement of Rome and St. Ignatius of Antioch.* ACW 1. Translated by James A. Kleist. Mahwah, NJ: Paulist, 1946.

Rendsburg, Gary A. *The Redaction of Genesis.* Winona Lake: Eisenbrauns, 1986.

Roberts, Jonathan, and Christopher Rowland. 'William Blake.' Pages 373–82 in Lemon et al., *Bible in English Literature.*

Rose, Seraphim. *Genesis, Creation and Early Man: The Orthodox Christian Vision.* Platina, CA: Saint Herman of Alaska Brotherhood, 2000.

Ruether, Rosemary R. 'The Western Tradition and Violence against Women.' Pages 31–41 in *Christianity, Patriarchy, and Abuse.* Edited by Joanne C. Brown and Carole R. Bohn. New York: Pilgrim, 1989.

Russell, Letty M., ed., *Feminist Interpretation of the Bible.* Philadelphia: Westminster, 1985.

Sanders, Theresa. *Approaching Eden: Adam and Eve in Popular Culture.* Lanham, MD: Rowman and Littlefield, 2009.

Sarna, Nahum M., et al. 'Abraham.' Pages 280–8 in vol. 1 of Berenbaum and Skolnik, *Encyclopaedia Judaica.*

Sarna, Nahum M., et al. 'Cain.' Pages 340–2 in vol. 4 of Berenbaum and Skolnik, *Encyclopaedia Judaica.*

Sarna, Nahum M., et al. 'Jacob.' Pages 17–25 in vol. 11 of Berenbaum and Skolnik, *Encyclopaedia Judaica.*

Sarna, Nahum M., et al. 'Joseph.' Pages 406–13 in vol. 11 of Berenbaum and Skolnik, *Encyclopaedia Judaica.*

Schearing. Linda S., and Valarie H. Ziegler. *Enticed by Eden: How Western Culture Uses, Confuses, (and Sometimes Abuses) Adam and Eve.* Waco: Baylor University Press, 2013.

Schmid, Konrad, and Christoph Riedweg, eds. *Beyond Eden: The Biblical Story of Paradise (Genesis 2–3) and Its Reception History.* FAT 2/34. Tübingen: Mohr Siebeck, 2008.

Scholem, Gershom. 'Lilith.' Pages 17–20 in vol. 13 of Berenbaum and Skolnik, *Encyclopaedia Judaica*.

Seidman, Naomi. 'Translation.' Pages 157–75 in Hendel, *Reading Genesis: Ten Methods*.

Seitz, Christopher R. *The Character of Christian Scripture: The Significance of a Two-Testament Bible*. STI; Grand Rapids: Baker Academic, 2011.

Shaked, Shaul. 'Zoroastrian Origins: Indian and Iranian Connections.' Pages 183–200 in *Axial Civilizations and World History*. JSRC 4. Edited by Johann P. Arnason, Shmuel N. Eisenstadt and Björn Wittrock. Leiden: Brill, 2005.

Shakespeare, William. *Hamlet*. Edited by Harold Jenkins. London: Thomson Learning, 2003.

Shaw, George B. *Back to Methuselah*. London: Constable, 1921.

Sicher, Efraim. 'Hard Times in Paradise: An Example of an Inverted Biblical Pattern.' Pages 165–72 in Hirsch and Aschkenasy, *Biblical Patterns*.

Siff, Myra J., Harold Louis Ginsberg and Israel Moses Ta-Shma. 'Babel, Tower of.' Pages 19–21 in vol. 3 of Berenbaum and Skolnik, *Encyclopaedia Judaica*.

Simon, Maurice. *Midrash Rabbah*. Translated by Harry Freedman. 3rd ed. 10 vols. London: Soncino, 1983.

Speiser, Ephraim A. *Genesis*. AB; Garden City, NY: Doubleday, 1964.

Steinbeck, John. *East of Eden*. New York: Viking, 1952. Reprint London: Penguin, 2000.

Sterling, Gregory E. 'When the Beginning Is the End: The Place of Genesis in the Commentaries of Philo.' Pages 427–46 in Evans, Lohr and Petersen, *The Book of Genesis*.

Stern, Max. *Bible and Music: Influences of the Old Testament on Western Music*. Jersey City, NJ: Ktav, 2011.

Strong, John T. 'Shattering the Image of God: A Response to Theodore Hiebert's Interpretation of the Story of the Tower of Babel.' *JBL* 127 (2008): 625–34.

Studer, Paul, ed. *Le Mystère d'Adam: An Anglo-Norman Drama of the Twelfth Century*. Manchester: Manchester University Press, 1928.

Tertullian. *Disciplinary, Moral and Ascetical Works*. FC 10. Translated by Rudolph Arbesmann, Emily J. Daly and Edwin A. Quain. Washington, DC: Catholic University of America Press, 1959.

Thistlethwaite, Susan B. 'A Gene for Violence? Genetic Determinism and Sin.' Pages 145–60 in Thistlethwaite, *Adam, Eve, and the Genome*.

Thistlethwaite, Susan B., ed. *Adam, Eve, and the Genome*. TSC. Minneapolis: Fortress, 2003.

Trible, Phyllis. *God and the Rhetoric of Sexuality*. OBT 2. Philadelphia: Fortress, 1978.

Trible, Phyllis and Letty M. Russell, eds. *Hagar, Sarah, and Their Children: Jewish, Christian, and Muslim Perspectives*. Louisville: Westminster John Knox, 2006.

Twain, Mark. *Adventures of Huckleberry Finn*. NCE 34. Edited by Sculley Bradley et al. New York: W. W. Norton and Company, 1962.

Visotzky, Burton L. 'Genesis in Rabbinic Interpretation.' Pages 579–606 in Evans, Lohr and Petersen, *The Book of Genesis*.

Von Rad, Gerhard. 'The Form Critical Problem of the Hexateuch.' Pages 1–58 in *From Genesis to Chronicles: Explorations in Old Testament Theology*. Edited by K. C. Hanson. Translated by E. W. Trueman Dicken. FCBS. Minneapolis: Fortress, 2005.

Waltke, Bruce K. *Genesis: A Commentary*. Grand Rapids: Zondervan, 2001.

Walton, John H. *Ancient Near Eastern Thought and the Old Testament: Introducing the Conceptual World of the Hebrew Bible*. Grand Rapids: Baker Academic, 2006.

Walton, John H. *Genesis*. NIVAC. Grand Rapids: Zondervan, 2001.

Walton, John H. *The Lost World of Adam and Eve: Genesis 2–3 and the Human Origins Debate*. Downers Grove: IVP Academic, 2015.

Wellhausen, Julius. *Prolegomena to the History of Israel*. Reprint of the 1885 ed. Atlanta: Scholars, 1994.

Wenham, Gordon J. 'The Coherence of the Flood Narrative.' *VT* 28 (1978): 336–48.

Wenham, Gordon J. *Genesis 1–15*. WBC. Dallas: Word, 1987.

Wenham, Gordon J. *Genesis 16–50*. WBC; Dallas: Word, 1994.

White, Lynn. 'The Historical Roots of Our Ecologic Crisis.' *Science* 155 (1967): 1203–7.

Whitehead, Christiania. 'Geoffrey Chaucer.' Pages 134–51 in Lemon et al., *Bible in English Literature*.

Whybray, R. Norman. *The Making of the Pentateuch: A Methodological Study*. JSOTSup 53. Sheffield: Sheffield Academic, 1987.

Williams, Delores S. 'Hagar in African American Biblical Appropriation.' Pages 171–84 in Trible and Russell, *Hagar, Sarah, and Their Children: Jewish, Christian, and Muslim Perspectives*.

Witzel, T. 'Roger Bacon.' NCE 13:111–16.

Wolff, Hans Walter. *Anthropology of the Old Testament*. London: SCM, 2011.

Wright, T. R. 'D. H. Lawrence.' Pages 654–66 in Lemon et al., *Bible in English Literature*.

Yonge, Charles D., trans. *The Works of Philo*. Peabody, MA: Hendrickson, 1993.

Young, Dwight, Elimelech Epstein Halevy and Haïm Z'ew Hirschberg. 'Noah.' Pages 287–90 in vol. 15 of Berenbaum and Skolnik, *Encyclopaedia Judaica*.

Zamyatin, Yevgeny. *We*. New York: E. P. Dutton, 1924.

Zerzan, John. *Twilight of the Machines*. Port Townsend, WA: Feral House, 2008.

Index of biblical references

Index of biblical references

Luke
9.62 21
10.1–16 127
17.31–32 21

John
1.29 150
3.16 150
8.31–47 135

Acts
7.9–16 170
15.17 4 n. 3

Romans
4.1–25 135
5.12–20 83

7.7 14
7.14 21
8.32 150
9.1–9 135
13.9 14
16.20 79 n. 1

1 Corinthians
15.12–58 83

2 Corinthians
11.3 81

Galatians
3.1–14 135
3.13–16 150

4.21–31 143
4.24 21

Ephesians
6.2–3 14

1 Timothy
2.14 81

2 Timothy
3.16 14

Hebrews
5.6 139
7.10 139
7.14 186
11.4 100

11.22 170
12.24 101

1 Peter
3.20–21 116

2 Peter
2.5 115 n. 7

1 John
3.12 100

Jude
7 141

Revelation
5.5 186

Index of pre-modern sources

Index of authors